足球竞赛规则 2021/2022

中国足球协会　审定

人民体育出版社

图书在版编目（CIP）数据

足球竞赛规则. 2021/2022 / 中国足球协会审定. --北京：人民体育出版社, 2022（2022.2重印）
ISBN 978-7-5009-6106-2

Ⅰ. ①足… Ⅱ. ①中… Ⅲ. ①足球运动–竞赛规则–2021-2022 Ⅳ. ①G843.4

中国版本图书馆CIP数据核字(2021)第224885号

*
人民体育出版社出版发行
北京中科印刷有限公司印刷
新　华　书　店　经　销
*
787×960　16开本　23印张　383千字
2022年1月第1版　2022年2月第2次印刷
印数：8,001—13,000册
*
ISBN 978-7-5009-6106-2
定价：86.00元

社址：北京市东城区体育馆路8号（天坛公园东门）
电话：67151482（发行部）　　邮编：100061
传真：67151483　　邮购：67118491
网址：www.sportspublish.cn
（购买本社图书，如遇有缺损页可与邮购部联系）

IFAB®

THE INTERNATIONAL FOOTBALL ASSOCIATION BOARD

国际足球理事会

地址：Münstergasse, 9, 8001 Zurich, Switzerland

电话：+41（0）44 245 1886

传真：+41（0）44 245 1887

网址：www.theifab.com

自2021年7月1日起生效。

前 言

国际足球理事会（IFAB）作为全球制定和修订足球竞赛规则的唯一决策机构，每年都要修订并发布新版本《足球竞赛规则》。中国足球协会每年对规则进行翻译和审定，出版发行《足球竞赛规则》的中英文对照版，受到国内广大裁判工作者、教练员、运动员，以及足球爱好者的广泛欢迎。

为使运动员、教练员、比赛官员等方面人员拥有更多时间去熟悉和准备新规则的执行，《足球竞赛规则》2021/2022版本于2021年6月发布，自2021年7月1日起生效并允许使用。

自从《足球竞赛规则》2019/2020中对手球犯规的条款全部内容进行重新编写以来，经过两年的实践，国际足球理事会意识到该条款在全世界范围内的执法应用和评估中容易造成误解和偏差，因此在《足球竞赛规则》2021/2022中再次对有关手球犯规的部分进行了重新措辞和描述，以求使足球界对于规则理解更加清晰，应用更加统一。手球犯规条款的重写也是本版本竞赛规则中最主要的修订之一。

除此之外，国际足球理事会自本版本开始，在竞赛规则中单独列出了“国际足联品质计划”。其中规定了足球比赛中所使用的各类产品、场地表面及技术设备的品质标准，在规则正文中的各相关章节的描述中直接导向该计划的相关内容。这使得竞赛规则更加规范化、模块化，并易于后续修订。

为与最新竞赛规则保持同步，确保规则执行的一致性，经国际足球理事会授权，中国足球协会翻译并出版了本书。书中包含了国际足球理事会《足球竞赛规则》2021/2022的全部章节和说明内容，并以原文和译文对照的形式呈现，以方便读者阅读和理解。我们保留并使用了原版规则中的图片展示、页边色块、黄色和黑色下划线（分别对应内容型调整和文字描述性调整）等设计模式，以提升中文竞赛规则的品质和易读性，并使读者能够更方便地检索规则调整部分。

中国足球协会与国际足球理事会、国际足球联合会及国内外各知名裁判专家和规则理论专家保持着持续的沟通和良好的合作，并根据国内足球界各方的意见，不断调整完善原有的竞赛规则用语。例如本版本中，将“球点球”（Penalty Kick）更改为“罚球点球”。

中国足球协会希望通过本书的出版，更好地服务于各类足球工作者，以及喜爱和关心足球运动的各界人士，并作为学习、掌握和正确运用足球竞赛规则的规范参考。

本次竞赛规则由段明洋翻译。审定过程听取了包括国际足球理事会规则编写负责人在内的国际、国内诸多裁判专家的宝贵意见与建议。

中国足球协会

2021年7月

Contents

目 录

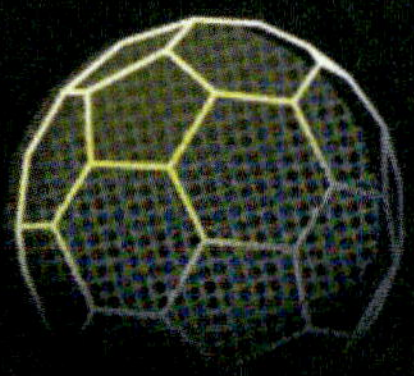

About the Laws

关于竞赛规则

The philosophy and spirit of the Laws

Football is the greatest sport on earth. It is played on every continent, in every country and at many different levels. The fact that the Laws of the Game are the same for all football throughout the world, from the FIFA World Cup™ through to a game between young children in a remote village, is a considerable strength which must continue to be harnessed for the good of football everywhere.

Football must have Laws which keep the game fair – this is a crucial foundation of the 'beautiful game' and a vital feature of the 'spirit' of the game. The best matches are those where the referee is rarely needed because the players play with respect for each other, the match officials and the Laws.

Football's Laws are relatively simple compared to most other team sports, but as many situations are subjective and match officials are human, some decisions will inevitably be wrong or cause debate and discussion. For some people, this discussion is part of the game's enjoyment and attraction but, whether decisions are right or wrong, the 'spirit' of the game requires that referees' decisions must always be respected. All those in authority, especially coaches and team captains, have a clear responsibility to the game to respect the match officials and their decisions.

The Laws cannot deal with every possible situation, so where there is no direct provision in the Laws, The IFAB expects the referee to make a decision within the 'spirit' of the game and the Laws – this often involves asking the question, "what would football want/expect?"

The Laws must also contribute to the safety and welfare of players. In recent years, player welfare has been the driving force behind a number of changes such as the possibility of allowing an additional substitute in extra time and the introduction of 'drinks' and 'cooling' breaks. Additionally, in response to

规则理念与精神

足球是世界第一运动，各国人民都乐享其中。从国际足联世界杯决赛，到偏僻乡村中的一场儿童比赛，都要遵循同一本《足球竞赛规则》。这一原则是足球运动的重要价值，必须予以保障和坚决执行，以促进世界各地足球的共同发展。

足球必须拥有一个使比赛公平公正的竞赛规则。“美丽足球”魅力的关键在于公平，这也是足球比赛“精神”的决定性特点。运动员在比赛中尊重对手、尊重比赛官员、尊重规则，不需要裁判员过多介入，一场精彩的比赛便由此而生。

与大多数其他团队体育项目相比，足球规则相对简单，但比赛中的许多情况需要进行主观判定，而裁判员也是人，一些判罚决定不可避免地会出现错误，或导致争议和讨论。对部分人士而言，这些讨论也是比赛的乐趣和魅力的一部分，但无论判罚决定正确与否，“足球比赛精神”要求永远尊重裁判员的判罚决定。所有相关授权人员，尤其是教练员与球队队长，在比赛中肩负着尊重比赛官员及其判罚决定的明确责任。

规则不可能涵盖所有的情形，所以当出现规则中未直接明确规定的情况时，国际足球理事会希望裁判员依照竞赛规则和足球比赛的“精神”做出判罚决定——这通常涉及一个问题，即“足球运动所要求/期望的是什么”。

规则还必须要有助于队员的安全和权益。近年来，规则的修订正是以队员权益问题作为原动力，例如允许加时赛额外的替换名额，以及引入“补水”暂停和“降温”暂停等。此外，为应对新冠疫情的影响，规则第三章又引入了允许竞赛方将最大替换人次数从3人提升为5人的修订内容。关于“脑震荡暂停”规则的测试也已开展，这项规则可以使队员发生脑震荡或疑似脑震荡情况时，权益得到优先保障，同时又不令其球队遭受人数上的损失。

the COVID-19 pandemic, a temporary amendment to Law 3 has been introduced to give top competitions the option of increasing the maximum number of substitutions from three to five. Trials have also started with additional 'concussion substitutes' so that teams can prioritise the welfare of a player who has an actual or suspected concussion without suffering a numerical disadvantage.

Accidents inevitably occur, but the Laws aim to help make the game as safe as possible, balancing player welfare and sporting fairness. This requires referees to use the Laws to deal strongly with those players whose actions are too aggressive or dangerous. The Laws embody the unacceptability of unsafe play in their disciplinary phrases, such as 'reckless challenge' and 'endangering the safety of an opponent' or 'using excessive force'.

虽然比赛中难免发生意外，但规则致力于尽可能让比赛安全进行，并在队员权益和比赛公平性之间力求平衡。这就需要裁判员运用规则，对比赛中具有侵害性和危险性的队员采取强有力的措施。规则中的纪律术语已经体现了对这些行为的不接受，如“鲁莽抢截”“危及对方安全”及“使用过分力量”等。

Managing changes to the Laws

Football must remain attractive and enjoyable for players, match officials and coaches, as well as spectators, fans and administrators, regardless of age, gender, race, religion, culture, ethnicity, sexual orientation or disability.

Therefore, for a Law to be changed, The IFAB and all its bodies that are involved in the decision-making process must be convinced that the change will benefit the game; this sometimes means that the potential change needs to be tested.

For every proposed change, the focus is on fairness, integrity, respect, safety, the enjoyment of participants and spectators and, where appropriate, using technology to enhance the game.

The IFAB will continue to engage with the global football community so changes to the Laws benefit football at all levels and in every corner of the world, and so the integrity of the game, the Laws and the match officials is respected, valued and protected.

规则变更的管理

足球必须保持对队员、比赛官员、教练员，以及观众、球迷、管理者等的吸引力和乐趣，无论其年龄、性别、种族、宗教、文化、民族、性取向如何，包括伤残人士等。

若规则需要调整与变更，国际足球理事会涉及决策程序的分支机构必须确保这些调整与变更有利于足球比赛。这意味着有时潜在的规则调整需要进行测试检验。

每次规则修订都是着眼于比赛的公平、诚信、尊重、安全、参与者及观众的体验，以及在适当的情况下，运用科技手段改进比赛。

国际足球理事会将继续与全球足球界紧密沟通，使规则的变更更有利于足球运动在世界每个角落和各个层面的发展，并且比赛的公正性、竞赛规则及比赛官员都能得到重视、保护与尊重。

The future

During 2021 and 2022, The IFAB will continue to work with its advisory panels and consult widely, with a special focus on player welfare in light of the pandemic and feedback from the 'concussion substitute' trial.

The IFAB greatly enjoys engaging with people throughout the world and we are always very pleased to receive suggestions or questions relating to the Laws of the Game. Indeed, many recent Law changes have originated from suggestions from people from many different parts of the world.

We hope to engage more easily and extensively in the future, so please check for details on our website: **www.theifab.com**.

Please continue to send your suggestions, ideas and questions to: **lawenquiries@theifab.com**.

未来规划

在2021年和2022年，国际足球理事会及其顾问组将继续展开广泛讨论，其中特别关注疫情影响之下有关队员权益的问题，以及“脑震荡暂停”的测试情况反馈。

国际足球理事会热诚期望与全球人士交流探讨，十分乐意听取关于竞赛规则的建议或问题。事实上，当前版本规则的许多变更正是来自世界不同地区人士的建议。

在未来，我们希望进行更便捷和广泛的交流。请访问我们的官方网址：www.theifab.com，以获取更多细节信息。

欢迎将您的建议、想法或问题发送至邮箱：lawenquiries@theifab.com。

Notes and modifications

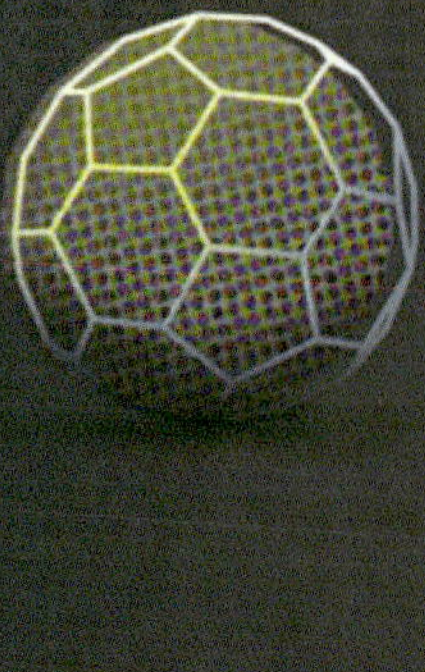

注解与调整

Notes on the Laws of the Game

Official languages

The IFAB publishes the Laws of the Game in English, French, German and Spanish. If there is any divergence in the wording, the English text is authoritative.

Other languages

National FAs which translate the Laws of the Game can obtain the layout template for the 2021/22 edition of the Laws from The IFAB by contacting: **info@theifab.com**.

National FAs which produce a translated version of the Laws of the Game using this format are invited to send a copy to The IFAB (stating clearly on the front cover that it is that national FA's official translation) so it can be posted on The IFAB website for use by others.

Measurements

If there is any divergence between metric and imperial units, the metric units are authoritative.

Applying the Laws

The same Laws apply in every match in every confederation, country, town and village and, apart from the modifications permitted by The IFAB (see 'General modifications'), the Laws must not be modified or changed, except with the permission of The IFAB.

Those who are educating match officials and other participants, should emphasise that:

- referees should apply the Laws within the 'spirit' of the game to help produce fair and safe matches

竞赛规则注解

官方语言

国际足球理事会使用英文、法文、德文和西班牙文发布《足球竞赛规则》，如果不同语言文字出现任何歧义，则以英文版文字为准。

其他语言

翻译此规则的国家足球协会，可以通过联络下列邮箱获得2021/2022版竞赛规则的设计模板：info@theifab.com。

欢迎以此模板制作本国语言版本竞赛规则的国家足球协会，将规则副本（在封面上标明由国家足球协会翻译审定）发给国际足球理事会，用以在其官方网站上发布。

计量单位

如果在公制单位和英制单位之间存在任何计量误差，一律以公制单位为准。

规则的执行

所有洲际联合会、国家、城市和乡村，都必须执行同样的竞赛规则。除国际足球理事会审定的可调整内容（见“规则调整”部分）外，不得修改或变更竞赛规则，除非获得国际足球理事会的许可。

在培训比赛官员或其他足球参与者时，应强调：

- 裁判员应该依照足球运动“精神”来执行竞赛规则，以创造公平和安全的比赛。

- everyone must respect the match officials and their decisions, remembering and respecting that referees are human and will make mistakes

Players have a major responsibility for the image of the game and the team captain should play an important role in helping to ensure that the Laws and referees' decisions are respected.

Key

The main Law changes are underlined in yellow and highlighted in the margin.
Editorial changes are underlined.
YC = yellow card (caution); RC = red card (sending-off).

- 所有人必须尊重比赛官员及其判罚决定，牢记并且尊重裁判员也是人、也会犯错误这一事实。

队员对于足球比赛的形象担负主要责任，球队队长在尊重规则和尊重裁判员判罚方面应扮演重要的角色。

提示

规则的主要变更部分在文中以黄色下划线的方式标出。文字描述性的调整用黑色下划线的方式标出。

General modifications

The universality of the Laws of the Game means that the game is essentially the same in every part of the world and at every level. As well as creating a 'fair' and safe environment in which the game is played, the Laws should also promote participation and enjoyment.

Historically, The IFAB has allowed national football associations (FAs) some flexibility to modify the 'organisational' Laws for specific categories of football. However, The IFAB strongly believes that national FAs should now be given more options to modify aspects of the way football is organised if it will benefit football in their own country.

How the game is played and refereed should be the same on every football field in the world from the FIFA World Cup™ final to the smallest village. However, the needs of a country's domestic football should determine how long the game lasts, how many people can take part and how some unfair behaviour is punished.

Consequently, the 131st AGM of The IFAB held in London on 3rd March 2017 unanimously agreed that national FAs (and confederations and FIFA) now have the option to modify all or some of the following organisational areas of the Laws of the Game for football for which they are responsible:

For youth, veterans, disability and grassroots football:

- size of the field of play
- size, weight and material of the ball
- width between the goalposts and height of the crossbar from the ground
- duration of the two (equal) halves of the game (and two equal halves of extra time)
- the use of return substitutes
- the use of temporary dismissals (sin bins) for some/all cautions (YCs)

一般性调整

竞赛规则的普适性意味着世界各地各个层面的足球比赛所执行的规则本质上是相同的。除了营造更为“公平”和安全的比赛环境外，竞赛规则还应促进比赛参与程度和乐趣的提升。

从历史上看，国际足球理事会已经允许国家足球协会针对特定类别的比赛具有调整一些“组织性”规则条款的灵活性。无论如何，国际足球理事会坚信，如果能对本国的足球运动有利，国家协会现在应该对于比赛组织方面的规则拥有更多调整的选择。

从世界杯赛的冠亚军决赛赛场，到最小的村镇，全世界每一块足球场上进行的比赛，其比赛进行的方式和裁判执法的方式都应该相同。然而，各国可以根据其国内情况的需要，来决定诸如比赛时长、球队人数、对不当行为的处罚等有关条款。

因此，2017年3月3日在伦敦召开的国际足球理事会第131次年度大会，一致通过了国家协会（包括洲际联合会以及国际足联）可以在其负责的赛事中，对下列涉及比赛组织方面的竞赛规则进行全部或部分调整：

对于青少年、年长人士、残障人士及草根足球：

- 比赛场地的大小。
- 比赛用球的大小、重量及制作材料。
- 两门柱间的宽度及地面到球门横梁的高度。
- 比赛两个半场（等时）的时长（以及加时赛两个等时半场的时长）。
- 使用返场替换。
- 对部分/全部应警告（黄牌）的情况使用暂时罚离（受罚席）。

For any level except competitions involving the 1st team of clubs in the top division or 'A' international teams:

- the number of substitutions each team is permitted to use up to a maximum of five, except in youth football where the maximum will be determined by the national association, confederation or FIFA

In addition, to allow national FAs further flexibility to benefit and develop their domestic football, The IFAB AGM approved the following changes relating to 'categories' of football:

- women's football is no longer a separate category and now has the same status as men's football
- the age limits for youth and veterans have been removed – national FAs, confederations and FIFA have the flexibility to decide the age restrictions for these categories
- each national FA will determine which competitions at the lowest levels of football are designated as 'grassroots' football

Permission for other modifications

National FAs have the option to approve different modifications for different competitions – there is no requirement to apply them universally or to apply them all. **However, no other modifications are allowed without the permission of The IFAB.**

National FAs are asked to inform The IFAB of their use of these modifications, and at which levels, as this information, and especially the reason(s) why the modifications are being used, may identify development ideas/strategies which The IFAB can share to assist the development of football in other national FAs.

The IFAB would also be very interested to hear about other potential modifications to the Laws of the Game which could increase participation, make football more attractive and promote its worldwide development.

除涉及最高级别俱乐部一线队或国家A队的比赛外，其他任何级别的赛事可以进行如下调整：

- 青少年比赛的最大替换人数由国家协会、洲际联合会和国际足联决定，除此之外的其他比赛可允许最大替换人数为5人。

此外，为使各国家协会进一步获得规则调整的灵活性，以利其国内足球发展，国际足球理事会批准了下列有关足球比赛“分类”的变更：

- 女子足球不再作为单独的类别，其与男子足球具有同等地位。
- 去除了关于青少年和年长人士的年龄规定——国家协会、洲际联合会以及国际足联可以灵活决定这些类别的年龄限制。
- 各国家协会自行决定哪些处于最低级别的赛事属于“草根”足球。

规则调整的许可

国家协会可以在其各项赛事中使用不同的规则调整，而不必在所有赛事中执行完全相同的规则。**但无论如何，未经国际足球理事会批准，不得对规则进行除上述以外的其他调整。**

国际足球理事会邀请各国家协会提供关于其赛事规则调整的信息，包括在哪些级别的赛事中进行了哪些调整，特别是进行这些调整的理由。通过这些信息，国际足球理事会可提炼出与其他国家协会分享的内容，以协助其足球发展。

国际足球理事会乐于听取能够扩大足球运动的参与程度、提升吸引力，以及促进足球运动在世界范围发展的其他潜在规则调整建议。

Guidelines for temporary dismissals (sin bins)

The 131st AGM of The IFAB held in London on 3rd March 2017 approved the use of temporary dismissals (sin bins) for all or some cautions/yellow cards (YCs) in youth, veterans, disability and grassroots football, subject to the approval of the competition's national FA, confederation or FIFA, whichever is appropriate.

Reference to temporary dismissals is found in:

Law 5 – The Referee (Powers and duties):
Disciplinary action

The referee has the power to show yellow or red cards and, where competition rules permit, temporarily dismiss a player, from entering the field at the start of the match until after the match has ended, including during the half-time interval, extra time and kicks from the penalty mark.

A temporary dismissal is when a player commits a cautionable (YC) offence and is punished by an immediate 'suspension' from participating in the next part of that match. The philosophy is that an 'instant punishment' can have a significant and immediate positive influence on the behaviour of the offending player and, potentially, the player's team.

The national FA, confederation or FIFA should approve (for publication in the competition rules) a temporary dismissal protocol within the following guidelines:

Players only

- Temporary dismissals apply to all players (including goalkeepers) but not for cautionable offences (YCs) committed by a substitute or substituted player

暂时罚离指南（受罚席）

2017年3月3日，在伦敦举行的国际足球理事会第131次年度大会上，批准了国家协会、洲际联合会以及国际足联可以在适当的青少年、年长人士、残障人士及草根足球比赛中，使用对全部或部分警告（黄牌）的情况实施暂时罚离（受罚席）规则。

关于暂时罚离的参考如下：

第五章　裁判员（权力和职责）

纪律处罚

从开赛前进入比赛场地直至比赛结束，包括中场休息、加时赛和罚球点球决胜期间，裁判员都有权出示红黄牌，以及在竞赛规程允许下，将队员暂时罚离。

暂时罚离是指队员在被警告（黄牌）时，受到的即时性“停止参加”接下来一段时间比赛的处罚形式。其理念是通过“即时的处罚”来对犯规队员乃至其球队产生有效的和立即的正面影响。

国家协会、洲际联合会及国际足联应以下列指南为准，（通过发布竞赛规程）实施暂时罚离规则：

仅用于场上队员

- 暂时罚离可适用于所有场上队员（包括守门员），但不适用于受到警告（黄牌）的替补队员或已替换下场的队员。

Referee's signal

- The referee will indicate a temporary dismissal by showing a yellow card (YC) and then clearly pointing with both arms to the temporary dismissal area (usually the player's technical area)

The temporary dismissal period

- The length of the temporary dismissal is the same for all offences
- The length of the temporary dismissal should be between 10–15% of the total playing time (e.g. 10 minutes in a 90-minute match; 8 minutes in an 80-minute match)
- The temporary dismissal period begins when play restarts after the player has left the field of play
- The referee should include in the temporary dismissal period any time 'lost' for a stoppage for which 'additional time' will be allowed at the end of the half (e.g. substitution, injury etc...)
- Competitions must decide who will help the referee time the dismissal period – it could be the responsibility of a delegate, 4th official or neutral assistant referee; conversely it could be a team official
- Once the temporary dismissal period has been completed, the player can return from the touchline with the referee's permission, which can be given while the ball is in play
- The referee has the final decision as to when the player can return
- A temporarily dismissed player cannot be substituted until the end of the temporary dismissal period (but not if the team has used all its permitted substitutes)
- If a temporary dismissal period has not been completed at the end of the first half (or the end of the second half when extra time is to be played) the remaining part of the temporary dismissal period is served from the start of the second half (start of extra time)
- A player who is still serving a temporary dismissal at the end of the match is permitted to take part in kicks from the penalty mark (penalties)

裁判员的示意信号

- 裁判员通过出示黄牌，随后清晰地用双臂指向暂时罚离区（通常是该队员一方的技术区域）的方式示意执行暂时罚离。

暂时罚离时段

- 所有暂时罚离的情形，罚离的时长相等。
- 暂时罚离的时长应为比赛总时长的10%~15%（例如总时长90分钟的比赛，暂时罚离时长可以是10分钟；80分钟的比赛，暂时罚离时长可以是8分钟）。
- 暂时罚离的计时，自罚离的队员离开比赛场地后、比赛恢复时开始。
- 裁判员需将暂时罚离时段中所有应计入本半场比赛“补时”的时间“损失”（例如换人、受伤等），补计入暂时罚离时长中。
- 竞赛方必须规定由谁帮助裁判员为暂时罚离进行计时，可以委派代表，或由第四官员、中立的助理裁判员负责；不得已时，可使用球队官员。
- 暂时罚离时段结束时，受罚队员需得到裁判员允许后从边线重新进入比赛场地，返场过程可以处于比赛进行中。
- 由裁判员决定受罚队员何时可以返场。
- 暂时罚离的队员，在罚离时段结束后才可被替换下场（如果该队已用完替换次数，则不能替换）。
- 如果暂时罚离在上半场比赛结束时（或下半场比赛结束，将进行加时赛比赛时）仍未执行完，则剩余的罚离时间从下半场比赛（或加时赛）开始时继续执行。
- 如果暂时罚离时段在比赛结束时仍未执行完，则该受罚队员可以参加罚球点球决胜。

Temporary dismissal area

- A temporarily dismissed player should remain within the technical area (where one exists) or with the team's coach/technical staff, unless 'warming up' (under the same conditions as a substitute)

Offences during a temporary dismissal

- A temporarily dismissed player who commits a cautionable (YC) or sending-off (RC) offence during their temporary dismissal period will take no further part in the match and may not be replaced or substituted

Further disciplinary action

- Competitions/national FAs will decide if temporary dismissals must be reported to the appropriate authorities and whether any further disciplinary action may be taken e.g. suspension for accumulating a number of temporary dismissals, as with cautions (YCs)

Temporary dismissal systems

A competition may use one of the following temporary dismissal systems:

- System A – for all cautions (YCs)
- System B – for some but not all cautions (YCs)

System A – temporary dismissal for all cautions (YCs)

- All cautions (YCs) are punished with a temporary dismissal
- A player who receives a second caution (YC) in the same match:
    - will receive a second temporary dismissal and then takes no further part in the match
    - may be replaced by a substitute at the end of the second temporary dismissal period if the player's team has not used its maximum number of substitutes (this is because the team has already been 'punished' by playing without that player for 2 x temporary dismissal periods)

暂时罚离区

- 暂时罚离的队员，除进行“热身活动”（热身活动的要求与其他替补队员相同）外，应始终留在技术区域（如果有）内，或者与其球队教练员/技术官员处于一处。

暂时罚离过程中的违规

- 处于暂时罚离阶段的受罚队员，犯有需警告（黄牌）或罚令出场（红牌）的犯规，将不得再次参与本场比赛，也不能被替换。

进一步的纪律措施

- 竞赛方 / 国家协会应决定是否需要向有关机构报告暂时罚离的情况，以及是否需要进一步的纪律措施，比如累计的暂时罚离是否需要参照警告（黄牌）的情况进行停赛处罚等。

暂时罚离体系

每个竞赛可以从下列暂时罚离体系中择一使用：

- 体系A——针对所有警告（黄牌）。
- 体系B——针对部分警告（黄牌）。

体系A——针对所有警告（黄牌）执行暂时罚离

- 所有受到警告（黄牌）的队员将被暂时罚离。
- 在同一场比赛中受到第二次警告（黄牌）的队员：
  - 执行第二次暂时罚离，并且不得再次参与本场比赛。
  - 如果其球队的替换次数尚未用完，可以在第二次暂时罚离时段结束时，被替补队员替换（这是因为受罚队员所在的球队已经在两个暂时罚离阶段受到了少一人的“惩罚”）。

System B – temporary dismissal for some but not all cautions (YCs)*

- A pre-defined list of cautionable (YC) offences will be punished by a temporary dismissal
- All other cautionable offences are punished with a caution (YC)
- A player who has been temporarily dismissed and then receives a caution (YC) continues playing
- A player who has received a caution (YC) and then receives a temporary dismissal can continue playing after the end of the temporary dismissal period
- A player who receives a second temporary dismissal in the same match will serve the temporary dismissal and then takes no further part in the match. The player may be replaced by a substitute at the end of the second temporary dismissal period if the player's team has not used its maximum number of substitutes but a player who has also received a non-temporary dismissal caution (YC) may not be replaced or substituted
- A player who receives a second caution (YC) in the same match will be sent off and takes no further part in the match and may not be replaced/substituted

**Some competitions may find it valuable to use temporary dismissals only for cautions (YCs) for offences relating to 'inappropriate' behaviour, e.g.*

- *Simulation*
- *Deliberately delaying the opposing team's restart of the match*
- *Dissent or verbal comments or gestures*
- *Stopping or interfering with a promising attack by holding, pulling, pushing or handball*
- *Kicker illegally feinting at a penalty kick*

体系B——针对部分而非全部的警告（黄牌）执行暂时罚离

- 需事先将被执行暂时罚离的警告（黄牌）情况列出。
- 此外的情况仍然执行警告（黄牌）。
- 已经受到过暂时罚离处罚的队员，在同一场比赛中再受到警告（黄牌），将继续比赛。
- 已经受到过警告（黄牌）的队员，在同一场比赛中再受到暂时罚离处罚，在罚离时段结束后，将继续比赛。
- 在同一场比赛中受到两次暂时罚离处罚的队员，不得再次参与本场比赛，但如果其球队的替换次数尚未用完，则在第二次暂时罚离时段结束时，该队员可以被替补队员替换。但如果该受罚队员已经受到过非暂时罚离的警告（黄牌），则不得被替代/替换。
- 在同一场比赛中受到两次警告（黄牌）的队员将被罚令出场，不得再次参与本场比赛，也不得被替代 / 替换。

**竞赛方可能会发现，仅针对涉及“不当行为”的警告（黄牌）执行暂时罚离，是非常有价值的处理方式。例如如下行为：*

- *佯装。*
- *故意延误对方球队恢复比赛。*
- *用语言或动作表示不满。*
- *以推、拉拽、拉扯对方队员或手球等方式，阻止或干扰了对方一次有希望的进攻。*
- *踢罚球点球时，罚球队员使用不合法的假动作。*

Guidelines for return substitutes

Following approval at the 131st AGM of The IFAB held in London on 3rd March 2017 the Laws of the Game now permit the use of return substitutes in youth, veterans, disability and grassroots football, subject to the approval of the competition's national FA, confederation or FIFA, whichever is appropriate.

Reference to return substitutions is found in:

Law 3 – The Players (Number of substitutions):
Return substitutions

- The use of return substitutions is only permitted in youth, veterans, disability and grassroots football, subject to the agreement of the national football association, confederation or FIFA.

A 'return substitute' is a player who has already played in the match and has been substituted (a substituted player) and later in the match returns to play by replacing another player.

Apart from the dispensation for a substituted player to return to play in the match, all other provisions of Law 3 and the Laws of the Game apply to return substitutes. In particular, the substitution procedure outlined in Law 3 must be followed.

返场替换指南

经2017年3月3日在伦敦召开的国际足球理事会第131次年度大会批准，足球竞赛规则允许国家协会、洲际联合会、国际足联或任何有关机构，可以在其主办的青少年、年长人士、残障人士，以及草根足球比赛中，使用返场替换规则。

关于返场替换的参考如下：

第三章　队员（替换人数）

返场替换

- 返场替换仅允许在青少年、年长人士、残障人士，以及草根足球比赛中使用，前提是得到国家足球协会、洲际联合会或国际足联许可。

“返场替换”指的是一名已经参与了比赛的场上队员在被替换下场后（即已被替换下场的队员），在同一场比赛中再次替换其他队员上场比赛。

除被替换下场而后返场这一点外，竞赛规则第三章的其他规定均适用于返场替换，尤其是替换的程序，必须遵从规则第三章的规定。

FIFA.com
13

FIFA.com

Laws of the Game

2021/22

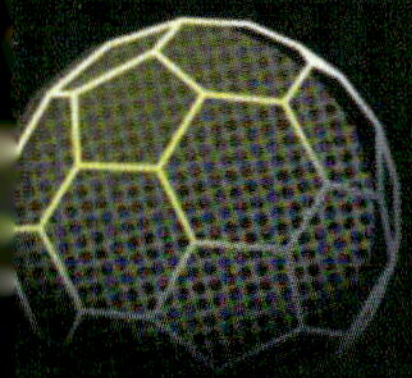

足球竞赛规则

2021/2022

01. The Field of Play

1. **Field surface**

   The field of play must be a wholly natural or, if competition rules permit, a wholly artificial playing surface except where competition rules permit an integrated combination of artificial and natural materials (hybrid system).

   The colour of artificial surfaces must be green.

   Where artificial surfaces are used in competition matches between representative teams of national football associations affiliated to FIFA or international club competition matches, the surface must meet the requirements of the FIFA Quality Programme for Football Turf, unless special dispensation is given by The IFAB.

2. **Field markings**

   The field of play must be rectangular and marked with continuous lines which must not be dangerous; artificial playing surface material may be used for the field markings on natural fields if it is not dangerous. These lines belong to the areas of which they are boundaries.

   Only the lines indicated in Law 1 are to be marked on the field of play. Where artificial surfaces are used, other lines are permitted provided they are a different colour and clearly distinguishable from the football lines.

   The two longer boundary lines are touchlines. The two shorter lines are goal lines.

   The field of play is divided into two halves by a halfway line, which joins the midpoints of the two touchlines.

   The centre mark is at the midpoint of the halfway line. A circle with a radius of 9.15 m (10 yds) is marked around it.

第一章　比赛场地

1. 场地表面

比赛场地必须为全天然草皮。若竞赛规程允许，可使用全人造草皮。此外，如果竞赛规程允许，可使用人造和天然结合材料制成的整体草皮（混合系统）。

人造草皮场地的表面必须为绿色。

除国际足球理事会特许外，在国际足联所属的国家协会代表队之间、国际俱乐部之间比赛中使用的人造草皮场地，必须达到《国际足联品质计划——足球场地》的要求。

2. 场地标识

比赛场地形状必须为长方形，且由不具危险性的连续标线标示。不具危险性的人造草皮材料可作为天然草皮场地的标记使用。这些标线作为边界线是其所标示区域的一部分。

只有在第一章中提及的标线可以标画在比赛场地内。在使用人造草皮场地时，允许场地上存在非足球运动的其他标线，但其颜色必须有别于足球比赛场地的标线，且区分明显。

两条较长的边界线为边线，两条较短的边界线为球门线。

比赛场地由一条连接两侧边线中点的中线划分为两个半场。

中线的中心位置为中点。以中点为圆心画一个半径为9.15米（10码）的圆圈。

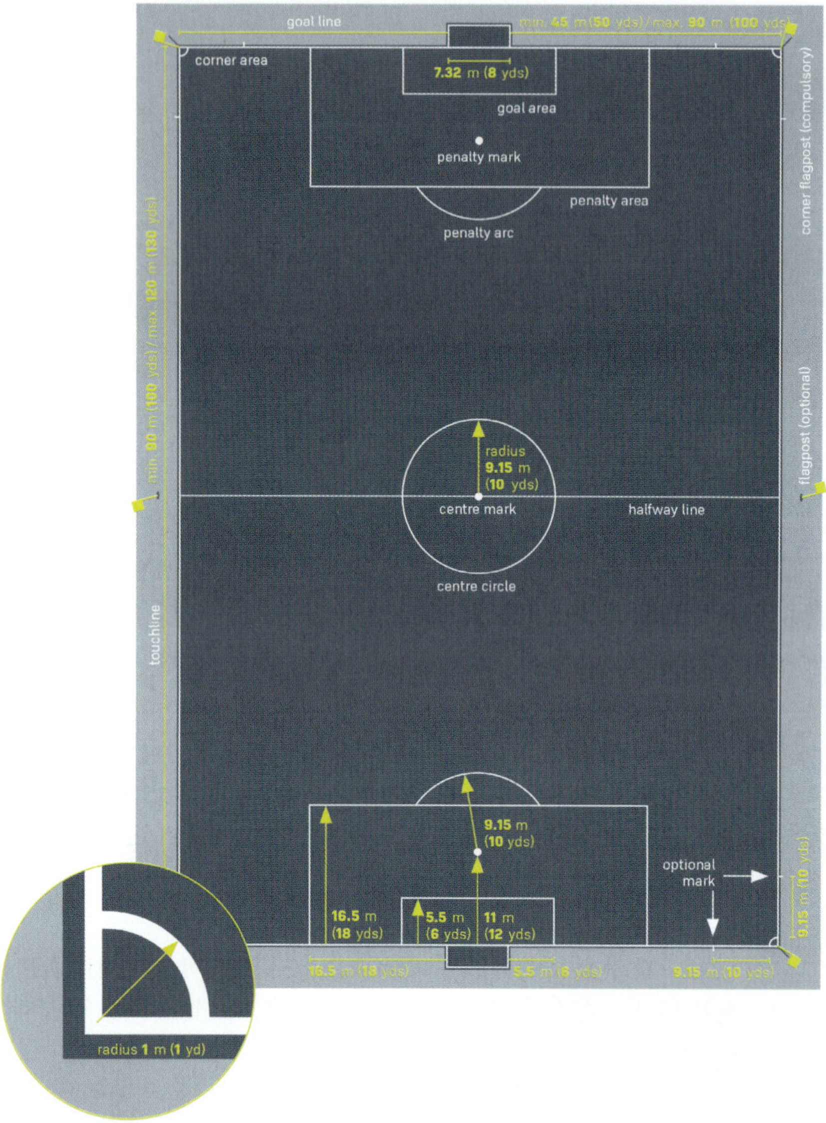

- Measurements are from the outside of the lines as the lines are part of the area they enclose.
- The penalty mark is measured from the centre of the mark to the back edge of the goal line.

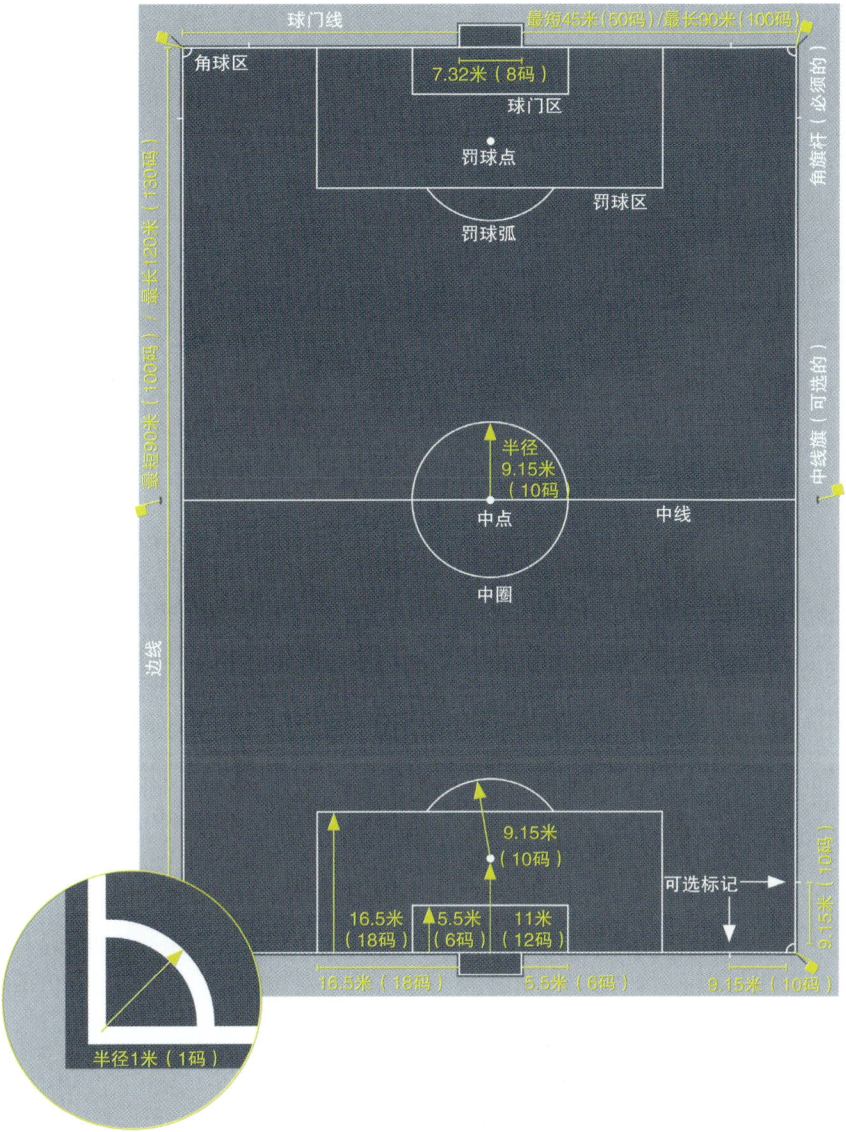

• 尺寸测量均以标线外侧为准，因为标线属于其所标示区域的一部分。

• 罚球点距球门的距离，是从罚球点中心到球门线外沿测量。

Marks may be made off the field of play 9.15 m (10 yds) from the corner arc at right angles to the goal lines and the touchlines.

All lines must be of the same width, which must not be more than 12 cm (5 ins). The goal lines must be of the same width as the goalposts and the crossbar.

A player who makes unauthorised marks on the field of play must be cautioned for unsporting behaviour. If the referee notices this being done during the match, the player is cautioned when the ball next goes out of play.

3. Dimensions

The touchline must be longer than the goal line.

- Length (touchline):
  minimum 90 m (100 yds)
  maximum 120 m (130 yds)
- Length (goal line):
  minimum 45 m (50 yds)
  maximum 90 m (100 yds)

Competitions may determine the length of the goal line and touchline within the above dimensions.

4. Dimensions for international matches

- Length (touchline):
  minimum 100 m (110 yds)
  maximum 110 m (120 yds)
- Length (goal line):
  minimum 64 m (70 yds)
  maximum 75 m (80 yds)

Competitions may determine the length of the goal line and touchline within the above dimensions.

可在比赛场地外，距角球弧9.15米（10码）处，分别做垂直于球门线和边线的标记。

所有标线宽度必须一致，且不得超过12厘米（5英寸）。球门线、球门柱和横梁的宽度必须一致。

在比赛场地内制造未经许可标记的队员，必须以非体育行为予以警告。如果裁判员在比赛进行中发现此类情况，则在随后比赛停止时警告相关队员。

3. 场地尺寸

边线必须长于球门线。

- 长度（边线）：
  最短 90米（100码）
  最长 120米（130码）
- 长度（球门线）：
  最短 45米（50码）
  最长 90米（100码）

竞赛方可以在上述尺寸范围内规定球门线和边线的长度。

4. 国际比赛场地尺寸

- 长度（边线）：
  最短 100米（110码）
  最长 110米（120码）
- 长度（球门线）：
  最短 64米（70码）
  最长 75米（80码）

竞赛方可以在上述尺寸范围内规定球门线和边线的长度。

5. **The goal area**

Two lines are drawn at right angles to the goal line, 5.5 m (6 yds) from the inside of each goalpost. These lines extend into the field of play for 5.5 m (6 yds) and are joined by a line drawn parallel with the goal line. The area bounded by these lines and the goal line is the goal area.

6. **The penalty area**

Two lines are drawn at right angles to the goal line, 16.5 m (18 yds) from the inside of each goalpost. These lines extend into the field of play for 16.5 m (18 yds) and are joined by a line drawn parallel with the goal line. The area bounded by these lines and the goal line is the penalty area.

Within each penalty area, a penalty mark is made 11 m (12 yds) from the midpoint between the goalposts.

An arc of a circle with a radius of 9.15 m (10 yds) from the centre of each penalty mark is drawn outside the penalty area.

7. **The corner area**

The corner area is defined by a quarter circle with a radius of 1 m (1 yd) from each corner flagpost drawn inside the field of play.

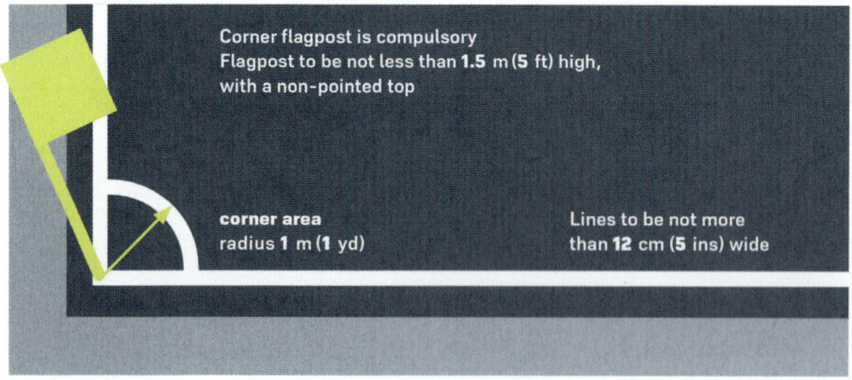

5. 球门区

从距两根球门柱内侧5.5米（6码）处，画两条垂直于球门线的标线。这两条标线向比赛场地内延伸5.5米（6码），与一条平行于球门线的标线相连接。由这些标线和球门线围成的区域是球门区。

6. 罚球区

从距两根球门柱内侧16.5米（18码）处，画两条垂直于球门线的标线。这两条标线向比赛场地内延伸16.5米（18码），与一条平行于球门线的标线相连接。由这些标线和球门线围成的区域是罚球区。

在每个罚球区内，距两根球门柱之间的中点11米（12码）处，设置一个罚球点。

在每个罚球区外，以罚球点为圆心，画一段半径为9.15米（10码）的圆弧。

7. 角球区

在比赛场地内，以各角旗杆为圆心，画一半径为1米的四分之一圆，这部分区域为角球区。

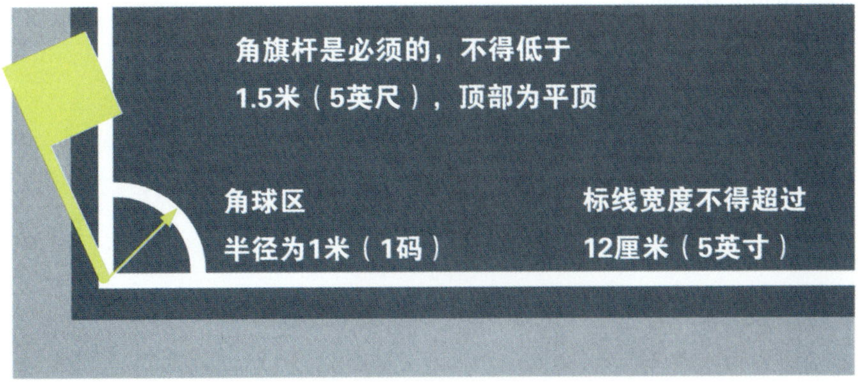

8. Flagposts

A flagpost, at least 1.5 m (5 ft) high, with a non-pointed top and a flag must be placed at each corner.

Flagposts may be placed at each end of the halfway line, at least 1 m (1 yd) outside the touchline.

9. The technical area

The technical area relates to matches played in stadiums with a designated sitting area for team officials, substitutes and substituted players as outlined below:

- the technical area should only extend 1 m (1 yd) on either side of the designated seated area and up to a distance of 1 m (1 yd) from the touchline
- markings should be used to define the area
- the number of persons permitted to occupy the technical area is defined by the competition rules
- the occupants of the technical area:
  - are identified before the start of the match in accordance with the competition rules
  - must behave in a responsible manner
  - must remain within its confines except in special circumstances, e.g. a physiotherapist/doctor entering the field of play, with the referee's permission, to assess an injured player
- only one person at a time is authorised to convey tactical instructions from the technical area

8. 旗杆

必须在比赛场地各角竖立高度不低于1.5米（5英尺）的平顶旗杆。

可在中线两端、边线外不少于1米（1码）处竖立旗杆。

9. 技术区域

技术区域是指设在场地内，与比赛相关，供球队官员、替补队员和已替换下场的队员使用的就坐区域，描述如下：

- 技术区域仅可从座席区域两侧向外扩展1米（1码），向前扩展到距边线至少1米（1码）。
- 应用标线标示出该区域。
- 允许占用技术区域的人员数量由竞赛规程决定。
- 占用技术区域的人员：
  - 需依据竞赛规程，在比赛开始前审核确认。
  - 举止必须得当。
  - 必须留在限定区域内。除特殊情况外，如理疗师 / 医生经裁判员许可后进入比赛场地内查看受伤队员伤情。
- 同一时刻仅允许1人在技术区域内进行战术指导。

10. Goals

A goal must be placed on the centre of each goal line.

A goal consists of two vertical posts equidistant from the corner flagposts and joined at the top by a horizontal crossbar. The goalposts and crossbar must be made of approved material and must not be dangerous. The goalposts and crossbar of both goals must be the same shape, which must be square, rectangular, round, elliptical or a hybrid of these options.

It is recommended that all goals used in an official competition organised under the auspices of FIFA or confederations meet the requirements of the FIFA Quality Programme for Football Goals.

The distance between the inside of the posts is 7.32 m (8 yds) and the distance from the lower edge of the crossbar to the ground is 2.44 m (8 ft).

The position of the goalposts in relation to the goal line must be in accordance with the graphics.

The goalposts and the crossbar must be white and have the same width and depth, which must not exceed 12 cm (5 ins).

If the crossbar becomes displaced or broken, play is stopped until it has been repaired or replaced in position. Play is restarted with a dropped ball. If it can not be repaired the match must be abandoned. A rope or any flexible or dangerous material may not replace the crossbar.

Nets may be attached to the goals and the ground behind the goal; they must be properly supported and must not interfere with the goalkeeper.

Safety

Goals (including portable goals) must be firmly secured to the ground.

11. Goal line technology (GLT)

GLT systems may be used to verify whether a goal has been scored to support the referee's decision.

The use of GLT must be stipulated in the competition rules.

10. 球门

必须在两条球门线的中央，各放置一个球门。

球门由两根距角旗杆等距离的直立球门柱和一根连接球门柱顶部的水平横梁组成。球门柱和横梁必须由经批准的材料制成，且不具危险性。两个球门的球门柱、横梁必须均为相同形状，即正方形、矩形、圆形、椭圆形或上述形状结合而成的一种形状。

建议国际足联或洲际联合会举办的正式赛事中的所有球门均符合《国际足联品质计划——足球球门》的要求。

两根球门柱内侧之间的距离为7.32米（8码），从横梁下沿至地面的距离为2.44米（8英尺）。

球门柱与球门线的位置关系必须符合图例所示（见下页）。

球门柱和横梁颜色必须为白色，且宽度和厚度必须一致，不得超过12厘米（5英寸）。

如果横梁移位或折损，则停止比赛直至横梁修复或归位。比赛以坠球方式恢复。如果无法修复，则必须中止比赛。不得用绳、任何弹性或危险性材料代替横梁使用。比赛以坠球方式恢复。

球门网可系在球门和球门后的地面上，并且必须适当撑开，不得影响守门员的活动。

安全性

球门（包括可移动式球门）必须牢固地固定在地面上。

11. 球门线技术（GLT）

球门线技术系统可以用于帮助裁判员判定进球与否。

如果使用球门线技术，必须在竞赛规程中注明。

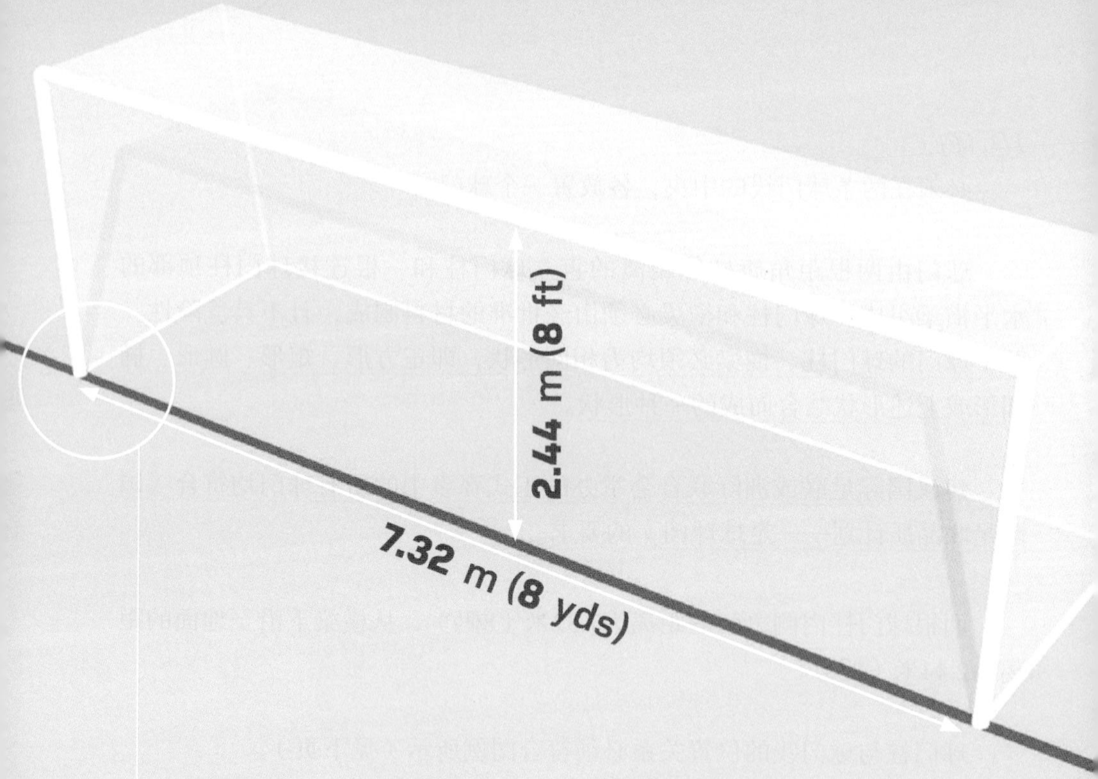

The position of the goalposts in relation to the goal line must be in accordance with the graphics below.

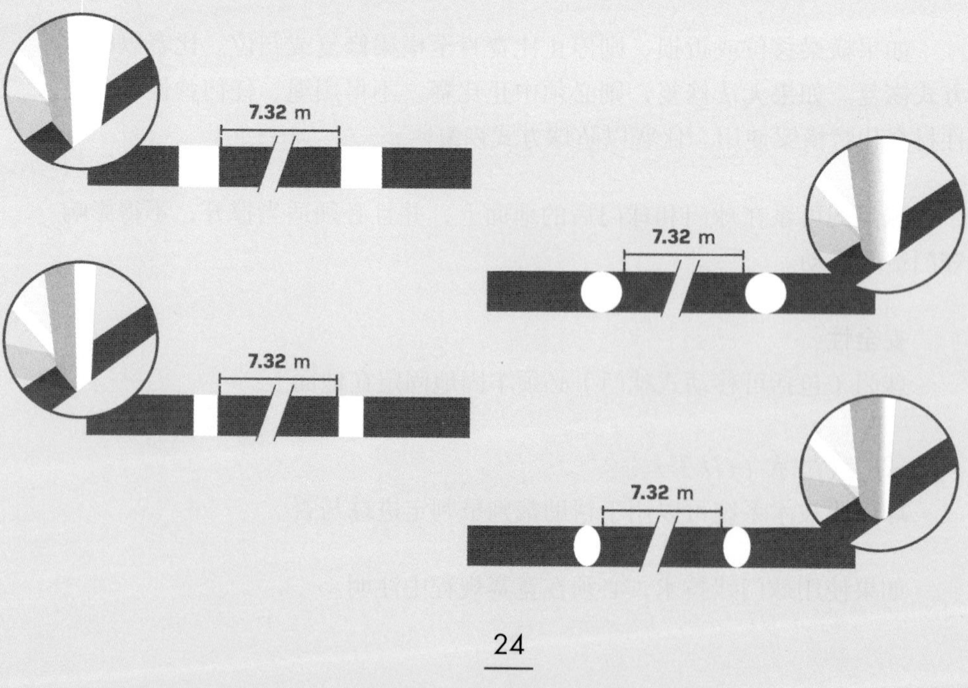

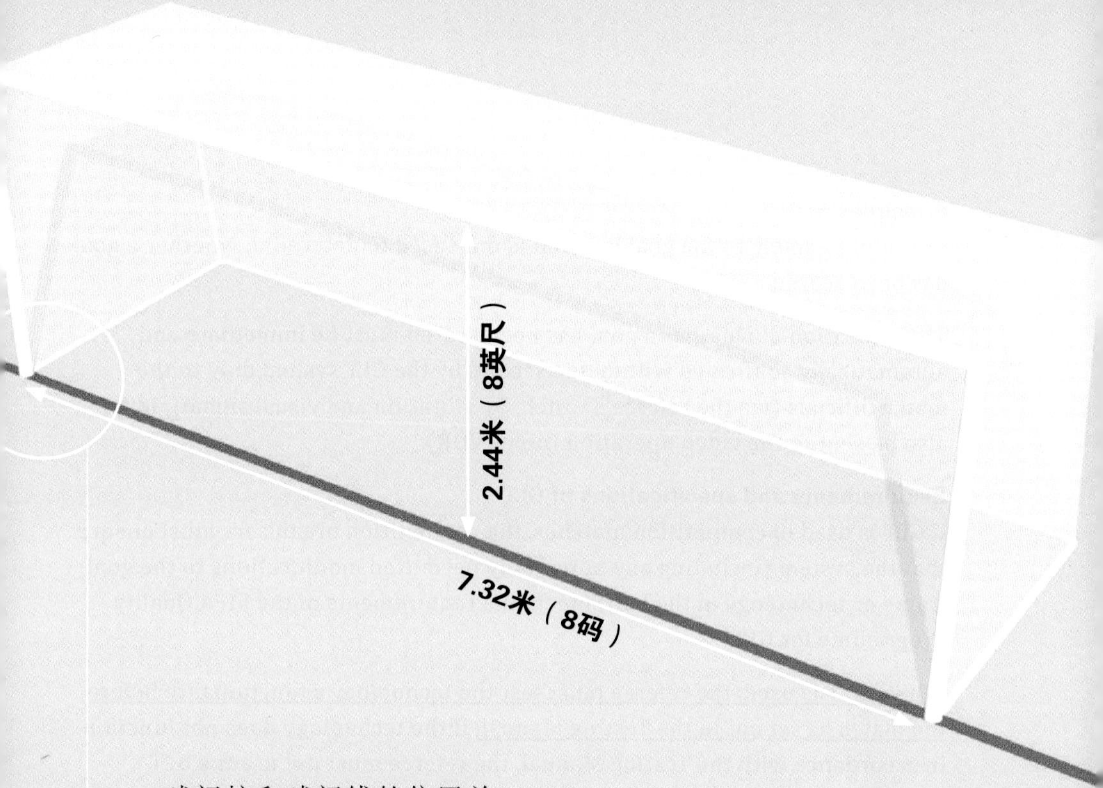

球门柱和球门线的位置关系必须符合如下图示：

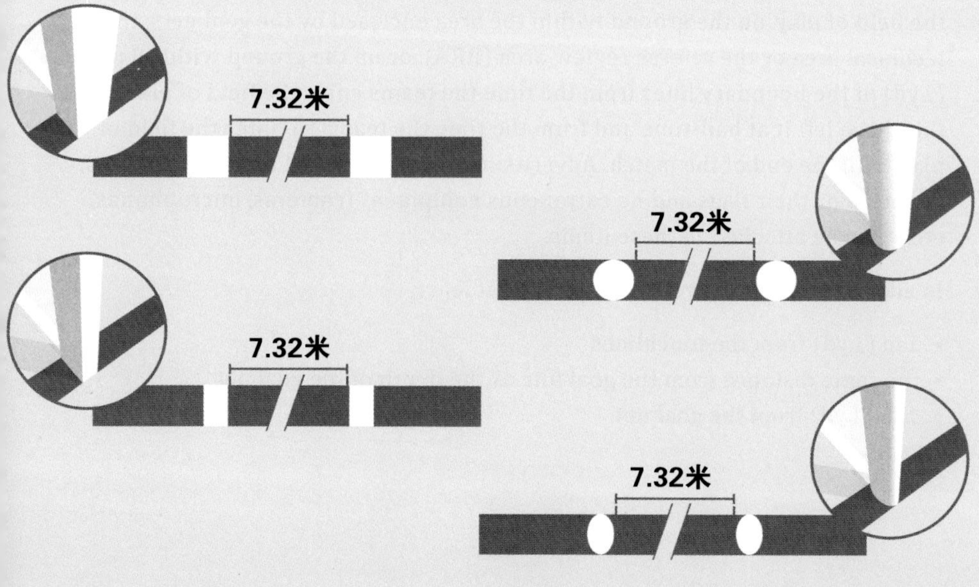

Principles of GLT

GLT applies solely to the goal line and is only used to determine whether a goal has been scored.

The indication of whether a goal has been scored must be immediate and automatically confirmed within one second by the GLT system only to the match officials (via the referee's watch, by vibration and visual signal); it may also be sent to the video operation room (VOR).

Requirements and specifications of GLT

If GLT is used in competition matches, the competition organisers must ensure that the system (including any potentially permitted modifications to the goal frame or technology in the ball) meets the requirements of the FIFA Quality Programme for GLT.

Where GLT is used, the referee must test the technology's functionality before the match as set out in the Testing Manual. If the technology does not function in accordance with the Testing Manual, the referee must not use the GLT system and must report this to the appropriate authorities.

12. Commercial advertising

No form of commercial advertising, whether real or virtual, is permitted on the field of play, on the ground within the area enclosed by the goal nets, the technical area or the referee review area (RRA), or on the ground within 1 m (1 yd) of the boundary lines from the time the teams enter the field of play until they have left it at half-time and from the time the teams re-enter the field of play until the end of the match. Advertising is not permitted on the goals, nets, flagposts or their flags and no extraneous equipment (cameras, microphones, etc.) may be attached to these items.

In addition, upright advertising must be at least:

- 1 m (1 yd) from the touchlines
- the same distance from the goal line as the depth of the goal net
- 1 m (1 yd) from the goal net

球门线技术原则

球门线技术仅用于在球门线上判定进球与否。

有关进球与否的提示信号，必须在1秒钟内由球门线技术系统即时自动确认，该信息仅可传送给比赛官员（通过裁判员手表的震动和可视信号）；同时也可以发送至视频操作室。

球门线技术规定及要求

如果在比赛中使用球门线技术，竞赛组织方必须确保该系统（包括有可能对球门框架进行的任何改造、比赛用球的任何科技成分等）符合《国际足联品质计划——球门线技术》的相关要求。

若要使用球门线技术，裁判员必须在比赛前依照测试手册对其功能性进行测试。如果该技术未能达到测试手册要求的功能，则裁判员不得使用该球门线技术系统，且必须向相关机构报告。

12. 商业广告

从球队进入比赛场地起至上半场结束离开，下半场重新进入比赛场地至比赛结束，任何形式的商业广告，无论是实体的还是虚拟的，都不允许出现在比赛场地内、球门网围合区域内的地面上、技术区域、裁判员回看分析区域，以及场地边界线外1米以内的地面上。同样，广告也不得出现在球门、球门网、旗杆或旗杆的旗帜上，也不可将外部设备（如照相机、麦克风等）附着在这些场地器材上。

此外，直立的广告必须：

- 距离边线至少1米（1码）。
- 距离球门线的距离至少等同于球门网的纵深。
- 距球门网至少1米（1码）。

13. Logos and emblems

The reproduction, whether real or virtual, of representative logos or emblems of FIFA, confederations, national football associations, competitions, clubs or other bodies is forbidden on the field of play, the goal nets and the areas they enclose, the goals, and the flagposts during playing time. They are permitted on the flags on the flagposts.

14. Video assistant referees (VARs)

In matches using VARs there must be a video operation room (VOR) and at least one referee review area (RRA).

Video operation room (VOR)

The VOR is where the video assistant referee (VAR), assistant VAR (AVAR) and replay operator (RO) work; it may be in/close to the stadium or at a more distant location. Only authorised persons are permitted to enter the VOR or communicate with the VAR, AVAR and RO during the match.

A player, substitute, substituted player or team official who enters the VOR will be sent off.

Referee review area (RRA)

In matches using VARs there must be at least one RRA where the referee undertakes an 'on-field review' (OFR). The RRA must be:

- in a visible location outside the field of play
- clearly marked

A player, substitute, substituted player or team official who enters the RRA will be cautioned.

13. 标志和图案

在比赛进行期间，国际足联、洲际足球联合会、国家足球协会、竞赛方、俱乐部，以及其他机构的代表性标志或图案的复制品，无论是实体还是虚拟形式，都禁止出现在比赛场地内、球门网及其围合区域、球门和旗杆上，但可出现在旗杆的旗帜上。

14. 视频助理裁判（VARs）

在使用视频助理裁判的比赛中，必须具备一个视频操作室以及至少一个裁判员回看分析区域。

视频操作室（VOR）

视频助理裁判员、助理视频助理裁判员以及回放操作员在视频操作室内工作；视频操作室可设在体育场内/附近或更远的地点。只有经授权的人员可在比赛过程中进入视频操作室或与视频助理裁判员、助理视频助理裁判员或回放操作员联络。

进入视频操作室的场上队员、替补队员、已替换下场的队员或球队官员，将被罚令出场。

裁判员回看分析区域（RRA）

在使用视频助理裁判员的比赛中，必须具备至少一个裁判员回看分析区域，以便裁判员执行“在场回看分析”。裁判员回看分析区域必须：

- 处于比赛场地外，并且可见。
- 清晰标注。

进入裁判员回看分析区域的场上队员、替补队员、已替换下场的队员或球队官员，将被警告。

02. The Ball

1. Qualities and measurements

All balls must be:

- spherical
- made of suitable material
- of a circumference of between 68 cm (27 ins) and 70 cm (28 ins)
- between 410 g (14 oz) and 450 g (16 oz) in weight at the start of the match
- of a pressure equal to 0.6–1.1 atmosphere (600–1,100 g/cm^2) at sea level (8.5 lbs/sq in–15.6 lbs/sq in)

All balls used in matches played in an official competition organised under the auspices of FIFA or confederations must meet the requirements and bear one of the marks of the FIFA Quality Programme for Footballs.

Each mark indicates that the ball has been officially tested and meets the specific technical requirements for that mark which are additional to the minimum specifications stipulated in Law 2 and must be approved by The IFAB.

National FA competitions may require the use of balls bearing one of these marks.

In matches played in an official competition organised under the auspices of FIFA, confederations or national FAs, no form of commercial advertising is permitted on the ball, except for the logo/emblem of the competition, the competition organiser and the authorised manufacturer's trademark. The competition regulations may restrict the size and number of such markings.

第二章　球

1. 质量与测量

所有比赛用球必须：

- 是球形。
- 由合适的材料制成。
- 周长为68厘米（27英寸）至70厘米（28英寸）。
- 重量在比赛开始时为410克（14盎司）至450克（16盎司）。
- 气压处于0.6～1.1个海平面（标准）大气压力（600～1100克/平方厘米、8.5～15.6磅/平方英寸）。

由国际足联、洲际联合会主办的正式赛事中，使用的所有比赛用球必须达到符合《国际足联品质计划——足球》的要求，并印有相关标志。

印有这些标志即表明该球已通过官方测试，符合与标志相对应的具体技术规定。这些标志是本章对比赛用球最低要求的补充，其使用也必须得到国际足球理事会批准。

国家足球协会的赛事可以要求使用印有这些标志之一的比赛用球。

在由国际足联、洲际联合会或国家足球协会主办的正式比赛中，除赛事标志和图案、赛事组织方和授权制造商商标外，任何形式的商业广告均不允许出现在比赛用球上。竞赛规程可限定这些标识的大小和数量。

2. Replacement of a defective ball

If the ball becomes defective:

- play is stopped and
- restarted with a dropped ball

If the ball becomes defective at a kick-off, goal kick, corner kick, free kick, penalty kick or throw-in, the restart is retaken.

If the ball becomes defective during a penalty kick or kicks from the penalty mark as it moves forward and before it touches a player, crossbar or goalposts the penalty kick is retaken.

The ball may not be changed during the match without the referee's permission.

3. Additional balls

Additional balls which meet the requirements of Law 2 may be placed around the field of play and their use is under the referee's control.

2. 坏球的更换

如果比赛用球出现破损：

- 停止比赛。
- 以坠球恢复比赛。

如果比赛用球在开球、球门球、角球、任意球、罚球点球或掷界外球时出现破损，则以重新执行的方式恢复比赛。

如果比赛用球在罚球点球或罚球点球决胜期间，在被踢出并向前移动后，触及队员、横梁或球门柱之前出现破损，则重踢该罚球点球。

在比赛中未经裁判员许可，不得更换比赛用球。

3. 其他比赛用球

符合第二章规定的其他比赛用球可放置在比赛场地周围，在裁判员管理下使用。

03. The Players

1. Number of players

A match is played by two teams, each with a maximum of eleven players; one must be the goalkeeper. A match may not start or continue if either team has fewer than seven players.

If a team has fewer than seven players because one or more players has deliberately left the field of play, the referee is not obliged to stop play and the advantage may be played, but the match must not resume after the ball has gone out of play if a team does not have the minimum number of seven players.

If the competition rules state that all players and substitutes must be named before kick-off and a team starts a match with fewer than eleven players, only the players and substitutes named on the team list may take part in the match upon their arrival.

2. Number of substitutions

Official competitions

The number of substitutes, up to a maximum of five, which may be used in any match played in an official competition will be determined by FIFA, the confederation or the national football association except for men's and women's competitions involving the 1st teams of clubs in the top division or senior 'A' international teams, where the maximum is three substitutes.

The competition rules must state:

- how many substitutes may be named, from three to a maximum of twelve
- whether one additional substitute may be used when a match goes into extra time (whether or not the team has already used the full number of permitted substitutes)

第三章　队员

1.场上队员人数

一场比赛由两队参加，每队最多可有11名上场队员，其中1名必须为守门员。如果任何一队场上队员人数少于7人，则比赛不得开始或继续。

如果某队因1名或多名场上队员故意离开比赛场地，而造成队员人数少于7人，则裁判员不必停止比赛，可掌握有利继续比赛，但随后比赛停止时，如果某队场上队员人数仍不足7人，则比赛不得恢复。

如果竞赛规程规定，在比赛开始前必须提交所有上场队员和替补队员名单，而一队以不足11名上场队员的情况开始比赛，则只有在提交名单内的上场队员和替补队员可在到达赛场后参加比赛。

2.替换人数

正式赛事

国际足联、各洲际联合会或各国足球协会可决定在其正式赛事中可使用的替补队员人数，但最多不能超过5人次替换。涉及顶级联赛球队一队及国家队A队的男子、女子赛事最多可进行3人次替换。

竞赛规程必须明确：

- 可提名的替补队员人数，从3名到最多不超过12名。
- 如果比赛进行至加时赛，是否可以多使用一名替补队员（不论该球队是否已用完规定的换人名额）。

Other matches

In national 'A' team matches, a maximum of twelve substitutes may be named of which a maximum of six may be used.

In all other matches, a greater number of substitutes may be used provided that:

- the teams reach agreement on a maximum number
- the referee is informed before the match

If the referee is not informed, or if no agreement is reached before the match, each team is allowed a maximum of six substitutes.

Return substitutions

The use of return substitutions is only permitted in youth, veterans, disability and grassroots football, subject to the agreement of the national football association, confederation or FIFA.

3. Substitution procedure

The names of the substitutes must be given to the referee before the start of the match. Any substitute not named by this time may not take part in the match.

To replace a player with a substitute, the following must be observed:

- the referee must be informed before any substitution is made
- the player being substituted:
    - receives the referee's permission to leave the field of play, unless already off the field, and must leave by the nearest point on the boundary line unless the referee indicates that the player may leave directly and immediately at the halfway line or another point (e.g. for safety/security or injury)
    - must go immediately to the technical area or dressing room and takes no further part in the match, except where return substitutions are permitted
- if a player who is to be substituted refuses to leave, play continues

其他比赛

在国家A队之间的比赛中，每队最多可提名12名、并最多可使用6名替补队员。

其他所有比赛，遵从如下规定即可增加替换人数：

- 双方球队就替换人数上限达成一致。
- 比赛开始前告知裁判员。

如果赛前未告知裁判员、双方球队未达成一致，则每队最多可使用6名替补队员。

返场替换（已替换下场的队员重新上场比赛）

返场替换仅允许在青少年、年长人士、残障人士，以及草根足球比赛中使用，前提是得到国家足球协会、洲际联合会或国际足联许可。

3. 替换程序

替补队员名单必须在赛前向裁判员提交。任何未在此阶段提交名单的替补队员不得参加该场比赛。

替补队员替换场上队员时，必须遵从如下规定：

- 替换前必须通知裁判员。
- 被替换的队员：
  - 经裁判员许可离开比赛场地，除非其已在比赛场地外，否则必须从距离最近的边界线处离场，除非裁判员示意其可以立即从中线或其他地点离场（例如考虑到安全和受伤因素）。
  - 必须立即前往技术区域或更衣室，且除非允许返场替换，否则不得再次参加该场比赛。
- 如果被替换的队员拒绝离开比赛场地，则比赛继续。

The substitute only enters:

- during a stoppage in play
- at the halfway line
- after the player being replaced has left
- after receiving a signal from the referee

The substitution is completed when a substitute enters the field of play; from that moment, the replaced player becomes a substituted player and the substitute becomes a player and can take any restart.

All substituted players and substitutes are subject to the referee's authority whether they play or not.

4. Changing the goalkeeper

Any of the players may change places with the goalkeeper if:

- the referee is informed before the change is made
- the change is made during a stoppage in play

5. Offences and sanctions

If a named substitute starts a match instead of a named player and the referee is not informed of this change:

- the referee allows the named substitute to continue playing
- no disciplinary action may be taken against the named substitute
- the named player can become a named substitute
- the number of substitutions is not reduced
- the referee reports the incident to the appropriate authorities

If a substitution is made during the half-time interval or before extra time, the procedure must be completed before the match restarts. If the referee is not informed, the named substitute may continue to play, no disciplinary action is taken and the matter is reported to the appropriate authorities.

替补队员遵从如下规定方可进入比赛场地：

- 在比赛停止时。
- 从中线处。
- 被替换的队员已离开比赛场地。
- 在得到裁判员信号后。

当替补队员进入比赛场地，替换程序即视为完成。从此时起，被替换的队员成为已替换下场的队员，替补队员成为场上队员并可执行任一恢复比赛的程序。

所有已替换下场的队员和替补队员，无论其是否上场参赛，裁判员均可对其行使职权。

4. 更换守门员

任何场上队员都可与守门员互换位置：

- 互换位置前告知裁判员。
- 在比赛停止时互换位置。

5. 违规与处罚

如果一名被提名的替补队员在未告知裁判员的情况下，取代被提名的上场队员开始比赛：

- 裁判员允许该名替补队员继续比赛。
- 不必对该名替补队员执行纪律措施。
- 原先被提名的上场队员视为被提名的替补队员。
- 替换人数不做削减。
- 裁判员向相关机构报告此事件。

如果在中场休息或加时赛开始前要进行队员替换，替换程序必须在比赛恢复前完成。如未告知裁判员，则提名的替补队员可以继续参加比赛，不执行纪律措施，此事件应报告给相关机构。

If a player changes places with the goalkeeper without the referee's permission, the referee:

- allows play to continue
- cautions both players when the ball is next out of play but not if the change occurred during half-time (including half-time of extra time) or the period between the end of the match and the start of extra time and/or kicks from the penalty mark

For any other offences:

- the players are cautioned
- play is restarted with an indirect free kick, from the position of the ball when play was stopped

6. Players and substitutes sent off

A player who is sent off:

- before submission of the team list cannot be named on the team list in any capacity
- after being named on the team list and before kick-off may be replaced by a named substitute, who cannot be replaced; the number of substitutions the team can make is not reduced
- after the kick-off cannot be replaced

A named substitute who is sent off before or after the kick-off may not be replaced.

7. Extra persons on the field of play

The coach and other officials named on the team list (with the exception of players or substitutes) are team officials. Anyone not named on the team list as a player, substitute or team official is an outside agent.

If a team official, substitute, substituted or sent-off player or outside agent enters the field of play, the referee must:

如果一名场上队员未经裁判员允许与守门员互换位置，裁判员：

- 允许比赛继续。
- 在随后比赛停止时警告这两名队员。如果在中场休息（包括加时赛的中场休息），或比赛结束后、加时赛和 / 或罚球点球决胜开始前互换位置，则无需警告。

对于其他任何违反本章条文的情况：

- 警告相关队员。
- 在比赛停止时球所在地点，以间接任意球恢复比赛。

6. 场上队员和替补队员被罚令出场

上场队员被罚令出场：

- 在球队名单提交前被罚令出场，不得以任何身份列入球队名单内。
- 在提交球队名单后，比赛开始前被罚令出场，可由被提名的替补队员取代，替补队员名单不得增补，球队的替换人数不做削减。
- 在比赛开始后被罚令出场，不得被替换。

被提名的替补队员在比赛开始前或比赛开始后被罚令出场，替补队员名单均不得增补。

7. 比赛场地内多出的人员

列入球队名单的教练员和其他官员（上场队员和替补队员除外）视为球队官员。除球队名单内的上场队员、替补队员以及球队官员外，其他任何人员视为场外因素。

如果球队官员、替补队员、已替换下场或被罚令出场的队员，以及场外因素进入比赛场地内，裁判员必须：

- only stop play if there is interference with play
- have the person removed when play stops
- take appropriate disciplinary action

If play is stopped and the interference was by:

- a team official, substitute, substituted or sent-off player, play restarts with a direct free kick or penalty kick
- an outside agent, play restarts with a dropped ball

If a ball is going into the goal and the interference does not prevent a defending player playing the ball, the goal is awarded if the ball enters the goal (even if contact was made with the ball) unless the interference was by the attacking team.

8. Player outside the field of play

If a player who requires the referee's permission to re-enter the field of play re-enters without the referee's permission, the referee must:

- stop play (not immediately if the player does not interfere with play or a match official or if the advantage can be applied)
- caution the player for entering the field of play without permission

If the referee stops play, it must be restarted:

- with a direct free kick from the position of the interference
- with an indirect free kick from the position of the ball when play was stopped if there was no interference

A player who crosses a boundary line as part of a playing movement does not commit an offence.

• 当存在干扰比赛的情况才可停止比赛。
• 在比赛停止时，责令无关人员离开比赛场地。
• 采取相应的纪律措施。

如果比赛停止是由如下干扰造成：

• 球队官员、替补队员、已替换下场或被罚令出场的队员，则以直接任意球或罚球点球恢复比赛。
• 场外因素，则以坠球恢复比赛。

如果球将要进门时，干扰因素没有阻止防守队员处理球，随后球进门，则进球有效（即便干扰因素与球发生接触），除非干扰因素来自攻方球队。

8. 比赛场地外的队员

如果一名场上队员需经裁判员许可方可返场，但未经许可即进入比赛场地内，裁判员必须：

• 停止比赛（如果该队员未干扰比赛或比赛官员，或出现可掌握有利的情况时，不必立即停止比赛）。
• 以未经允许进入比赛场地为由警告该名队员。

如果裁判员停止比赛，比赛必须：

• 在该队员干扰比赛的地点以直接任意球恢复。
• 如果该队员没有干扰比赛，则在比赛停止时球所在的地点以间接任意球恢复。

场上队员在正常比赛移动中越过边界线，不应视为违反规则。

9. Goal scored with an extra person on the field of play

If, after a goal is scored, the referee realises, before play restarts, that an extra person was on the field of play when the goal was scored:

- the referee must disallow the goal if the extra person was:
  - a player, substitute, substituted player, sent-off player or team official of the team that scored the goal; play is restarted with a direct free kick from the position of the extra person
  - an outside agent who interfered with play unless a goal results as outlined above in 'extra persons on the field of play'; play is restarted with a dropped ball
- the referee must allow the goal if the extra person was:
  - a player, substitute, substituted player, sent-off player or team official of the team that conceded the goal
  - an outside agent who did not interfere with play

In all cases, the referee must have the extra person removed from the field of play.

If, after a goal is scored and play has restarted, the referee realises an extra person was on the field of play when the goal was scored, the goal cannot be disallowed. If the extra person is still on the field the referee must:

- stop play
- have the extra person removed
- restart with a dropped ball or free kick as appropriate

The referee must report the incident to the appropriate authorities.

10. Team captain

The team captain has no special status or privileges but has a degree of responsibility for the behaviour of the team.

9. 比赛场地内多出人员时出现进球

如果裁判员在进球后，比赛恢复前意识到进球时比赛场地内有多出的人员：

- 如果多出的人员是如下人员，裁判员必须判定进球无效：
  - 进球队一方的场上队员、替补队员、已替换下场或被罚令出场的队员及球队官员；在多出人员所处的位置以直接任意球恢复比赛。
  - 干扰了比赛的场外因素，则以坠球恢复比赛，除非进球符合本章第7条“比赛场地内多出的人员”的说明。

- 如果多出的人员是如下人员，裁判员必须判定进球有效：
  - 被进球队一方的场上队员、替补队员、已替换下场或被罚令出场的队员及球队官员。
  - 没有干扰比赛的场外因素。

无论何种情况，裁判员必须责令多出的人员离开比赛场地。

如果裁判员在出现进球，且已经恢复比赛后意识到发生进球时比赛场地内有多出的人员，则不得取消进球。如果多出的人员仍在比赛场地内，裁判员必须：

- 停止比赛。
- 责令多出的人员离开比赛场地。
- 以坠球或相应的任意球方式恢复比赛。

裁判员必须向相关机构报告此事件。

10. 球队队长

球队队长并不享有特殊身份或权力，但对球队的行为需承担一定责任。

FIFA

FIFA
9

04. The Players' Equipment

1. Safety

A player must not use equipment or wear anything that is dangerous.

All items of jewellery (necklaces, rings, bracelets, earrings, leather bands, rubber bands, etc.) are forbidden and must be removed. Using tape to cover jewellery is not permitted.

The players must be inspected before the start of the match and substitutes before they enter the field of play. If a player is wearing or using unauthorised/ dangerous equipment or jewellery, the referee must order the player to:

- remove the item
- leave the field of play at the next stoppage if the player is unable or unwilling to comply

A player who refuses to comply or wears the item again must be cautioned.

2. Compulsory equipment

The compulsory equipment of a player comprises the following separate items:

- a shirt with sleeves
- shorts
- socks – tape or any material applied or worn externally must be the same colour as that part of the sock it is applied to or covers
- shinguards – these must be made of a suitable material to provide reasonable protection and covered by the socks
- footwear

Goalkeepers may wear tracksuit bottoms.

第四章　队员装备

1. 安全性

队员不得使用或佩戴具有危险性的装备或任何物件。

禁止佩戴任何类型的珠宝首饰（项链、指环、手镯、耳坠、皮质带、橡胶带等），如有佩戴必须移除。不允许用胶带覆盖珠宝首饰。

上场队员必须在比赛开始前、替补队员则在进入比赛场地前接受检查。如果场上队员穿戴或使用了未授权/具有危险性的装备或珠宝首饰，裁判员必须令其：

- 移除相关物件。
- 如果队员暂时无法或不愿将物件摘除，则需在随后比赛停止时，离开比赛场地摘除。

拒绝摘除或再次穿戴相关物件的队员，必须对其予以警告。

2. 必要装备

场上队员的必要装备包括如下单独分开的物件：

- 有袖上衣。
- 短裤。
- 护袜——胶带或任何附着、外套的材料，其颜色必须与所附着或包裹部分的护袜颜色一致。
- 护腿板——护腿板必须由能提供一定保护的合适材料制成，由护袜完全包裹。
- 鞋子。

守门员可穿着长裤。

A player whose footwear or shinguard is lost accidentally must replace it as soon as possible and no later than when the ball next goes out of play; if before doing so the player plays the ball and/or scores a goal, the goal is awarded.

3. Colours

- The two teams must wear colours that distinguish them from each other and the match officials
- Each goalkeeper must wear colours that are distinguishable from the other players and the match officials
- If the two goalkeepers' shirts are the same colour and neither has another shirt, the referee allows the match to be played

Undershirts must be:

- a single colour which is the same colour as the main colour of the shirt sleeve

or

- a pattern/colours which exactly replicate(s) the shirt sleeve

Undershorts/tights must be the same colour as the main colour of the shorts or the lowest part of the shorts – players of the same team must wear the same colour.

4. Other equipment

Non-dangerous protective equipment, for example headgear, facemasks and knee and arm protectors made of soft, lightweight padded material is permitted as are goalkeepers' caps and sports spectacles.

Head covers

Where head covers (excluding goalkeepers' caps) are worn, they must:

- be black or the same main colour as the shirt (provided that the players of the same team wear the same colour)
- be in keeping with the professional appearance of the player's equipment
- not be attached to the shirt

意外脱落鞋子或护腿板的场上队员，必须在随后比赛停止前尽快整理好装备，如果该名队员在整理好装备前触球且 / 或射门得分，则进球有效。

3. 着装颜色

- 队员的着装颜色必须有别于对方球队和比赛官员。
- 双方守门员着装颜色必须有别于其他场上队员和比赛官员。
- 如果双方守门员的上衣颜色相同且无法更换，裁判员允许比赛进行。

上衣内衣颜色必须：

- 如果为单色，则必须与衣袖主色一致，或者
- 如果带图案，则必须与衣袖图案一致。

内衬裤/紧身裤颜色必须与短裤主色或短裤底部颜色一致——同队场上队员必须颜色统一。

4. 其他装备

可允许佩戴不具危险性的保护器具，如软性、轻质材料制成的头罩、面具、护膝和护臂，类似的还包括守门员球帽和运动眼镜等。

头巾

如需佩戴头巾（守门员球帽除外），其必须：

- 为黑色或与上衣主色一致（同队场上队员必须颜色统一）。
- 设计合乎队员装备专业形象。
- 不得与上衣相连。

- not be dangerous to the player wearing it or any other player (e.g. opening/closing mechanism around neck)
- not have any part(s) extending out from the surface (protruding elements)

Electronic communication
Players (including substitutes/substituted and sent-off players) are not permitted to wear or use any form of electronic or communication equipment (except where EPTS is allowed). The use of any form of electronic communication by team officials is permitted where it directly relates to player welfare or safety or for tactical/coaching reasons but only small, mobile, handheld equipment (e.g. microphone, headphone, earpiece, mobile phone/smartphone, smartwatch, tablet, laptop) may be used. A team official who uses unauthorised equipment or who behaves in an inappropriate manner as a result of the use of electronic or communication equipment will be sent off.

Electronic performance and tracking systems (EPTS)
Where wearable technology (WT) as part of electronic performance and tracking systems (EPTS) is used in matches played in an official competition organised under the auspices of FIFA, confederations or national football associations, the competition organiser must ensure that the technology attached to the players' equipment is not dangerous and meets the requirements for wearable EPTS under the FIFA Quality Programme for EPTS.

Where EPTS are provided by the match or competition organiser, it is the responsibility of that match or competition organiser to ensure that the information and data transmitted from EPTS to the technical area during matches played in an official competition are reliable and accurate.

The FIFA Quality Programme for EPTS supports competition organisers with the approval process of reliable and accurate electronic performance and tracking systems.

5. Slogans, statements, images and advertising
Equipment must not have any political, religious or personal slogans, statements or images. Players must not reveal undergarments that show political, religious, personal slogans, statements or images, or advertising other than the

- 不会对佩戴者个人和其他队员构成危险（如在颈部有可开合的装置）。
- 不能有任何部分凸出头巾表面（突出表面的部件）。

电子通信

不允许队员（包括替补队员、已替换下场队员和已罚令出场队员）穿戴或使用任何形式的电子或通信设备（表现跟踪电子系统除外）。允许球队官员使用任何关乎队员福祉与安全、或用于战术/指导的电子通信设备，但只能使用小巧、可移动、便携（例如麦克风、耳机、耳麦、手机/智能手机、智能手表、平板电脑、笔记本电脑等）的设备。球队官员如果使用违规设备，或使用设备方式及行为不当，将被驱逐出技术区域。

表现跟踪电子系统（EPTS）

在由国际足联、洲际联合会或国家足球协会主办的正式比赛中，可穿戴技术作为表现跟踪电子系统的一部分，竞赛组织方必须确保队员所装备的技术设备不具有危险性，且满足《国际足联品质标准——EPTS》中对于可穿戴EPTS的要求。

在正式赛事的比赛中，若竞赛组织方提供EPTS，则该系统传输至技术区域的信息与数据的可靠性和准确性由竞赛组织方负责保证。

《国际足联品质计划——EPTS》可以为竞赛组织方对于表现跟踪电子系统的可靠性和准确性的认证过程提供支持。

5. 标语、言论、图像及广告

队员装备不得带有任何政治性、宗教性、个人化的标语、言论或图像。队员不得展示内衣、裤上带有任何政治性、宗教性、个人化的标语、

manufacturer's logo. For any offence the player and/or the team will be sanctioned by the competition organiser, national football association or by FIFA.

Principles

- Law 4 applies to all equipment (including clothing) worn by players, substitutes and substituted players; its principles also apply to all team officials in the technical area
- The following are (usually) permitted:
  - the player's number, name, team crest/logo, initiative slogans/emblems promoting the game of football, respect and integrity as well as any advertising permitted by competition rules or national FA, confederation or FIFA regulations
  - the facts of a match: teams, date, competition/event, venue
- Permitted slogans, statements or images should be confined to the shirt front and/or armband
- In some cases, the slogan, statement or image might only appear on the captain's armband

Interpreting the Law

When interpreting whether a slogan, statement or image is permissible, note should be taken of Law 12 (Fouls and Misconduct), which requires the referee to take action against a player who is guilty of:

- using offensive, insulting or abusive language and/or action(s)
- acting in a provocative, derisory or inflammatory way

Any slogan, statement or image which falls into any of these categories is not permitted.

Whilst 'religious' and 'personal' are relatively easily defined, 'political' is less clear but slogans, statements or images related to the following are not permitted:

言论或图像，以及生产商标志以外的广告。任何违反规定的队员和 / 或球队将由赛事组织方、国家足球协会或国际足联处理。

原则

- 第四章的相关规定适用于场上队员、替补队员和已替换下场队员穿戴的所有装备（包括服装）；这些原则同样适用于技术区域内的所有球队官员。
- 以下内容（通常）是允许的：
  - 队员的号码、名字、球队徽章/标志、意在推广足球运动的倡议标语/图案、有关尊重与诚信精神的内容，以及国际足联、洲际联合会或国家足球协会竞赛规程中允许的任何广告。
  - 比赛信息：包括球队、日期、赛事名称、比赛地点等。
- 经许可的标语、言论及图像仅可出现在上衣正面和/或臂章位置。
- 某些情况下，标语、言论及图像仅可出现在队长袖标上。

规则解读

在判断某个标语、言论及图像是否应被允许时，需考虑第十二章（犯规与不正当行为）中的相关规定，裁判员需要对队员的如下行为采取措施：

- 使用攻击性、侮辱性或辱骂性的语言和/或行为。
- 做出挑衅、嘲讽或煽动性质的行为。

任何属于上述范畴的标语、言论及图像都是不被允许的。

宗教性质及个人性质的标语、言论及图像相对比较容易辨认，而政治性内容有时并不明确，但如果涉及下列内容，则不被允许：

- any person(s), living or dead (unless part of the official competition name)
- any local, regional, national or international political party/organisation/group, etc.
- any local, regional or national government or any of its departments, offices or functions
- any organisation which is discriminatory
- any organisation whose aims/actions are likely to offend a notable number of people
- any specific political act/event

When commemorating a significant national or international event, the sensibilities of the opposing team (including its supporters) and the general public should be carefully considered.

Competition rules may contain further restrictions/limitations, particularly in relation to the size, number and position of permitted slogans, statements and images. It is recommended that disputes relating to slogans, statements or images be resolved prior to a match/competition taking place.

6. Offences and sanctions

For any offence, play need not be stopped and the player:

- is instructed by the referee to leave the field of play to correct the equipment
- leaves when play stops, unless the equipment has already been corrected

A player who leaves the field of play to correct or change equipment must:

- have the equipment checked by a match official before being allowed to re-enter
- only re-enter with the referee's permission (which may be given during play)

A player who enters without permission must be cautioned, and if play is stopped to issue the caution, an indirect free kick is awarded from the position of the ball when play was stopped, unless there was interference, in which case a direct free kick (or penalty kick) is awarded from the position of the interference.

- 任何在世或已故的人（除非属于官方赛事名称的一部分）。
- 任何本地的、地区性的、国家性的或国际性的政党/政治组织/政治团体等。
- 任何本地的、地区性的或国家性的政府及其任何部门、机构或职能。
- 任何带有歧视性的组织。
- 任何以冒犯大量人群为目的或有此类行动的组织。
- 任何特殊政治行为/事件。

当纪念国家或国际重大事件时，必须谨慎考虑到对方球队（包括其支持者）及公众的感受。

竞赛规程可以包含进一步的规定/限制，特别是有关标语、言论及图像的尺寸、数量和位置。建议在比赛/赛事开始前解决有关标语、言论及图像的分歧。

6. 违规与处罚

无需为任何违反本章条文的行为停止比赛，违规的场上队员：

- 由裁判员引导离开比赛场地调整装备。
- 除非已经调整好装备，否则需在比赛停止时离开比赛场地。

离开比赛场地调整或更换装备的队员必须：

- 由一名比赛官员在其被许可重新进入比赛场地前检查好装备。
- 只可在裁判员许可后重新进入比赛场地（可在比赛进行中）。

未经裁判员允许进入比赛场地的队员必须予以警告，如果因警告而停止比赛，则在比赛停止时球所在地点以间接任意球恢复比赛。如果该队员干扰了比赛，则在干扰地点判罚直接任意球（或罚球点球）。

05. The Referee

1. **The authority of the referee**

   Each match is controlled by a referee who has full authority to enforce the Laws of the Game in connection with the match.

2. **Decisions of the referee**

   Decisions will be made to the best of the referee's ability according to the Laws of the Game and the 'spirit of the game' and will be based on the opinion of the referee, who has the discretion to take appropriate action within the framework of the Laws of the Game.

   The decisions of the referee regarding facts connected with play, including whether or not a goal is scored and the result of the match, are final. The decisions of the referee, and all other match officials, must always be respected.

   The referee may not change a restart decision on realising that it is incorrect or on the advice of another match official if play has restarted or the referee has signalled the end of the first or second half (including extra time) and left the field of play or abandoned the match. However, if at the end of the half, the referee leaves the field of play to go to the referee review area (RRA) or to instruct the players to return to the field of play, this does not prevent a decision being changed for an incident which occurred before the end of the half.

   Except as outlined in Law 12.3 and the VAR protocol, a disciplinary sanction may only be issued after play has restarted if another match official had identified and attempted to communicate the offence to the referee before play restarted; the restart associated with the sanction does not apply.

   If a referee is incapacitated, play may continue under the supervision of the other match officials until the ball is next out of play.

第五章　裁判员

1. 裁判员的职权

每场比赛由一名裁判员掌控。裁判员拥有全部权力去执行与比赛相关的竞赛规则。

2. 裁判员的决定

裁判员依据足球竞赛规则和“足球比赛精神”，尽自身最大能力,在规则框架内酌情考量，做出自己认为最合适的决定。

裁判员根据与比赛相关的事实所做出的决定，包括进球与否以及比赛的结果，都是最终的决定。必须无条件地尊重裁判员及其他所有比赛官员的决定。

如果裁判员本人，或经其他比赛官员建议后意识到恢复比赛的方式的决定发生错误，而比赛已经恢复，或裁判员已经示意上下半场结束（包括加时赛）并离开比赛场地，或已经中止了比赛，则不可更改该决定。但如果在某半场比赛结束时，裁判员离开比赛场地前往裁判员回看分析区域，或要求队员回到比赛场地，则针对该半场比赛结束前发生的事件所做出的判罚决定仍可以更改。

除规则第十二章第3条以及视频助理裁判操作规范所列的相关情形外，仅当比赛恢复前，其他比赛官员已经识别出了违规行为，并在已经尝试与裁判员沟通的情况下，才可以在比赛已经恢复后实施纪律处罚，且不执行该纪律处罚所对应的比赛恢复方式。

如果裁判员无法继续执法，比赛可在其他比赛官员的监管下继续进行，直到随后比赛停止。

3. **Powers and duties**

The referee:

- enforces the Laws of the Game
- controls the match in cooperation with the other match officials
- acts as timekeeper, keeps a record of the match and provides the appropriate authorities with a match report, including information on disciplinary action and any other incidents that occurred before, during or after the match
- supervises and/or indicates the restart of play

Advantage

- allows play to continue when an offence occurs and the non-offending team will benefit from the advantage, and penalises the offence if the anticipated advantage does not ensue at that time or within a few seconds

Disciplinary action

- punishes the more serious offence, in terms of sanction, restart, physical severity and tactical impact, when more than one offence occurs at the same time
- takes disciplinary action against players guilty of cautionable and sending-off offences
- has the authority to take disciplinary action from entering the field of play for the pre-match inspection until leaving the field of play after the match ends (including kicks from the penalty mark). If, before entering the field of play at the start of the match, a player commits a sending-off offence, the referee has the authority to prevent the player taking part in the match (see Law 3.6); the referee will report any other misconduct
- has the power to show yellow or red cards and, where competition rules permit, temporarily dismiss a player, from entering the field of play at the start of the match until after the match has ended, including during the half-time interval, extra time and kicks from the penalty mark
- takes action against team officials who fail to act in a responsible manner and warns or shows a yellow card for a caution or a red card for a sending-off from the field of play and its immediate surrounds, including the technical area; if the offender cannot be identified, the senior coach present

3. 权力和职责

裁判员：

- 执行足球竞赛规则。
- 与其他比赛官员协作管理比赛。
- 记录比赛时间、比赛成绩、并向相关机构提交比赛报告，报告内容包括赛前、赛中、赛后发生的纪律处罚信息及任何其他事件。
- 监管和 / 或示意比赛恢复。

有利

- 当犯规或违规情况发生时，未犯规或违规的一队能从有利原则中获益，则允许比赛继续。如果预期的有利没有在那一时刻或随后几秒内出现，则判罚最初的犯规或违规。

纪律措施

- 当多种犯规同时发生时，从纪律处罚、比赛恢复方式、身体接触程度和战术影响等方面考量，判罚相对严重的犯规。
- 对应被警告和罚令出场的队员执行纪律措施。
- 从进入比赛场地开始赛前检查直至比赛结束（包括罚球点球决胜）离开比赛场地，裁判员均有权执行纪律措施。如果在开赛进入场地前，一名上场队员犯有可被罚令出场的犯规，裁判员有权阻止其参加该场比赛（详见第三章第6条），并将任何其他不正当行为上报。
- 从开赛前进入比赛场地直至比赛结束，包括中场休息、加时赛和罚球点球决胜期间，裁判员都有权出示红黄牌，以及在竞赛规程允许下，将队员暂时罚离。
- 对对自己行为不负责任的球队官员进行劝诫，或向其出示黄牌警告，或出示红牌将其驱逐出比赛场地及周边，包括技术区域。如果违规人员无法被辨别确认，则该球队技术区域内最高职务的教练员将接受此纪律措施。球队医护人员犯有可罚令出场的违规行为时，如该队无其他医护人员可用，则该医护人员可以留下，并在队员需要治疗时执行工作。

in the technical area will receive the sanction. A medical team official who commits a sending-off offence may remain if the team has no other medical person available, and act if a player needs medical attention

- acts on the advice of other match officials regarding incidents that the referee has not seen

Injuries

- allows play to continue until the ball is out of play if a player is only slightly injured
- stops play if a player is seriously injured and ensures that the player is removed from the field of play. An injured player may not be treated on the field of play and may only re-enter after play has restarted; if the ball is in play, re-entry must be from the touchline but if the ball is out of play, it may be from any boundary line. Exceptions to the requirement to leave the field of play are only when:
    - a goalkeeper is injured
    - a goalkeeper and an outfield player have collided and need attention
    - players from the same team have collided and need attention
    - a severe injury has occurred
    - a player is injured as the result of a physical offence for which the opponent is cautioned or sent off (e.g. reckless or serious foul challenge), if the assessment/treatment is completed quickly
    - a penalty kick has been awarded and the injured player will be the kicker
- ensures that any player bleeding leaves the field of play. The player may only re-enter on receiving a signal from the referee, who must be satisfied that the bleeding has stopped and there is no blood on the equipment
- if the referee has authorised the doctors and/or stretcher bearers to enter the field of play the player must leave on a stretcher or on foot. A player who does not comply must be cautioned for unsporting behaviour
- if the referee has decided to caution or send off a player who is injured and has to leave the field of play for treatment, the card must be shown before the player leaves
- if play has not been stopped for another reason, or if an injury suffered by a player is not the result of an offence, play is restarted with a dropped ball

- 对于自己未看到的情况，根据其他比赛官员的建议做出判罚决定。

受伤

- 如果队员仅是轻微受伤，则允许比赛继续直至比赛停止。
- 如果队员严重受伤，则停止比赛，确保受伤队员离开比赛场地。受伤队员不可在比赛场地内接受治疗，在比赛恢复后才可重新进入比赛场地；如果比赛在进行中，受伤队员必须从边线处入场；比赛停止时，则可从任一边界线入场。当发生如下情况时，不必遵循离场治疗的规定：

  - 守门员受伤时。
  - 守门员与其他队员发生碰撞，需要引起关注时。
  - 同队队员发生碰撞，需要引起关注时。
  - 出现严重受伤时。
  - 场上队员因遭受对方队员有身体接触，且可被警告或罚令出场的犯规（如鲁莽或严重犯规性质的抢截）而受伤，其伤情能够在短时间完成评估 / 得到治疗时。
  - 裁判员判罚了罚球点球，且罚球点球将由受伤的队员主罚时。

- 确保任何流血的队员离开比赛场地。必须在其流血已被止住、装备没有血迹的情况下，经裁判员示意后，才可重新进入比赛场地。
- 如果裁判员已经指示医生和 / 或担架手进入比赛场地，受伤队员必须在担架上或自行离开比赛场地。未遵从该条文的受伤队员必须以非体育行为予以警告。
- 如果裁判员已经决定要对需要离场接受治疗的受伤队员予以警告或罚令出场，必须在其离场前出示红黄牌。
- 如果不是因为类似原因而暂停比赛，或队员受伤并不是因违反竞赛规则造成的，则以坠球恢复比赛。

Outside interference

- stops, suspends or abandons the match for any offences or because of outside interference e.g. if:
  - the floodlights are inadequate
  - an object thrown by a spectator hits a match official, a player or team official, the referee may allow the match to continue, or stop, suspend or abandon it depending on the severity of the incident
  - a spectator blows a whistle which interferes with play – play is stopped and restarted with a dropped ball
  - an extra ball, other object or animal enters the field of play during the match, the referee must:
    - stop play (and restart with a dropped ball) only if it interferes with play – unless the ball is going into the goal and the interference does not prevent a defending player playing the ball; the goal is awarded if the ball enters the goal (even if contact was made with the ball) unless the interference was by the attacking team
    - allow play to continue if it does not interfere with play and have it removed at the earliest possible opportunity
- allows no unauthorised persons to enter the field of play

4. Video assistant referee (VAR)

The use of video assistant referees (VARs) is only permitted where the match/competition organiser has fulfilled all Implementation Assistance and Approval Programme (IAAP) requirements as set out in FIFA's IAAP documents, and has received written permission from FIFA.

The referee may be assisted by a video assistant referee (VAR) only in the event of a 'clear and obvious error' or 'serious missed incident' in relation to:

- goal/no goal
- penalty/no penalty
- direct red card (not second caution)
- mistaken identity when the referee cautions or sends off the wrong player of the offending team

场外干扰

- 裁判员可就任何违反规则的情况或场外干扰等原因暂停、中断或中止比赛，如：

  - 比赛场地照明灯光不足。
  - 观众掷入的物品击中比赛官员、参赛队员或球队官员，裁判员就事件的严重程度决定继续、暂停、中断或中止比赛。
  - 观众鸣哨干扰比赛——裁判员停止比赛，随后以坠球恢复比赛。
  - 比赛进行中，多余的球、其他物品或动物出现在场内，裁判员必须：
    > 只有当其干扰了比赛，裁判员才停止比赛（随后以坠球恢复比赛），除非球将要进门，干扰因素没有阻止防守队员处理球，且随后球进门，则视为进球有效（即便干扰因素与球发生接触），除非干扰因素来自攻方球队。
    > 如果其未干扰比赛，则裁判员允许比赛继续，并尽早将其移出比赛场地。
- 未经授权的人员不得进入比赛场地。

4. 视频助理裁判（VAR）

只有当比赛/竞赛方完全满足了视频助理裁判协助实施和审核项目（IAAP）的要求（国际足联IAAP文件所述内容），且得到国际足联书面许可后，方可使用视频助理裁判。

仅当裁判员在有关以下各类事件的判罚存在“清晰而明显的错误”或“遗漏的严重事件”时，视频助理裁判员方可进行协助：

- 进球/未进球。
- 罚球点球/不是罚球点球。
- 直接红牌（不包括第二次警告）。
- 裁判员对违规球队执行警告或罚令出场时出现处罚对象错误。

The assistance from the video assistant referee (VAR) will relate to using replay(s) of the incident. The referee will make the final decision which may be based solely on the information from the VAR and/or the referee reviewing the replay footage directly ('on-field review').

Except for a 'serious missed incident', the referee (and where relevant other 'on-field' match officials) must always make a decision (including a decision not to penalise a potential offence); this decision does not change unless it is a 'clear and obvious error'.

Reviews after play has restarted
If play has stopped and restarted, the referee may only undertake a 'review', and take the appropriate disciplinary sanction, for mistaken identity or for a potential sending-off offence relating to violent conduct, spitting, biting or extremely offensive, insulting and/or abusive action(s).

5. Referee's equipment

Compulsory equipment
Referees must have the following equipment:

- Whistle(s)
- Watch(es)
- Red and yellow cards
- Notebook (or other means of keeping a record of the match)

Other equipment
Referees may be permitted to use:

- Equipment for communicating with other match officials – buzzer/beep flags, headsets etc.
- EPTS or other fitness monitoring equipment

Referees and other 'on-field' match officials are prohibited from wearing jewellery or any other electronic equipment, including cameras.

视频助理裁判员通过回看事件视频获取有关信息从而提供协助。裁判员基于视频助理裁判员提供的信息和/或自己直接回看视频画面（“在场回看分析”）做出最终的决定。

除“遗漏的严重事件”情况外，裁判员（以及其他有关的“在场”比赛官员）必须先做出一个决定（此决定也包括不对潜在的违规行为进行判罚）；此决定不可更改，除非属于“清晰而明显的错误”。

在比赛已经恢复后进行回看分析

如果比赛停止，又已经恢复，则裁判员只可针对纪律处罚对象错误或涉及到的暴力行为、吐口水、咬人或极具攻击性、侮辱性和/或辱骂性的行为潜在的罚令出场事件执行“回看分析”，并执行相应的纪律处罚。

5. 裁判员的装备

必要装备

裁判员必须有如下装备：

- 一个或多个口哨。
- 一块或多块手表。
- 红黄牌。
- 记录簿（或其他可记录比赛情况的用具）。

其他装备

可允许裁判员使用：

- 与其他比赛官员进行交流的设备——振动 / 蜂鸣信号旗、耳麦等。
- 表现跟踪电子系统或其他体质监测设备。

禁止裁判员和其他“在场”比赛官员佩戴珠宝首饰或任何其他电子设备，包括摄影摄像设备。

6. Referee signals

Refer to graphics for approved referee signals.

Penalty kick

Indirect free kick

Direct free kick

6. 裁判员的示意信号

参见裁判员示意信号图例。

罚球点球

间接任意球

直接任意球

Advantage (1)

Advantage (2)

Corner kick

Goal kick

有利（1）

有利（2）

角球

球门球

Red and **yellow** card

Check: finger to ear,
other hand/arm extended

Review: "TV signal"

红牌、黄牌

查看　一手手指指耳，另一手臂张开

回看分析　电视示意信号

7. Liability of match officials

A referee or other match official is not held liable for:

- any kind of injury suffered by a player, official or spectator
- any damage to property of any kind
- any other loss suffered by any individual, club, company, association or other body, which is due or which may be due to any decision taken under the terms of the Laws of the Game or in respect of the normal procedures required to hold, play and control a match

Such decisions may include a decision:

- that the condition of the field of play or its surrounds or that the weather conditions are such as to allow or not to allow a match to take place
- to abandon a match for whatever reason
- as to the suitability of the field equipment and ball used during a match
- to stop or not to stop a match due to spectator interference or any problem in spectator areas
- to stop or not to stop play to allow an injured player to be removed from the field of play for treatment
- to require an injured player to be removed from the field of play for treatment
- to allow or not to allow a player to wear certain clothing or equipment
- where the referee has the authority, to allow or not to allow any persons (including team or stadium officials, security officers, photographers or other media representatives) to be present in the vicinity of the field of play
- any other decision taken in accordance with the Laws of the Game or in conformity with their duties under the terms of FIFA, confederation, national football association or competition rules or regulations under which the match is played

7. 比赛官员的责任

裁判员或其他比赛官员不对如下情况承担责任：

- 参赛队员、官员或观众任何形式的受伤。
- 任何形式的财产损失。
- 由于或可能由于根据竞赛规则，或按照正常程序要求做出的维持、继续和管理比赛的决定，对任何个人、俱乐部、公司、协会或其他机构所造成的任何损失。

这些决定可能包括：

- 就比赛场地及其周边环境，或天气状况决定是否进行比赛。
- 因无论何种原因决定中止比赛。
- 比赛场地器材和比赛用球是否适合在比赛中使用。
- 根据观众的影响或观众区域的任何问题，决定是否停止比赛。
- 是否停止比赛将受伤队员移至场外治疗。
- 要求受伤队员移至场外治疗。
- 是否允许队员穿着某种服装或佩戴某种设备。
- 在有权时，决定是否允许任何人员（包括球队或球场官员、安保人员、摄像师或者其他媒体代表）出现在比赛场地附近区域。
- 根据竞赛规则或国际足联、洲际联合会、国家足球协会条款，或比赛所涉及的竞赛规程履行职责时所做出的决定。

06. The Other Match Officials

Other match officials (two assistant referees, fourth official, two additional assistant referees, reserve assistant referee, video assistant referee (VAR) and at least one assistant VAR (AVAR)) may be appointed to matches. They will assist the referee in controlling the match in accordance with the Laws of the Game but the final decision will always be taken by the referee.

The referee, assistant referees, fourth official, additional assistant referees and reserve assistant referee are the 'on-field' match officials.

The VAR and AVAR are the 'video' match officials (VMOs) and assist the referee in accordance with the Laws of the Game and the VAR protocol.

The match officials operate under the direction of the referee. In the event of undue interference or improper conduct, the referee will relieve them of their duties and make a report to the appropriate authorities.

With the exception of the reserve assistant referee, the 'on-field' match officials assist the referee with offences when they have a clearer view than the referee and they must submit a report to the appropriate authorities on any serious misconduct or other incident that occurred out of the view of the referee and the other match officials. They must advise the referee and other match officials of any report being made.

The 'on-field' match officials assist the referee with inspecting the field of play, the balls and players' equipment (including if problems have been resolved) and maintaining records of time, goals, misconduct etc.

Competition rules must state clearly who replaces a match official who is unable to start or continue and any associated changes. In particular, it must be clear whether, if the referee is unable to start or continue, the fourth official or the senior assistant referee or senior additional assistant referee takes over.

第六章　其他比赛官员

可选派其他比赛官员（两名助理裁判员、一名第四官员、两名附加助理裁判员、候补助理裁判员、视频助理裁判员，以及至少一名助理视频助理裁判员）执法比赛。他们根据竞赛规则协助裁判员管理比赛，但最终决定必须由裁判员做出。

裁判员、助理裁判员、第四官员、附加助理裁判员，以及候补助理裁判员统称为“在场”比赛官员。

视频助理裁判员和助理视频助理裁判员统称为视频比赛官员（VMOs），并依照竞赛规则及视频助理裁判操作规范协助裁判员。

比赛官员在裁判员的领导下履行各自职责。如果出现不当的干涉或行为，裁判员可解除其职权，并向相关机构提交报告。

除候补助理裁判员外，当其他“在场”比赛官员的观察角度比裁判员更好时，需提示裁判员发生的犯规和违规情况，并就裁判员或其他比赛官员视线范围外发生的任何严重不当行为或其他事件，向有关机构提交报告。在完成报告前，必须与裁判员和其他比赛官员商议。

其他“在场”比赛官员协助裁判员检查比赛场地、比赛用球及队员装备（包括再次检查相关问题是否已被解决），以及记录比赛时间、进球、不正当行为等。

竞赛规程必须明确由谁替换不能开始或继续执法的比赛官员，以及任何相应产生的更替。尤其要明确，当裁判员不能继续执法时，是由第四官员、第一助理裁判员，还是第一附加助理裁判员替换。

1. **Assistant referees**
   They indicate when:

   - the whole of the ball leaves the field of play and which team is entitled to a corner kick, goal kick or throw-in
   - a player in an offside position may be penalised
   - a substitution is requested
   - at penalty kicks, the goalkeeper moves off the goal line before the ball is kicked and if the ball crosses the line; if additional assistant referees have been appointed the assistant referee takes a position in line with the penalty mark

   The assistant referee's assistance also includes monitoring the substitution procedure.

   The assistant referee may enter the field of play to help control the 9.15 m (10 yards) distance.

2. **Fourth official**
   The fourth official's assistance also includes:

   - supervising the substitution procedure
   - checking a player's/substitute's equipment
   - the re-entry of a player following a signal/approval from the referee
   - supervising the replacement balls
   - indicating the minimum amount of additional time the referee intends to play at the end of each half (including extra time)
   - informing the referee of irresponsible behaviour by any technical area occupant

1. 助理裁判员

当出现如下情况时，给予示意：

- 球的整体离开比赛场地，应由哪一队踢角球、球门球或掷界外球。
- 处于越位位置的队员可被判罚越位。
- 申请队员替换。
- 在踢罚球点球时，守门员是否在球被踢出前离开球门线，以及球是否越过球门线。如果比赛选派附加助理裁判员，则助理裁判员的选位应在与罚球点齐平的位置上。

助理裁判员的协助也包括监管队员替换程序。

助理裁判员可进入比赛场地管理9.15米（10码）的距离。

2. 第四官员

第四官员的协助包括：

- 监管队员替换程序。
- 检查场上队员/替补队员的装备。
- 在裁判员示意/同意后让场上队员重新进入比赛场地。
- 监管用于更换使用的比赛用球。
- 在各半场（包括加时赛）结束时，展示裁判员将要补足的最短补时时间。
- 将技术区域人员的不当行为告知裁判员。

3. **Additional assistant referees**

The additional assistant referees may indicate:

- when the whole of the ball passes over the goal line, including when a goal is scored
- which team is entitled to a corner kick or goal kick
- whether, at penalty kicks, the goalkeeper moves off the goal line before the ball is kicked and if the ball crosses the line

4. **Reserve assistant referee**

The only duty of a reserve assistant referee is to replace an assistant referee or fourth official who is unable to continue.

5. **Video match officials**

A video assistant referee (VAR) is a match official who may assist the referee to make a decision using replay footage only for a 'clear and obvious error' or 'serious missed incident' relating to a goal/no goal, penalty/no penalty, direct red card (not a second caution) or a case of mistaken identity when the referee cautions or sends off the wrong player of the offending team.

An assistant video assistant referee (AVAR) is a match official who helps the VAR primarily by:

- watching the television footage while the VAR is busy with a 'check' or a 'review'
- keeping a record of VAR-related incidents and any communication or technology problems
- assisting the VAR's communication with the referee, especially communicating with the referee when the VAR is undertaking a 'check'/'review', e.g. to tell the referee to 'stop play' or 'delay the restart' etc.
- recording the time 'lost' when play is delayed for a 'check' or a 'review'
- communicating information about a VAR-related decision to relevant parties

3. 附加助理裁判员

附加助理裁判员需示意：

- 当球的整体越过球门线，包括进球得分时。
- 哪一队踢角球或球门球。
- 在踢罚球点球时，守门员是否在球被踢出前离开球门线，以及球是否越过球门线。

4. 候补助理裁判员

候补助理裁判员的唯一任务是替换不能继续执法的助理裁判员或第四官员。

5. 视频比赛官员

视频助理裁判员作为比赛官员，仅当裁判员在涉及进球/未进球、罚球点球/不是罚球点球、直接红牌（不包括第二次警告）或裁判员在对违规球队执行警告或罚令出场时出现处罚对象错误的决定中，出现“清晰而明显的错误”或“严重的遗漏事件”时，使用视频回放画面协助裁判员做出正确决定。

助理视频助理裁判员作为比赛官员，主要在以下方面协助视频助理裁判员：

- 在视频助理裁判员进行“查看”或“回看分析”时，观看电视画面。
- 记录与视频助理裁判员相关的时间以及任何沟通或技术问题。
- 协助裁判员与视频助理裁判员的沟通，特别是当视频助理裁判员执行“查看”/“回看分析”时，与裁判员沟通，例如告知裁判员需“停止比赛”或“延迟恢复比赛”等。
- 记录每次“查看”或“回看分析”造成的时间“损耗”。
- 就与视频助理裁判员相关的决定信息，与有关方面进行沟通。

6. Assistant referee signals

Refer to graphics for approved assistant referee signals.

Substitution

Free kick for **attacking team**

Free kick for **defending team**

6. 助理裁判员的信号

参见助理裁判员示意信号图例。

替换队员

攻方踢任意球

守方踢任意球

Throw-in for **attacking team**

Throw-in for **defending team**

Corner kick

Goal kick

攻方掷界外球

守方掷界外球

角球

球门球

Offside

Offside on the
near side of the field

Offside in the
middle of the field

Offside on the
far side of the field

越位

近端越位

中端越位

远端越位

7. Additional assistant referee signals

Goal
(unless the ball has very clearly passed over the goal line)

7. 附加助理裁判员的信号

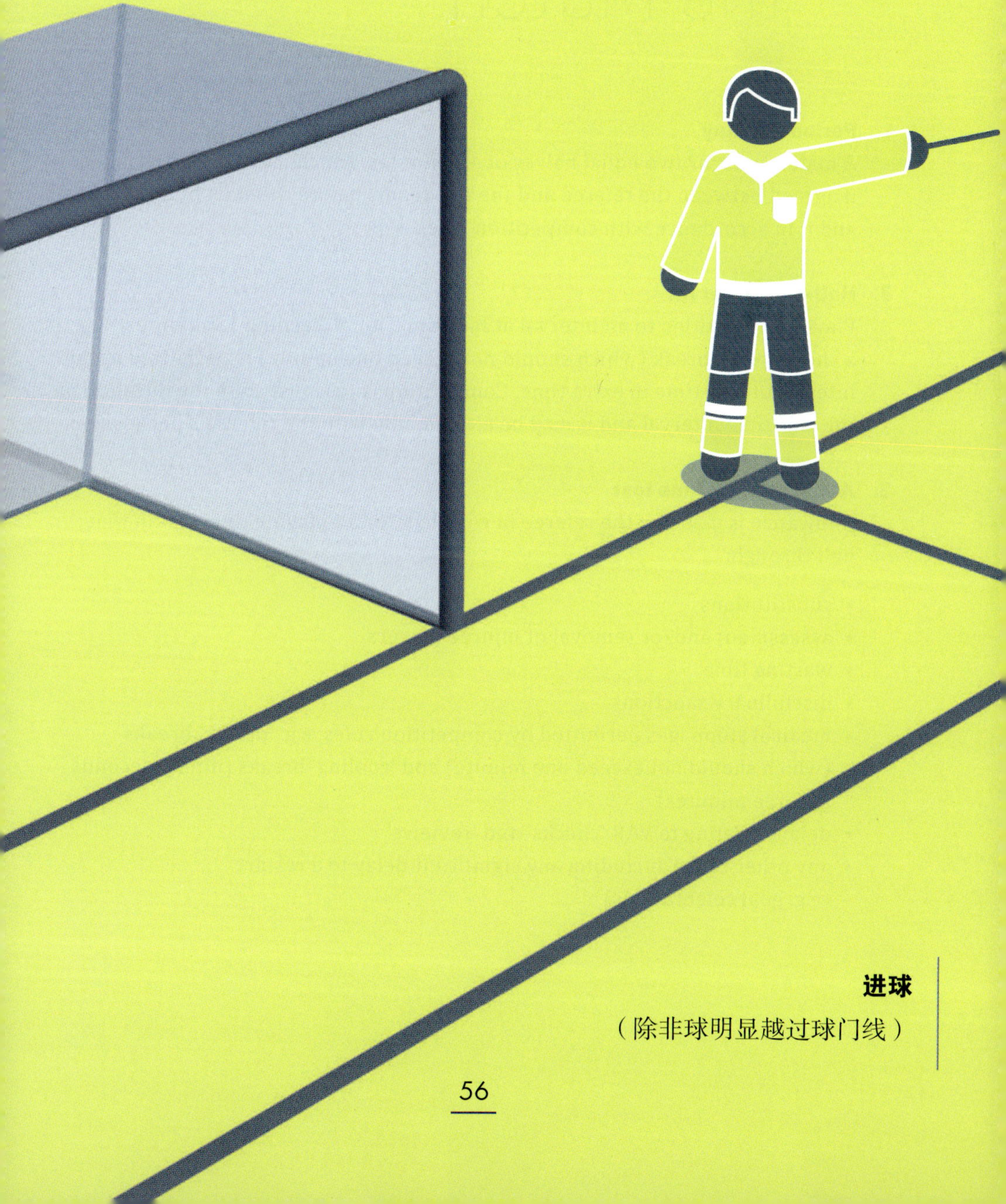

进球

（除非球明显越过球门线）

07. The Duration of the Match

1. **Periods of play**

   A match lasts for two equal halves of 45 minutes, which may only be reduced if agreed between the referee and the two teams before the start of the match and if in accordance with competition rules.

2. **Half-time interval**

   Players are entitled to an interval at half-time, not exceeding 15 minutes; a short drinks break (which should not exceed one minute) is permitted at the interval of half-time in extra time. Competition rules must state the duration of the half-time interval and it may be altered only with the referee's permission.

3. **Allowance for time lost**

   Allowance is made by the referee in each half for all playing time lost in that half through:

   - substitutions
   - assessment and/or removal of injured players
   - wasting time
   - disciplinary sanctions
   - medical stoppages permitted by competition rules, e.g. 'drinks' breaks (which should not exceed one minute) and 'cooling' breaks (ninety seconds to three minutes)
   - delays relating to VAR 'checks' and 'reviews'
   - any other cause, including any significant delay to a restart (e.g. goal celebrations)

第七章 比赛时间

1. 比赛阶段

一场比赛分为两个45分钟相同时长的半场。依照竞赛规程，在比赛开始前经裁判员和双方球队同意后，方可缩短各半场比赛时长。

2. 中场休息

队员享有中场休息的权利，休息时间不得超过15分钟。加时赛中场阶段可短暂补水（时长不超过一分钟）。竞赛规程必须明确中场休息的时长，在经裁判员许可的情况下方可调整中场休息时长。

3. 对损耗时间的补足

裁判员对每半场所有因如下情况而损耗的比赛时间予以补足：

- 队员替换。
- 对受伤队员的伤情评估和/或将其移出比赛场地。
- 浪费的时间。
- 纪律处罚。
- 竞赛规程允许的医疗暂停。例如“补水”暂停（不超过1分钟）和“降温”暂停（90秒至3分钟）。
- 与视频助理裁判员“查看”及“回看分析”有关的延误。
- 任何其他原因，包括任何明显延误比赛恢复的情况（如庆祝进球）。

The fourth official indicates the minimum additional time decided by the referee at the end of the final minute of each half. The additional time may be increased by the referee but not reduced.

The referee must not compensate for a timekeeping error during the first half by changing the length of the second half.

4. Penalty kick

If a penalty kick has to be taken or retaken, the half is extended until the penalty kick is completed.

5. Abandoned match

An abandoned match is replayed unless the competition rules or organisers determine otherwise.

第四官员在每半场最后一分钟结束时展示裁判员决定的最短补时时间。裁判员可增加补时时间，但不得减少。

裁判员不得因上半场计时失误而改变下半场的比赛时长。

4. 罚球点球

如需执行罚球点球或重踢罚球点球，应延长该半场时长直至罚球点球程序完成。

5. 中止的比赛

除非竞赛规程规定，或主办方另有决议，否则中止的比赛需进行重赛。

FIFA
REFEREE
2021
FIFA
REFEREE
2021
44
hummel

FIFA
REFEREE
2021
FIFA
REFEREE
2021
44
hummel

08. The Start and Restart of Play

A kick-off starts both halves of a match, both halves of extra time and restarts play after a goal has been scored. Free kicks (direct or indirect), penalty kicks, throw-ins, goal kicks and corner kicks are other restarts (see Laws 13–17). A dropped ball is the restart when the referee stops play and the Law does not require one of the above restarts.

If an offence occurs when the ball is not in play, this does not change how play is restarted.

1. Kick-off

Procedure

- the team that wins the toss of a coin decides which goal to attack in the first half or to take the kick-off
- depending on the above, their opponents take the kick-off or decide which goal to attack in the first half
- the team that decided which goal to attack in the first half takes the kick-off to start the second half
- for the second half, the teams change ends and attack the opposite goals
- after a team scores a goal, the kick-off is taken by their opponents

For every kick-off:

- all players, except the player taking the kick-off, must be in their own half of the field of play
- the opponents of the team taking the kick-off must be at least 9.15 m (10 yds) from the ball until it is in play
- the ball must be stationary on the centre mark
- the referee gives a signal
- the ball is in play when it is kicked and clearly moves

第八章　比赛开始与恢复

一场比赛各半场、加时赛各半场、进球后均以开球恢复比赛。任意球（直接或间接任意球）、罚球点球、掷界外球、球门球和角球是其他恢复比赛的方式（详见规则第十三章至第十七章）。当裁判员暂停比赛，而规则未明确以上述任何一种方式恢复比赛时，以坠球恢复比赛。

比赛停止时发生的违规违例行为，不会改变随后恢复比赛的方式。

1. 开球

程序

- 掷硬币猜中的一队决定本方上半场进攻方向，或者由本方开球。
- 根据上一条的选择结果，另一队开球，或者决定本方上半场进攻方向。
- 选择了本方上半场进攻方向的一队，在下半场开球开始比赛。
- 下半场，双方球队交换半场和进攻方向。
- 当一队进球后，由另一队开球。

所有的开球：

- 除开球队员外，所有场上队员必须处在本方半场内。
- 开球队的对方队员必须距球至少9.15米（10码）直至比赛开始。
- 球必须放定在中点上。
- 裁判员给出信号。
- 当球被踢且明显移动时，比赛即为开始。

- a goal may be scored directly against the opponents from the kick-off; if the ball directly enters the kicker's goal, a corner kick is awarded to the opponents

Offences and sanctions

If the player taking the kick-off touches the ball again before it has touched another player, an indirect free kick, or for a handball offence, a direct free kick, is awarded.

In the event of any other kick-off procedure offence, the kick-off is retaken.

2. Dropped ball

Procedure

- The ball is dropped for the defending team goalkeeper in their penalty area if, when play was stopped:
  - the ball was in the penalty area or
  - the last touch of the ball was in the penalty area
- In all other cases, the referee drops the ball for one player of the team that last touched the ball at the position where it last touched a player, an outside agent or, as outlined in Law 9.1, a match official
- All other players (of both teams) must remain at least 4 m (4.5 yds) from the ball until it is in play

The ball is in play when it touches the ground.

Offences and sanctions

The ball is dropped again if it:

- touches a player before it touches the ground
- leaves the field of play after it touches the ground, without touching a player

If a dropped ball enters the goal without touching at least two players, play is restarted with:

- a goal kick if it enters the opponents' goal
- a corner kick if it enters the team's goal

• 开球可直接射入对方球门得分；如果直接射入了本方球门，则判给对方角球。

违规与处罚

如果开球队员在其他场上队员触及球前再次触球，则判罚间接任意球，如果手球犯规，则判罚直接任意球。

对于其他任何违反开球程序的情况，应重新开球。

2. 坠球

程序

• 如果比赛被停止的时刻：

- 球处于罚球区内，或
- 比赛停止前球最后一次被触及的地点处于罚球区内。

则坠球给守方球队的守门员，坠球地点在罚球区内。

• 其他所有情况，裁判员坠球给最后触球的球队的一名场上队员。坠球地点在球最后一次被队员、场外因素或比赛官员（参照第九章第1条）触及的位置。

• 其他所有队员（包括双方队员）必须处于距离球不少于4米（4.5码）的位置，直至比赛恢复。

当球触及地面，比赛即为恢复。

违规与处罚

出现如下情况时，需重新坠球：

• 球在触及地面前被队员触及。
• 球在触及地面后，未经队员触及而离开比赛场地。

如果坠球后，球未经至少两名场上队员触及而进入球门：

• 球进入对方球门，则以球门球恢复比赛。
• 球进入本方球门，则以角球恢复比赛。

REFEREE

REFEREE
JFA
adidas

09. The Ball in and out of Play

1. **Ball out of play**

   The ball is out of play when:

   - it has wholly passed over the goal line or touchline on the ground or in the air
   - play has been stopped by the referee
   - it touches a match official, remains on the field of play and:
     - a team starts a promising attack or
     - the ball goes directly into the goal or
     - the team in possession of the ball changes

   In all these cases, play is restarted with a dropped ball.

2. **Ball in play**

   The ball is in play at all other times when it touches a match official and when it rebounds off a goalpost, crossbar or corner flagpost and remains on the field of play.

第九章　比赛进行与停止

1. 比赛停止

当出现如下情况时，比赛即为停止：

- 球的整体从地面或空中越过球门线或边线。
- 裁判员停止了比赛。
- 球接触了比赛官员后仍在比赛场地内，并且：
  - 任一队开始了一次有希望的进攻，或
  - 直接进入了球门，或
  - 控球球队发生了转换。

上述情况下，比赛以坠球恢复。

2. 比赛进行

所有其他时间，如果球接触了比赛官员，或从球门柱、横梁、角旗杆弹回并且仍在比赛场地内，均为比赛进行中。

10. Determining the Outcome of a Match

1. **Goal scored**

   A goal is scored when the whole of the ball passes over the goal line, between the goalposts and under the crossbar, provided that no offence has been committed by the team scoring the goal.

   If the goalkeeper throws the ball directly into the opponents' goal, a goal kick is awarded.

   If a referee signals a goal before the ball has passed wholly over the goal line, play is restarted with a dropped ball.

2. **Winning team**

   The team scoring the greater number of goals is the winner. If both teams score no goals or an equal number of goals, the match is drawn.

   When competition rules require a winning team after a drawn match or home-and-away tie, the only permitted procedures to determine the winning team are:

   - away goals rule
   - two equal periods of extra time not exceeding 15 minutes each
   - kicks from the penalty mark

   A combination of the above procedures may be used.

3. **Kicks from the penalty mark**

   Kicks from the penalty mark are taken after the match has ended and unless otherwise stated, the relevant Laws of the Game apply. A player who has been sent off during the match is not permitted to take part; warnings and cautions issued during the match are not carried forward into kicks from the penalty mark.

第十章　确定比赛结果

1. 进球得分

当球的整体从球门柱之间及横梁下方越过球门线，且进球队未犯规或违规时，即为进球得分。

如果守门员手抛球直接进入对方球门，则由对方踢球门球。

如果裁判员在球的整体还未越过球门线时示意进球，则以坠球恢复比赛。

2. 获胜队

进球数较多的队伍为获胜队。如果双方球队没有进球或进球数相等，则该场比赛为平局。

当竞赛规程规定一场比赛出现平局，或主客场进球数相同时必须有一方取胜，仅允许采取如下方式决定获胜队：

- 客场进球规则。
- 加时赛。加时赛上下半场时长相等且均不超过15分钟。
- 罚球点球决胜。

可将上述各方式组合使用。

3. 罚球点球决胜

在比赛结束后执行罚球点球决胜程序，除非有其他规定，否则按竞赛规则相关内容执行。在比赛中已被罚令出场的队员不得参与罚球点球决胜；在比赛中已执行的劝诫与警告，不带入罚球点球决胜阶段。

Goal
No goal
No goal
goal
line
Goal
goal
line

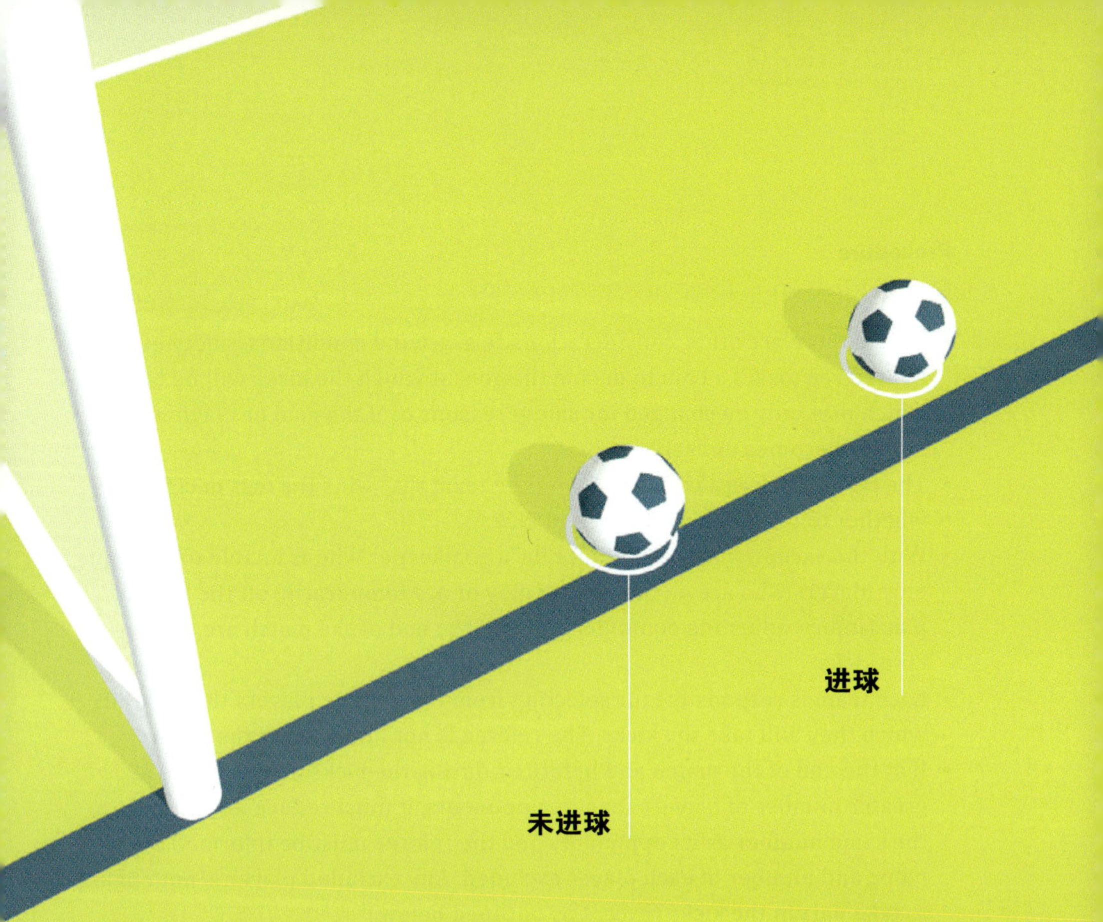
进球
未进球

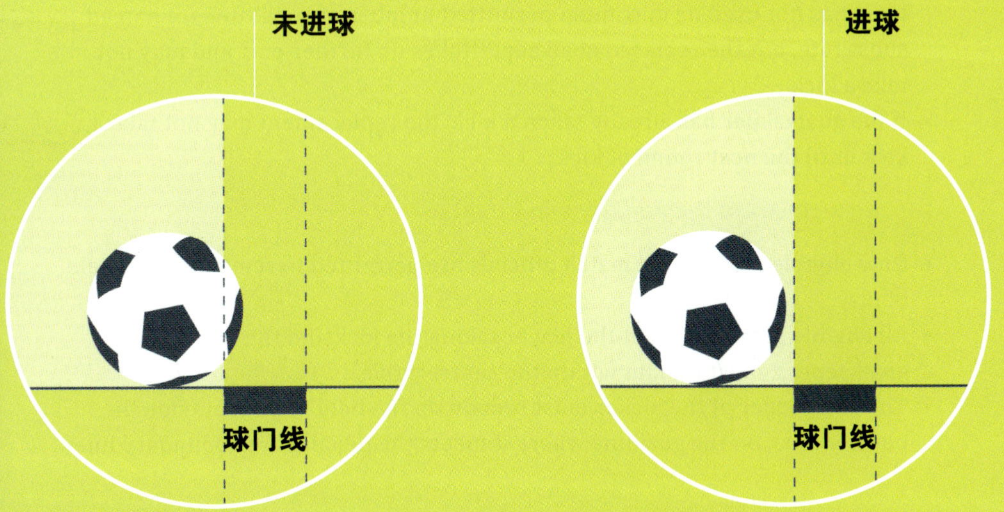
未进球
进球
球门线
球门线

Procedure

Before kicks from the penalty mark start

- Unless there are other considerations (e.g. ground conditions, safety etc.), the referee tosses a coin to decide the goal at which the kicks will be taken which may only be changed for safety reasons or if the goal or playing surface becomes unusable
- The referee tosses a coin again, and the team that wins the toss decides whether to take the first or second kick
- With the exception of a substitute for a goalkeeper who is unable to continue, only players who are on the field of play or are temporarily off the field of play (injury, adjusting equipment etc.) at the end of the match are eligible to take kicks
- Each team is responsible for selecting from the eligible players the order in which they will take the kicks. The referee is not informed of the order
- If at the end of the match and before or during the kicks one team has a greater number of players than its opponents, it must reduce its numbers to the same number as its opponents and the referee must be informed of the name and number of each player excluded. Any excluded player is not eligible to take part in the kicks (except as outlined below)
- A goalkeeper who is unable to continue before or during the kicks may be replaced by a player excluded to equalise the number of players or, if their team has not used its maximum permitted number of substitutes, a named substitute, but the replaced goalkeeper takes no further part and may not take a kick
- If the goalkeeper has already taken a kick, the replacement may not take a kick until the next round of kicks

During kicks from the penalty mark

- Only eligible players and match officials are permitted to remain on the field of play
- All eligible players, except the player taking the kick and the two goalkeepers, must remain within the centre circle
- The goalkeeper of the kicker must remain on the field of play, outside the penalty area, on the goal line where it meets the penalty area boundary line

程序

罚球点球决胜开始前

- 裁判员通过掷硬币决定罚球点球决胜使用的球门，除非有其他考虑（如场地条件、安全性等）。只有因为安全原因，或在球门、场地草皮无法正常使用的情况下，才可更换罚球点球决胜使用的球门。
- 裁判员再次掷硬币，猜中的一队决定先踢或后踢。
- 除替补队员替换无法继续比赛的守门员的情况外，只有在比赛结束时在比赛场地内，或暂时离场（受伤、调整装备等）的场上队员有资格参加罚球点球决胜。
- 各队负责安排有资格的场上队员踢罚球点球的顺序，罚球队员顺序不必告知裁判员。
- 如果在比赛结束时、罚球点球决胜开始前或进行中，一队场上队员人数多于另一队，则必须削减队员人数以与对方保持一致，且必须告知裁判员被削减的队员姓名及号码。被削减的队员不得参加罚球点球决胜（除下述情况外）。
- 在罚球点球决胜开始前或进行中，如果一队守门员无法继续比赛，则守门员可由为保持人数一致而被削减的场上队员替换，或如果该队替换名额还未用完时，由一名提名的替补队员替换。被替换的守门员不得再次参加罚球点球决胜或踢罚球点球。
- 如果守门员已经踢了罚球点球，则替换该守门员的队员在下一轮踢罚球点球之前，不得踢罚球点球。

罚球点球决胜进行中

- 只有符合资格的场上队员和比赛官员可以留在比赛场地内。
- 除踢罚球点球的队员和两名守门员外，所有符合资格的场上队员必须留在中圈内。
- 踢球队员一方的守门员必须留在比赛场地内、在罚球区外球门线与罚球区线交汇的位置。

- An eligible player may change places with the goalkeeper
- The kick is completed when the ball stops moving, goes out of play or the referee stops play for any offence; the kicker may not play the ball a second time
- The referee keeps a record of the kicks
- If the goalkeeper commits an offence and, as a result, the kick is retaken, the goalkeeper is warned for the first offence and cautioned for any subsequent offence(s)
- If the kicker is penalised for an offence committed after the referee has signalled for the kick to be taken, that kick is recorded as missed and the kicker is cautioned
- If both the goalkeeper and the kicker commit an offence at the same time, the kick is recorded as missed and the kicker is cautioned

Subject to the conditions explained below, both teams take five kicks

- The kicks are taken alternately by the teams
- Each kick is taken by a different player, and all eligible players must take a kick before any player can take a second kick
- If, before both teams have taken five kicks, one has scored more goals than the other could score, even if it were to complete its five kicks, no more kicks are taken
- If, after both teams have taken five kicks, the scores are level, kicks continue until one team has scored a goal more than the other from the same number of kicks
- The above principle continues for any subsequent sequence of kicks but a team may change the order of kickers
- Kicks from the penalty mark must not be delayed for a player who leaves the field of play. The player's kick will be forfeited (not scored) if the player does not return in time to take a kick

Substitutions and sendings-off during kicks from the penalty mark

- A player, substitute or substituted player may be cautioned or sent off
- A goalkeeper who is sent off must be replaced by an eligible player
- A player other than the goalkeeper who is unable to continue may not be replaced
- The referee must not abandon the match if a team is reduced to fewer than seven players

- 符合资格的场上队员可与守门员互换位置。
- 当球停止移动、离开比赛场地，或因发生任何违规的情况而裁判员停止比赛时，视为罚球完成。主罚队员不得再次触球 / 补射。
- 裁判员记录罚球点球决胜情况。
- 因守门员违规而造成重踢罚球点球时，如果守门员是首次违规，则对其实施劝诫，之后其所有违规均需实施警告。
- 裁判员示意执行罚球点球后，主罚队员违规，则警告主罚队员，此球记为罚失。
- 守门员与主罚队员同时违规，则警告该主罚队员，并记为罚失。

双方球队各踢5轮罚球点球，并遵循如下规定：

- 双方球队轮流踢球。
- 每次踢球由不同的场上队员执行，直至双方符合资格的队员均踢过一次后，同一名队员才可踢第二次。
- 在双方球队各踢完5次罚球点球前，如果一队进球数已经超过另一队罚满5次可能的进球数，则不再继续执行罚球点球决胜程序。
- 在双方球队踢完5轮罚球点球后，如果进球数相同，则继续踢球，直到出现踢完相同次数时，一队比另一队多进一球的情况为止。
- 在全部队员踢完之后接下来的踢球中都应遵从上述条款，但球队可以更换踢球队员顺序。
- 不得因一名场上队员离场而拖延罚球点球决胜。如果队员未及时返场踢罚球点球，则视为丧失本次踢球资格（射失）。

罚球点球决胜阶段的队员替换与罚令出场

- 场上队员、替补队员或已替换下场的队员均可被警告或罚令出场。
- 被罚令出场的守门员必须由一名符合资格的场上队员替换。
- 除守门员外的其他无法继续参加罚球点球决胜的场上队员不可被替换。
- 如果一队场上队员人数少于7人，裁判员不得中止比赛。

RUI PATRÍCIO
1

20
RUI PATRÍCIO
1

11. Offside

1. Offside position

It is not an offence to be in an offside position.

A player is in an offside position if:

- any part of the head, body or feet is in the opponents' half (excluding the halfway line) and
- any part of the head, body or feet is nearer to the opponents' goal line than both the ball and the second-last opponent

The hands and arms of all players, including the goalkeepers, are not considered. For the purposes of determining offside, the upper boundary of the arm is in line with the bottom of the armpit.

A player is not in an offside position if level with the:

- second-last opponent or
- last two opponents

2. Offside offence

A player in an offside position at the moment the ball is played or touched* by a team-mate is only penalised on becoming involved in active play by:

- interfering with play by playing or touching a ball passed or touched by a team-mate or
- interfering with an opponent by:
  - preventing an opponent from playing or being able to play the ball by clearly obstructing the opponent's line of vision or
  - challenging an opponent for the ball or

**The first point of contact of the 'play' or 'touch' of the ball should be used*

第十一章　越位

1. 越位位置

处于越位位置并不意味着构成越位犯规。

队员处于越位位置，如果其：

- 头、躯干或脚的任何部分处在对方半场（不包含中线），且
- 头、躯干或脚的任何部分较球和对方倒数第二名队员更接近于对方球门线。

所有队员包括守门员的手和臂部不在越位位置判定范围内。在判定越位位置时，臂部的上端边界定义为与腋窝底部齐平。

队员不处于越位位置，如果其：

- 与对方倒数第二名队员齐平或
- 与对方最后两名队员齐平。

2. 越位犯规

一名队员在同队队员传球或触球*的一瞬间处于越位位置，该队员随后以如下方式参与了实际比赛，才被判罚越位犯规：

- 在同队队员传球或触球后得球或触及球，从而干扰了比赛，或

- 干扰对方队员，包括：
  - 通过明显阻碍对方队员视线，以妨碍对方队员处理球，或影响其处理球的能力，或
  - 与对方队员争抢球，或

** 应使用传球或触球的第一接触点。*

- clearly attempting to play a ball which is close when this action impacts on an opponent or
- making an obvious action which clearly impacts on the ability of an opponent to play the ball

or

- gaining an advantage by playing the ball or interfering with an opponent when it has:
    - rebounded or been deflected off the goalpost, crossbar, match official or an opponent
    - been deliberately saved by any opponent

A player in an offside position receiving the ball from an opponent who deliberately plays the ball, including by deliberate handball, is not considered to have gained an advantage, unless it was a deliberate save by any opponent.

A 'save' is when a player stops, or attempts to stop, a ball which is going into or very close to the goal with any part of the body except the hands/arms (unless the goalkeeper within the penalty area).

In situations where:

- a player moving from, or standing in, an offside position is in the way of an opponent and interferes with the movement of the opponent towards the ball this is an offside offence if it impacts on the ability of the opponent to play or challenge for the ball; if the player moves into the way of an opponent and impedes the opponent's progress (e.g. blocks the opponent), the offence should be penalised under Law 12
- a player in an offside position is moving towards the ball with the intention of playing the ball and is fouled before playing or attempting to play the ball, or challenging an opponent for the ball, the foul is penalised as it has occurred before the offside offence
- an offence is committed against a player in an offside position who is already playing or attempting to play the ball, or challenging an opponent for the ball, the offside offence is penalised as it has occurred before the foul challenge

- 有明显的试图触及近处的来球的举动，且该举动影响了对方队员，或
- 做出影响对方队员处理球能力的明显举动。

或

- 在如下情况发生后触球或干扰对方队员，从而获得利益：
  - 球从球门柱、横梁、比赛官员或对方队员处反弹或折射过来。
  - 球从任一对方队员有意救球后而来。

处于越位位置的队员，在对方队员有意触球，其中包括故意手球之后得球，不被视为获得利益，除非对方队员属于主动救球。

“救球”是指队员用除手 / 臂以外（守门员在本方罚球区内除外）的身体任何部位，阻止或试图阻止将要进入球门或极为接近球门的球。

在如下情况中：

- 队员站在越位位置，或自越位位置移动到对方队员的行进路线中，干扰了对方队员向球的方向移动，影响了对方队员处理球或争抢球的能力时，应被判罚越位犯规。如果该队员向对方队员的行进路线中移动，阻碍了对方队员移动时（如阻挡对方队员），应按照第十二章条款判罚犯规。
- 处于越位位置的队员以控球为目的朝球的方向移动，在其触球或试图触球前，或与对方队员争抢球前被犯规，则应判罚犯规在先，该犯规发生在越位犯规之前。
- 处于越位位置的队员在已经触球或试图触球后，或已与对方队员争抢球后被犯规，则应判罚越位犯规在先，越位犯规发生在另一犯规之前。

3. No offence

There is no offside offence if a player receives the ball directly from:

- a goal kick
- a throw-in
- a corner kick

4. Offences and sanctions

If an offside offence occurs, the referee awards an indirect free kick where the offence occurred, including if it is in the player's own half of the field of play.

A defending player who leaves the field of play without the referee's permission shall be considered to be on the goal line or touchline for the purposes of offside until the next stoppage in play or until the defending team has played the ball towards the halfway line and it is outside its penalty area. If the player left the field of play deliberately, the player must be cautioned when the ball is next out of play.

An attacking player may step or stay off the field of play not to be involved in active play. If the player re-enters from the goal line and becomes involved in play before the next stoppage in play or the defending team has played the ball towards the halfway line and it is outside its penalty area, the player shall be considered to be positioned on the goal line for the purposes of offside. A player who deliberately leaves the field of play and re-enters without the referee's permission and is not penalised for offside and gains an advantage must be cautioned.

If an attacking player remains stationary between the goalposts and inside the goal as the ball enters the goal, a goal must be awarded unless the player commits an offside offence or a Law 12 offence, in which case play is restarted with an indirect or direct free kick.

3. 不存在越位犯规

如果队员直接从下列情况得球，不存在越位犯规：

- 球门球。
- 掷界外球。
- 角球。

4. 违规与处罚

如果出现越位犯规，裁判员在越位犯规发生的地点判罚间接任意球，这包括发生在越位队员的本方半场。

就越位而言，未经裁判员许可离开比赛场地的防守队员，应视为处于球门线或边线上，直到比赛停止，或防守方已将球向中线方向处理且球已在防守方罚球区外。如果一名队员故意离开比赛场地，在比赛停止时，裁判员必须警告该名队员。

攻方队员为了不卷入实际比赛可以移步至比赛场地外或留在比赛场地外。就越位而言，如果该攻方队员在随后比赛停止，或防守方已将球向中线方向处理且球已在防守方罚球区外之前，从球门线重新进入比赛场地内，并卷入实际比赛，应视其处于球门线上。未经裁判员许可故意离开比赛场地又重新回场的攻方队员，虽不被判罚越位，但从其位置获得了利益，裁判员必须警告该名队员。

如果球进门时，一名攻方队员在球门柱之间的球门内保持不动，进球必须视为有效，除非该名队员越位或违反规则第十二章条文，这种情况下，裁判员以间接或直接任意球恢复比赛。

12. Fouls and Misconduct

Direct and indirect free kicks and penalty kicks can only be awarded for offences committed when the ball is in play.

1. **Direct free kick**

A direct free kick is awarded if a player commits any of the following offences against an opponent in a manner considered by the referee to be careless, reckless or using excessive force:

- charges
- jumps at
- kicks or attempts to kick
- pushes
- strikes or attempts to strike (including head-butt)
- tackles or challenges
- trips or attempts to trip

If an offence involves contact, it is penalised by a direct free kick.

- Careless is when a player shows a lack of attention or consideration when making a challenge or acts without precaution. No disciplinary sanction is needed
- Reckless is when a player acts with disregard to the danger to, or consequences for, an opponent and must be cautioned
- Using excessive force is when a player exceeds the necessary use of force and/or endangers the safety of an opponent and must be sent off

A direct free kick is awarded if a player commits any of the following offences:

- a handball offence (except for the goalkeeper within their penalty area)

第十二章 犯规与不正当行为

只有在比赛进行中犯规或违规，才可判罚直接或间接任意球，以及罚球点球。

1. 直接任意球

如果裁判员认为，一名场上队员草率地、鲁莽地或使用过分力量对对方队员实施如下犯规，则判罚直接任意球：

- 冲撞。
- 跳向。
- 踢或企图踢。
- 推搡。
- 打或企图打（包括用头顶撞）。
- 用脚或其他部位抢截。
- 绊或企图绊。

如果是有身体接触的犯规，则判罚直接任意球。

- 草率是指队员在争抢时没有预防措施，缺乏注意力或考虑。这种情况不必给予纪律处罚。
- 鲁莽是指队员的行为没有顾及到可能对对方造成的危险或后果。这种情况下必须对队员予以警告。
- 使用过分力量是指队员使用了超出自身所需要的力量，危及了对方的安全。这种情况必须将队员罚令出场。

如果场上队员实施如下犯规时，判罚直接任意球：

- 手球犯规（守门员在本方罚球区内除外）。

- holds an opponent
- impedes an opponent with contact
- bites or spits at someone on the team lists or a match official
- throws an object at the ball, an opponent or a match official, or makes contact with the ball with a held object

See also offences in Law 3.

Handling the ball

For the purposes of determining handball offences, the upper boundary of the arm is in line with the bottom of the armpit. Not every touch of a player's hand/arm with the ball is an offence.

It is an offence if a player:

- deliberately touches the ball with their hand/arm, for example moving the hand/arm towards the ball
- touches the ball with their hand/arm when it has made their body unnaturally bigger. A player is considered to have made their body unnaturally bigger when the position of their hand/arm is not a consequence of, or justifiable by, the player's body movement for that specific situation. By having their hand/arm in such a position, the player takes a risk of their hand/arm being hit by the ball and being penalised
- scores in the opponents' goal:
  - directly from their hand/arm, even if accidental, including by the goalkeeper
  - immediately after the ball has touched their hand/arm, even if accidental

The goalkeeper has the same restrictions on handling the ball as any other player outside the penalty area. If the goalkeeper handles the ball inside their penalty area when not permitted to do so, an indirect free kick is awarded but there is no disciplinary sanction. However, if the offence is playing the ball a second time (with or without the hand/arm) after a restart before it touches another player, the goalkeeper must be sanctioned if the offence stops a promising attack or denies an opponent or the opposing team a goal or an obvious goal-scoring opportunity.

- 拉扯对方队员。
- 在身体接触的情况下阻碍对方队员移动。
- 对在比赛名单上的人员或比赛官员实施咬人或吐口水。
- 向球、对方队员或比赛官员扔掷物品，或用手中的物品触及球。

以及规则第三章涉及的其他犯规行为。

手球

在判定手球犯规时，臂部的上端边界定义为与腋窝底部齐平。队员的手/臂部触球，并非每次都是犯规。

以下行为属于手球犯规：

- 故意用手/臂部触球，例如手/臂部向球移动。
- 当手/臂部触球时，其位置使身体不自然地扩大。使身体不自然扩大，是指队员的手/臂部的位置并非此情形下其身体的动作形成的正当结果或合理位置。队员将手/臂部置于此位置，是冒了被球击中并被判罚犯规的风险。
- 球进入对方球门：
  - 队员（包括守门员）手/臂部触球后，球直接进入了对方球门，即使是意外手球。
  - 队员手/臂部触球后（即使是意外手球），立即进球得分。

在本方罚球区外，守门员和所有其他场上队员在手球上具有同等限制。如果守门员在本方罚球区内以违规方式手球，将判罚间接任意球，不执行纪律处罚。但是，如果由守门员恢复比赛后，守门员在其他队员触球前违规二次触球（不论是否使用手/臂部），而且该违规行为阻止了一次有希望的进攻，或者破坏了对方的进球或明显的进球得分机会，则必须对守门员实施相应的纪律处罚。

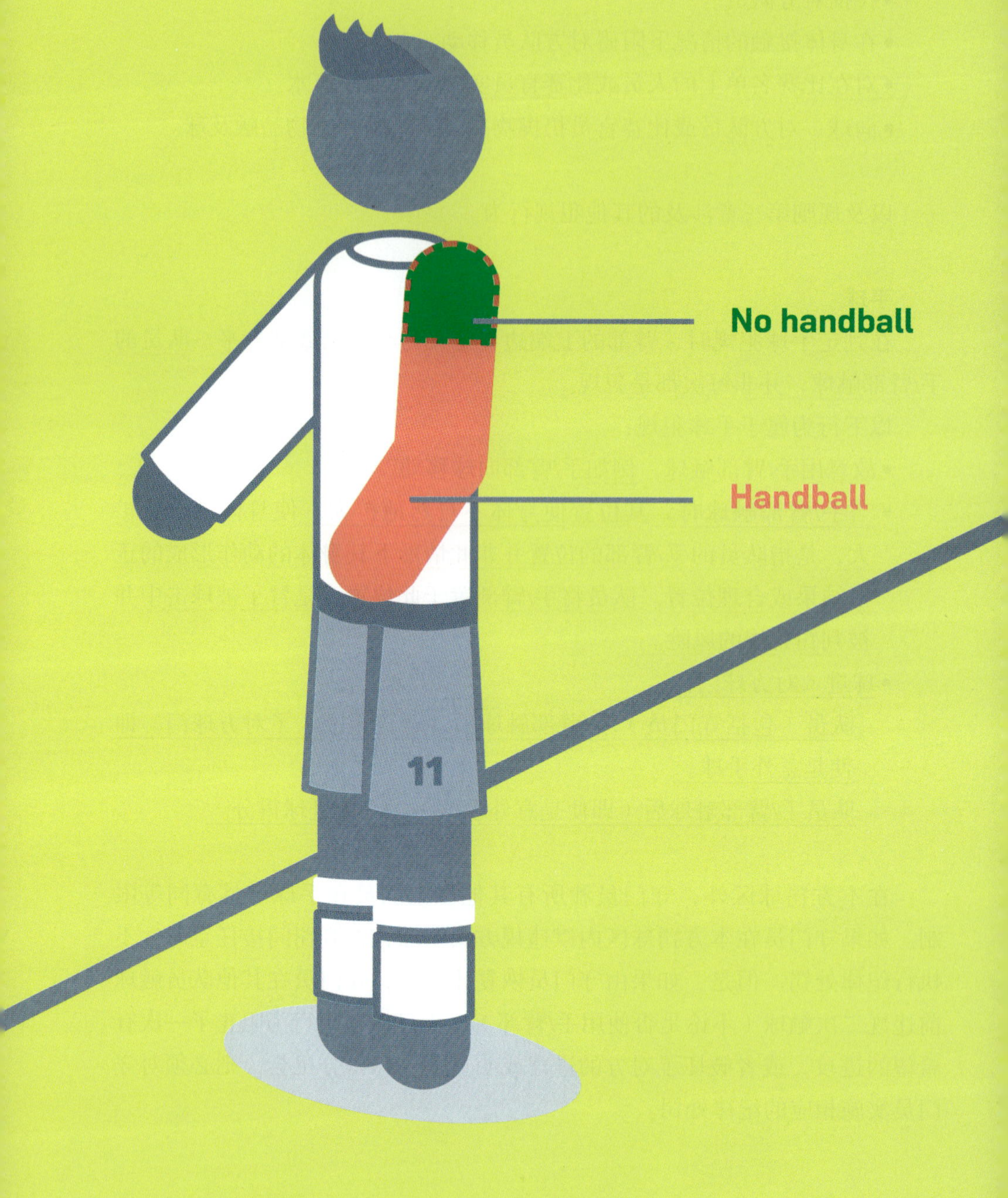
No handball
Handball

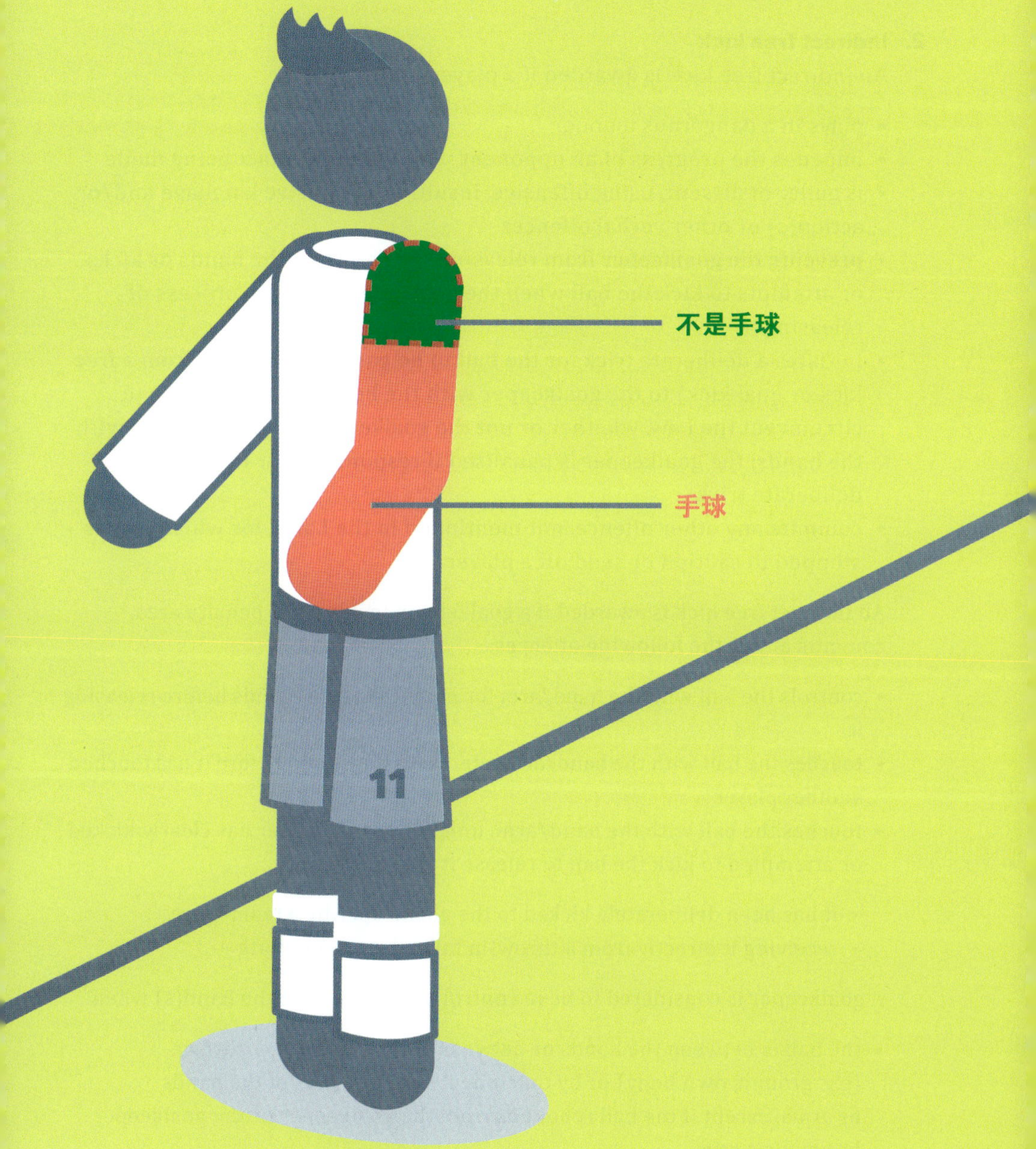
不是手球
手球
11

2. Indirect free kick

An indirect free kick is awarded if a player:

- plays in a dangerous manner
- impedes the progress of an opponent without any contact being made
- is guilty of dissent, using offensive, insulting or abusive language and/or action(s) or other verbal offences
- prevents the goalkeeper from releasing the ball from the hands or kicks or attempts to kick the ball when the goalkeeper is in the process of releasing it
- initiates a deliberate trick for the ball to be passed (including from a free kick or goal kick) to the goalkeeper with the head, chest, knee etc. to circumvent the Law, whether or not the goalkeeper touches the ball with the hands; the goalkeeper is penalised if responsible for initiating the deliberate trick
- commits any other offence, not mentioned in the Laws, for which play is stopped to caution or send off a player

An indirect free kick is awarded if a goalkeeper, inside their penalty area, commits any of the following offences:

- controls the ball with the hand/arm for more than six seconds before releasing it
- touches the ball with the hand/arm after releasing it and before it has touched another player
- touches the ball with the hand/arm, unless the goalkeeper has clearly kicked or attempted to kick the ball to release it into play, after:
    - it has been deliberately kicked to the goalkeeper by a team-mate
    - receiving it directly from a throw-in taken by a team-mate

A goalkeeper is considered to be in control of the ball with the hand(s) when:

- the ball is between the hands or between the hand and any surface (e.g. ground, own body) or by touching it with any part of the hands or arms, except if the ball rebounds from the goalkeeper or the goalkeeper has made a save

2. 间接任意球

如果一名场上队员犯有如下行为时，则判罚间接任意球：

- 以危险方式进行比赛。
- 在没有身体接触的情况下阻碍对方行进。
- 以语言表示不满，使用攻击性、侮辱性或辱骂性的语言和/或行为，或其他口头的违规行为。
- 在守门员发球过程中，阻止守门员从手中发球、踢或准备踢球。
- 故意发起施诡计用头、胸、膝等部位将球传递给守门员以逃避规则相关条款处罚的行为（包括在踢任意球或球门球时），无论守门员是否用手触球。如果该行为由守门员发起，则处罚守门员。
- 犯有规则中没有提及的，又需裁判员停止比赛予以警告或罚令出场的任何其他犯规。

如果守门员在本方罚球区内犯有如下行为时，则判罚间接任意球：

- 在发出球前，用手/臂部控制球超过6秒。
- 在发出球后、其他场上队员触球前，用手/臂部触球：
- 在下列情况之后用手/臂部触球，除非守门员已经清晰地将球踢出或试图踢出：
  - 同队队员故意将球踢给守门员。
  - 接同队队员直接掷来的界外球。

当出现下列情况时，视为守门员用手控制球：

- 球在双手之间，或手与任何表面（如地面、自己的身体）之间，以及用手或臂部的任何部分触球，除非球从守门员身上反弹出来，或守门员做出扑救的情况。

- holding the ball in the outstretched open hand
- bouncing it on the ground or throwing it in the air

A goalkeeper cannot be challenged by an opponent when in control of the ball with the hand(s).

Playing in a dangerous manner

Playing in a dangerous manner is any action that, while trying to play the ball, threatens injury to someone (including the player themself) and includes preventing a nearby opponent from playing the ball for fear of injury.

A scissors or bicycle kick is permissible provided that it is not dangerous to an opponent.

Impeding the progress of an opponent without contact

Impeding the progress of an opponent means moving into the opponent's path to obstruct, block, slow down or force a change of direction when the ball is not within playing distance of either player.

All players have a right to their position on the field of play; being in the way of an opponent is not the same as moving into the way of an opponent.

A player may shield the ball by taking a position between an opponent and the ball if the ball is within playing distance and the opponent is not held off with the arms or body. If the ball is within playing distance, the player may be fairly charged by an opponent.

3. Disciplinary action

The referee has the authority to take disciplinary action from entering the field of play for the pre-match inspection until leaving the field of play after the match ends (including kicks from the penalty mark).

If, before entering the field of play at the start of the match, a player or team official commits a sending-off offence, the referee has the authority to prevent the player or team official taking part in the match (see Law 3.6); the referee will report any other misconduct.

A player or team official who commits a cautionable or sending-off offence, either on or off the field of play, is disciplined according to the offence.

- 用伸展开的手持球。
- 向地面拍球或向空中抛球。

守门员在用手控制球的情况下，对方不得与其争抢球。

以危险方式进行比赛

以危险方式进行比赛是指在尝试争球的过程中做出的任何动作，存在对对方（包括自己）造成伤害的危险，包括使附近的对方队员因为害怕受伤而不敢争抢球。

剪刀脚和倒钩动作如果不会对对方造成危险，则允许使用。

在没有身体接触的情况下阻碍对方行进

阻碍对方行进是指当球不在双方的合理争抢范围时，移动至对方的行进路线上以阻碍、阻挡、减缓或迫使对方改变行进方向。

所有队员有权在比赛场地内选择自己的位置。已处在对方行进路线上和移动至对方行进路线上是不同的概念。

如果球在一名队员的合理争抢范围内，且其没有用臂部或身体阻拦对方队员争球，则该名队员可以在对方队员和球之间选好位置护球。如果球在双方的合理争抢范围内，队员可用合理冲撞的方式与对方争抢球。

3. 纪律措施

裁判员从进入比赛场地进行赛前检查开始，至比赛结束（包括罚球点球决胜）离开比赛场地，均有权执行纪律措施。

如果上场队员或球队官员在开赛进入比赛场地前，犯有可被罚令出场的违规行为，裁判员有权阻止该队员或球队官员参加比赛（参见第三章第6条），裁判员将就任何其他不正当行为提交报告。

一名队员或球队官员，无论是在场内还是场外，犯有可被警告或罚令出场的违规行为，均将受到相应的处罚。

The yellow card communicates a caution and the red card communicates a sending-off.

Only a player, substitute, substituted player or team official may be shown the red or yellow card.

Players, substitutes and substituted players

Delaying the restart of play to show a card

Once the referee has decided to caution or send off a player, play must not be restarted until the sanction has been administered, unless the non-offending team takes a quick free kick, has a clear goal-scoring opportunity and the referee has not started the disciplinary sanction procedure. The sanction is administered at the next stoppage; if the offence was denying the opposing team an obvious goal-scoring opportunity, the player is cautioned; if the offence interfered with or stopped a promising attack, the player is not cautioned.

Advantage

If the referee plays the advantage for an offence for which a caution/sending-off would have been issued had play been stopped, this caution/sending-off must be issued when the ball is next out of play. However, if the offence was denying the opposing team an obvious goal-scoring opportunity, the player is cautioned for unsporting behaviour; if the offence was interfering with or stopping a promising attack, the player is not cautioned.

Advantage should not be applied in situations involving serious foul play, violent conduct or a second cautionable offence unless there is a clear opportunity to score a goal. The referee must send off the player when the ball is next out of play, but if the player plays the ball or challenges/interferes with an opponent, the referee will stop play, send off the player and restart with an indirect free kick, unless the player committed a more serious offence.

If a defender starts holding an attacker outside the penalty area and continues holding inside the penalty area, the referee must award a penalty kick.

黄牌代表警告，红牌代表罚令出场。

只可对场上队员、替补队员、已替换下场的队员或球队官员出示红黄牌。

场上队员、替补队员和被替换下场的队员

因出示红黄牌而延迟恢复比赛

一旦裁判员决定对队员予以警告或罚令出场，在处罚程序执行完成前，不得恢复比赛，除非在裁判员执行纪律处罚程序之前，未违规球队快速发出任意球，并且出现清晰的进球得分机会。上述情况下，在接下来比赛停止时执行纪律处罚；如果违规行为属于破坏对方明显进球得分机会的情况，则执行警告；如果违规行为属于干扰或阻止了有希望的进攻，则不警告违规队员。

有利

如果裁判员在出现可警告或罚令出场的犯规时，没有停止比赛而掌握有利，则必须在随后比赛停止时执行该警告/罚令出场。但如果该违规行为属于破坏对方明显进球得分机会的情况，则以非体育行为警告相关队员；如果违规行为属于干扰或阻止了有希望的进攻，则不警告违规队员。

在出现严重犯规、暴力行为或可被第二次警告的犯规时不应掌握有利，除非有明显的进球机会。裁判员必须在随后比赛停止时将相关队员罚令出场，但如果该队员触球或与对方队员争抢或干扰对方队员，裁判员则停止比赛，将该队员罚令出场，并以间接任意球恢复比赛，除非该队员出现了更严重的违规。

如果防守队员在罚球区外就开始拉扯对方队员，并持续至罚球区内，裁判员必须判罚球点球。

Cautionable offences

A player is cautioned if guilty of:

- delaying the restart of play
- dissent by word or action
- entering, re-entering or deliberately leaving the field of play without the referee's permission
- failing to respect the required distance when play is restarted with a dropped ball, corner kick, free kick or throw-in
- persistent offences (no specific number or pattern of offences constitutes 'persistent')
- unsporting behaviour
- entering the referee review area (RRA)
- excessively using the 'review' (TV screen) signal

A substitute or substituted player is cautioned if guilty of:

- delaying the restart of play
- dissent by word or action
- entering or re-entering the field of play without the referee's permission
- unsporting behaviour
- entering the referee review area (RRA)
- excessively using the 'review' (TV screen) signal

Where two separate cautionable offences are committed (even in close proximity), they should result in two cautions, for example if a player enters the field of play without the required permission and commits a reckless tackle or stops a promising attack with a foul/handball, etc.

Cautions for unsporting behaviour

There are different circumstances when a player must be cautioned for unsporting behaviour, including if a player:

- attempts to deceive the referee, e.g. by feigning injury or pretending to have been fouled (simulation)
- changes places with the goalkeeper during play or without the referee's permission (see Law 3)

可警告的犯规行为

场上队员犯有如下行为时，应被警告：

- 延误比赛恢复。
- 以语言或行动表示不满。
- 未经裁判员许可进入、重新进入或故意离开比赛场地。
- 当比赛以坠球、角球、任意球或掷界外球恢复时，未退出规定距离。
- 持续违反规则（对“持续”的定义并没有明确的次数和犯规类型）。
- 非体育行为。
- 进入裁判员回看分析区域。
- 过分地做出要求回看分析（比划电视屏幕）的信号。

替补队员或已替换下场的队员犯有如下行为时，应被警告：

- 延误比赛恢复。
- 以语言或行动表示不满。
- 未经裁判员许可进入、重新进入比赛场地。
- 非体育行为。
- 进入裁判员回看分析区域。
- 过分地做出要求回看分析（比划电视屏幕）的信号。

如果出现两个独立的、可警告的犯规行为（即使发生在相距很近的时间或距离内），应进行两次警告（黄牌），例如一名队员在需要裁判员允许才可进入比赛场地的情况下，未经允许进入场地，随后实施了一次鲁莽犯规或通过犯规/手球阻止了对方有希望的进攻等。

对非体育行为的警告

在一些情况下必须以非体育行为警告相关队员，例如：

- 试图用假装受伤或假装被犯规（佯装）欺骗裁判员。
- 在比赛进行中，未经裁判员许可与守门员互换位置（详见第三章）。

- commits in a reckless manner a direct free kick offence
- handles the ball to interfere with or stop a promising attack
- commits any other offence which interferes with or stops a promising attack, except where the referee awards a penalty kick for an offence which was an attempt to play the ball
- denies an opponent an obvious goal-scoring opportunity by an offence which was an attempt to play the ball and the referee awards a penalty kick
- handles the ball in an attempt to score a goal (whether or not the attempt is successful) or in an unsuccessful attempt to prevent a goal
- makes unauthorised marks on the field of play
- plays the ball when leaving the field of play after being given permission to leave
- shows a lack of respect for the game
- initiates a deliberate trick for the ball to be passed (including from a free kick or goal kick) to the goalkeeper with the head, chest, knee etc. to circumvent the Law, whether or not the goalkeeper touches the ball with the hands; the goalkeeper is cautioned if responsible for initiating the deliberate trick
- verbally distracts an opponent during play or at a restart

Celebration of a goal

Players can celebrate when a goal is scored, but the celebration must not be excessive; choreographed celebrations are not encouraged and must not cause excessive time-wasting.

Leaving the field of play to celebrate a goal is not a cautionable offence but players should return as soon as possible.

A player must be cautioned, even if the goal is disallowed, for:

- climbing onto a perimeter fence and/or approaching the spectators in a manner which causes safety and/or security issues
- acting in a provocative, derisory or inflammatory way
- covering the head or face with a mask or other similar item
- removing the shirt or covering the head with the shirt

- 以鲁莽的方式犯有可判直接任意球的犯规。
- 通过手球的方式干扰或阻止有希望的进攻。
- 通过其他任何违规的方式干扰或阻止有希望的进攻，除非裁判员判了罚球点球而且犯规的意图是争抢球或触球。
- 在意图争抢球或触球时出现犯规，破坏对方明显进球得分机会，并被判罚球点球。
- 用手球的方式试图得分（无论进球与否）或阻止进球未果。
- 在比赛场地上制造未经许可的标记。
- 在经许可离场的过程中触球。
- 表现出对比赛缺乏尊重。
- 故意发起施诡计用头、胸、膝等部位将球传递给守门员以逃避规则相关条款处罚（包括在踢任意球或球门球时），无论守门员是否用手触球。如果该行为由守门员发起，则警告守门员。
- 在比赛进行中或比赛恢复时，用语言干扰对方队员。

庆祝进球

队员可以在进球得分后进行庆祝，但庆祝活动不得过度。不鼓励在庆祝进球时表演自编舞蹈，这种庆祝不得过度浪费时间。

离开场地庆祝进球无需予以警告，但场上队员应尽快返场。

队员必须被警告的行为（无论进球有效与否）：

- 攀爬上周边的围栏，并 / 或以可能引发安全和 / 或安保问题的方式接近观众。
- 做出挑衅、嘲讽或煽动性质的动作或表现。
- 用面具或类似器物遮住头部或面部。
- 脱去上衣或用上衣遮住头部。

Delaying the restart of play

Referees must caution players who delay the restart of play by:

- appearing to take a throw-in but suddenly leaving it to a team-mate to take
- delaying leaving the field of play when being substituted
- excessively delaying a restart
- kicking or carrying the ball away, or provoking a confrontation by deliberately touching the ball after the referee has stopped play
- taking a free kick from the wrong position to force a retake

Sending-off offences

A player, substitute or substituted player who commits any of the following offences is sent off:

- denying the opposing team a goal or an obvious goal-scoring opportunity by a handball offence (except a goalkeeper within their penalty area)
- denying a goal or an obvious goal-scoring opportunity to an opponent whose overall movement is towards the offender's goal by an offence punishable by a free kick (unless as outlined below)
- serious foul play
- biting or spitting at someone
- violent conduct
- using offensive, insulting or abusive language and/or action(s)
- receiving a second caution in the same match
- entering the video operation room (VOR)

A player, substitute or substituted player who has been sent off must leave the vicinity of the field of play and the technical area.

Denying a goal or an obvious goal-scoring opportunity

Where a player denies the opposing team a goal or an obvious goal-scoring opportunity by a handball offence, the player is sent off wherever the offence occurs.

Where a player commits an offence against an opponent within their own penalty area which denies an opponent an obvious goal-scoring opportunity and the referee awards a penalty kick, the offender is cautioned if the offence

延误比赛恢复

裁判员必须警告以下列方式延误比赛恢复的队员：

- 看似要掷界外球，但突然将球交给同队队员掷球。
- 在被替换下场时延误离场时间。
- 过度地拖延比赛恢复。
- 在裁判员停止比赛后，故意将球踢走或拿走，引发冲突。
- 在错误的地点踢任意球以造成重踢。

罚令出场的犯规

场上队员、替补队员或已替换下场的队员犯有如下行为时，应被罚令出场：

- 通过手球犯规破坏对方球队进球或明显的进球得分机会（守门员在本方罚球区内除外）。
- 通过可判罚任意球的犯规，破坏对方的进球或总体上朝犯规方球门方向移动的明显的进球得分机会（本章下述“破坏进球或明显进球得分机会”中说明的相关情况除外）。
- 严重犯规。
- 咬人或向任何人吐口水。
- 暴力行为。
- 使用攻击性、侮辱性或辱骂性的语言和/或行为。
- 在同一场比赛中得到第二次警告。
- 进入视频操作室。

被罚令出场的场上队员、替补队员或已替换下场的队员，必须离开比赛场地周边区域及技术区域。

破坏进球或明显进球得分机会

无论发生在何处，当队员用手球犯规破坏对方进球或明显进球得分机会时应被罚令出场。

当队员在本方罚球区内对对方犯规，破坏了对方明显的进球得分机会，裁判员判罚球点球。如果是在意图争抢球时造成犯规，则警告犯规队

was an attempt to play the ball; in all other circumstances (e.g. holding, pulling, pushing, no possibility to play the ball etc.) the offending player must be sent off.

A player, sent-off player, substitute or substituted player who enters the field of play without the required referee's permission and interferes with play or an opponent and denies the opposing team a goal or an obvious goal-scoring opportunity is guilty of a sending-off offence.

The following must be considered:

- distance between the offence and the goal
- general direction of the play
- likelihood of keeping or gaining control of the ball
- location and number of defenders

Serious foul play

A tackle or challenge that endangers the safety of an opponent or uses excessive force or brutality must be sanctioned as serious foul play.

Any player who lunges at an opponent in challenging for the ball from the front, from the side or from behind using one or both legs, with excessive force or endangers the safety of an opponent is guilty of serious foul play.

Violent conduct

Violent conduct is when a player uses or attempts to use excessive force or brutality against an opponent when not challenging for the ball, or against a team-mate, team official, match official, spectator or any other person, regardless of whether contact is made.

In addition, a player who, when not challenging for the ball, deliberately strikes an opponent or any other person on the head or face with the hand or arm, is guilty of violent conduct unless the force used was negligible.

Team officials

Where an offence is committed and the offender cannot be identified, the senior team coach present in the technical area will receive the sanction.

员。除此以外的所有犯规（如拉扯、拉拽、推搡、没有触球的可能性等情况），必须将犯规队员罚令出场。

场上队员、已被罚令出场的队员、替补队员或已替换下场的队员，未经裁判员许可进入比赛场地内，干扰了比赛或对方队员，并破坏对方球队进球或明显进球得分机会的行为，应视为可被罚令出场的犯规。

必须考虑如下情况：

- 犯规发生地点与球门间的距离。
- 比赛发展的大致方向。
- 控制球或得到控球权的可能性。
- 防守队员的位置和人数。

严重犯规

危及到对方队员安全或使用过分力量或野蛮方式的抢截，必须视为严重犯规加以处罚。

任何队员用单腿或双腿从对方身前、侧向或后方，使用过分力量或危及对方安全的蹬踹动作，应视为严重犯规。

暴力行为

暴力行为是指队员的目的不是争抢球，而是对对方队员或同队队员、球队官员、比赛官员、观众或任何其他人，使用或企图使用过分力量或野蛮动作，无论是否与他人发生身体接触。

除此之外，队员的目的不是争抢球，而是故意用手或臂部击打对方队员，以及任何其他人的头或面部时，应视为暴力行为，除非所使用的力量非常轻微，足以忽略。

球队官员

如果无法准确辨别是哪名球队官员违规，则该违规行为及纪律处罚将由该队技术区域内最高职位的教练员承担。

Warning

The following offences should usually result in a warning; repeated or blatant offences should result in a caution or sending-off:

- entering the field of play in a respectful/non-confrontational manner
- failing to cooperate with a match official e.g. ignoring an instruction/request from an assistant referee or the fourth official
- minor/low-level disagreement (by word or action) with a decision
- occasionally leaving the confines of the technical area without committing another offence

Caution

Caution offences include (but are not limited to):

- clearly/persistently not respecting the confines of their team's technical area
- delaying the restart of play by their team
- deliberately entering the technical area of the opposing team (non-confrontational)
- dissent by word or action including:
  - throwing/kicking drinks bottles or other objects
  - action(s) which show(s) a clear lack of respect for the match official(s) e.g. sarcastic clapping
- entering the referee review area (RRA)
- excessively/persistently gesturing for a red or yellow card
- excessively showing the "TV signal" for a VAR 'review'
- acting in a provocative or inflammatory manner
- persistent unacceptable behaviour (including repeated warning offences)
- showing a lack of respect for the game

Sending-off

Sending-off offences include (but are not limited to):

- delaying the restart of play by the opposing team e.g. holding onto the ball, kicking the ball away, obstructing the movement of a player
- deliberately leaving the technical area to:

劝诫

下列违规行为通常应进行劝诫，如果反复或过于明显地违规，则应警告或罚令出场：

- 以有礼貌/非对抗的态度进入比赛场地。
- 不配合比赛官员。例如无视助理裁判员或第四官员的指令/要求。
- 轻微/较低程度地（以语言或行动）对裁判员的决定表示异议。
- 偶尔离开技术区域，且无其他违规行为。

警告

应警告的违规行为包括（但不仅限于）：

- 清晰/持续地违反技术区域的限制。
- 延误本方球队恢复比赛。
- 故意进入对方技术区域（非对抗性地）。
- 以语言或行动表示异议，包括：
  - 扔/踢饮料瓶或其他物品。
  - 做出明显对比赛官员缺乏尊重的行为。例如讽刺性地鼓掌等。
- 进入裁判员回看分析区域。
- 过分/持续地做出出示红牌或黄牌的动作。
- 过分地做出要求回看分析（比划电视屏幕）的信号。
- 做出挑衅或煽动性的行为。
- 持续做出不可接受的行为。
- 表现出对比赛缺乏尊重。

罚令出场

应罚令出场的违规行为包括（但不仅限于）：

- 延误对方球队恢复比赛。例如持球、将球踢走、妨碍队员的移动等。
- 故意离开技术区域并且：

  - show dissent towards, or remonstrate with, a match official
  - act in a provocative or inflammatory manner

- entering the opposing technical area in an aggressive or confrontational manner
- deliberately throwing/kicking an object onto the field of play
- entering the field of play to:

  - confront a match official (including at half-time and full-time)
  - interfere with play, an opposing player or a match official

- entering the video operation room (VOR)
- physical or aggressive behaviour (including spitting or biting) towards an opposing player, substitute, team official, match official, spectator or any other person (e.g. ball boy/girl, security or competition official etc.)
- receiving a second caution in the same match
- using offensive, insulting or abusive language and/or action(s)
- using unauthorised electronic or communication equipment and/or behaving in an inappropriate manner as the result of using electronic or communication equipment
- violent conduct

Offences where an object (or the ball) is thrown

In all cases, the referee takes the appropriate disciplinary action:

- reckless – caution the offender for unsporting behaviour
- using excessive force – send off the offender for violent conduct

4. Restart of play after fouls and misconduct

If the ball is out of play, play is restarted according to the previous decision. If the ball is in play and a player commits a physical offence inside the field of play against:

- an opponent – an indirect or direct free kick or penalty kick
- a team-mate, substitute, substituted or sent-off player, team official or a match official – a direct free kick or penalty kick

All verbal offences are penalised with an indirect free kick.

- 抗议或指责比赛官员。
- 表现出挑衅或嘲讽的态度。
- 以侵略性或对抗性的态度故意进入对方技术区域。
- 故意向场内扔/踢物品。
- 进入比赛场地并且：
  - 与比赛官员进行对抗（包括在半场及全场比赛结束时）。
  - 干扰比赛、对方队员或比赛官员。
- 进入视频操作室。
- 对对方场上队员、替补队员、球队官员、比赛官员、观众或任何其他人（例如球童、安保人员或竞赛官员等）实施肢体侵犯或侵略性行为（包括吐口水或咬人）。
- 在一场比赛中受到第二次警告。
- 使用攻击性、侮辱性或辱骂性的语言和/或行为。
- 使用未经授权的电子或通信设备和/或在使用电子或通信设备时做出不当行为。
- 暴力行为。

投掷物品（或比赛用球）的违规行为

裁判员根据事件情况做出恰当的纪律处罚：
- 鲁莽的——以非体育行为警告违规人员。
- 使用过分力量的——以暴力行为将违规人员罚令出场。

4. 犯规与不正当行为出现后的比赛恢复方式

如果比赛此前已经停止，则以之前的决定恢复比赛。

如果比赛进行中，场上队员在比赛场地内，以身体行为对如下人员实施犯规：
- 对方场上队员——以间接或直接任意球、罚球点球恢复比赛。
- 同队队员、替补队员、已替换下场或已罚令出场的队员、球队官员或比赛官员——以直接任意球或罚球点球恢复比赛。

所有口头的违规行为，均判罚间接任意球。

If the referee stops play for an offence committed by a player, inside or outside the field of play, against an outside agent, play is restarted with a dropped ball, unless a free kick is awarded for leaving the field of play without the referee's permission.

If, when the ball is in play:

- a player commits an offence against a match official or an opposing player, substitute, substituted or sent-off player, or team official outside the field of play or
- a substitute, substituted or sent-off player, or team official commits an offence against, or interferes with, an opposing player or match official outside the field of play,

play is restarted with a free kick on the boundary line nearest to where the offence/interference occurred; for direct free kick offences, a penalty kick is awarded if this is within the offender's penalty area.

If an offence is committed outside the field of play by a player against a player, substitute, substituted player or team official of their own team, play is restarted with an indirect free kick on the boundary line closest to where the offence occurred.

If a player makes contact with the ball with an object (boot, shinguard etc.) held in the hand, play is restarted with a direct free kick (or penalty kick).

If a player who is on or off the field of play throws or kicks an object (other than the match ball) at an opposing player, or throws or kicks an object (including a ball) at an opposing substitute, substituted or sent-off player, team official, or a match official or the match ball, play is restarted with a direct free kick from the position where the object struck or would have struck the person or the ball. If this position is off the field of play, the free kick is taken on the nearest point on the boundary line; a penalty kick is awarded if this is within the offender's penalty area.

If a substitute, substituted or sent-off player, player temporarily off the field of play or team official throws or kicks an object onto the field of play and it

如果一名场上队员，在比赛场地内或场地外，对场外因素实施犯规，裁判员停止了比赛，则以坠球恢复比赛，除非裁判员以队员未经允许离开比赛场地为由判罚任意球。

如果比赛进行中：

- 场上队员在比赛场地外对比赛官员或对方场上队员、替补队员、已替换下场或已罚令出场的队员、球队官员实施犯规，或
- 替补队员、已替换下场或已罚令出场的队员、球队官员在比赛场地外对对方场上队员或比赛官员实施犯规或造成了干扰，

则在距犯规/干扰地点最近的边界线上以任意球恢复比赛。如果该地点位于犯规方罚球区内且该犯规可被判直接任意球，则判罚球点球。

如果一名场上队员在比赛场地外对同队队员、替补队员、已替换下场的队员或球队官员犯规，则在距离犯规发生地点最近的场地边界线上以间接任意球恢复比赛。

如果队员使用手中的物品（例如球鞋、护腿板等）触球，则以直接任意球（或罚球点球）恢复比赛。

如果处于比赛场地内或比赛场地外的场上队员，向对方场上队员扔掷或踢（除比赛用球外的）物品，或向对方替补队员、已替换下场或已罚令出场的队员、球队官员、比赛官员或比赛用球扔掷或踢物品（包括比赛用球），则在相关人员或比赛用球被物品击中或可能被击中的地点以直接任意球恢复比赛。如果该地点在比赛场地外，则在距该地点最近的边界线上以直接任意球恢复比赛；如果发生在犯规方罚球区内，则判罚球点球。

如果替补队员、已替换下场或已罚令出场的队员，以及暂时离场的场上队员或球队官员向比赛场地内扔掷或踢出物品，干扰了比赛、对方队员

interferes with play, an opponent or match official, play is restarted with a direct free kick (or penalty kick) where the object interfered with play or struck or would have struck the opponent, match official or the ball.

或比赛官员，则在该物品干扰比赛地点，或对方队员、比赛官员、比赛用球被击中或可能被击中的地点，以直接任意球（或罚球点球）恢复比赛。

NEYMAR JR
10

NEYMAR JR
10

13. Free Kicks

1. Types of free kick

Direct and indirect free kicks are awarded to the opposing team of a player, substitute, substituted or sent-off player, or team official guilty of an offence.

Indirect free kick signal

The referee indicates an indirect free kick by raising the arm above the head; this signal is maintained until the kick has been taken and the ball touches another player, goes out of play or it is clear that a goal cannot be scored directly.

An indirect free kick must be retaken if the referee fails to signal that the kick is indirect and the ball is kicked directly into the goal.

Ball enters the goal

- if a direct free kick is kicked directly into the opponents' goal, a goal is awarded
- if an indirect free kick is kicked directly into the opponents' goal, a goal kick is awarded
- if a direct or indirect free kick is kicked directly into the team's own goal, a corner kick is awarded

2. Procedure

All free kicks are taken from the place where the offence occurred, except:

- indirect free kicks to the attacking team for an offence inside the opponents' goal area are taken from the nearest point on the goal area line which runs parallel to the goal line
- free kicks to the defending team in their goal area may be taken from anywhere in that area

第十三章　任意球

1. 任意球的种类

当场上队员、替补队员、已替换下场的队员、已罚令出场的队员或者球队官员犯规或违规时，判由对方球队罚直接或间接任意球。

间接任意球示意信号

裁判员单臂上举过头，示意间接任意球，并保持这种姿势直到球踢出后被其他队员触及、比赛停止或球已经明显不可能直接进入球门为止。

如果裁判员未正确示意间接任意球，而球被直接踢入球门，则必须重罚间接任意球。

球进门

- 如果直接任意球直接踢入对方球门，则判为进球得分。
- 如果间接任意球直接踢入对方球门，则判为球门球。
- 如果直接或间接任意球直接踢入本方球门，则判为角球。

2. 程序

所有任意球均应在犯规或违规的地点罚球，但下列情况除外：

- 攻方球队在对方球门区内获得的间接任意球，应在与球门线平行的，离犯规地点最近的球门区线上执行罚间接任意球。
- 守方球队在本方球门区内获得的任意球可在球门区内的任意地点罚球。

- free kicks for offences involving a player entering, re-entering or leaving the field of play without permission are taken from the position of the ball when play was stopped. However, if a player commits an offence off the field of play, play is restarted with a free kick taken on the boundary line nearest to where the offence occurred; for direct free kick offences, a penalty kick is awarded if this is within the offender's penalty area
- where the Law designates another position (see Laws 3, 11, 12)

The ball:

- must be stationary and the kicker must not touch the ball again until it has touched another player
- is in play when it is kicked and clearly moves

Until the ball is in play, all opponents must remain:

- at least 9.15 m (10 yds) from the ball, unless they are on their own goal line between the goalposts
- outside the penalty area for free kicks inside the opponents' penalty area

Where three or more defending team players form a 'wall', all attacking team players must remain at least 1 m (1 yd) from the 'wall' until the ball is in play.

A free kick can be taken by lifting the ball with a foot or both feet simultaneously.

Feinting to take a free kick to confuse opponents is permitted as part of football.

If a player, while correctly taking a free kick, deliberately kicks the ball at an opponent in order to play the ball again but not in a careless or reckless manner or using excessive force, the referee allows play to continue.

- 场上队员未经裁判员允许进入、重新进入或离开比赛场地而被判罚的任意球，应在比赛停止时球所在地点罚球。然而，如果一名场上队员在比赛场地外犯规，则应在距犯规发生地点最近的边界线上以任意球恢复比赛。如果该地点位于犯规方罚球区内，且该犯规可被判罚直接任意球，则判罚球点球。
- 规则规定的其他地点（详见第三章、第十一章、第十二章）。

球：

- 必须放定，且罚球队员不得在其他队员触及球前再次触球。
- 当球被踢且明显移动，则为比赛恢复。

在比赛恢复前，所有对方队员必须：

- 距球至少9.15米（10码），除非已经处在本方球门柱之间的球门线上。
- 守方队员在本方罚球区内罚任意球时，处在罚球区外。

当守方组成“人墙”的队员人数为3人或3人以上时，攻方队员必须距离“人墙”至少1米（1码），直至比赛恢复。

任意球可以用单脚或双脚同时挑起的方式罚出。

作为比赛的一部分，允许用假动作罚任意球迷惑对方。

如果一名队员在以正确方式罚任意球的过程中，故意将球踢向对方以再次获得球权，但并未使用草率的、鲁莽的方式或过分的力量，裁判员允许比赛继续。

3. **Offences and sanctions**

If, when a free kick is taken, an opponent is closer to the ball than the required distance, the kick is retaken unless the advantage can be applied; but if a player takes a free kick quickly and an opponent who is less than 9.15 m (10 yds) from the ball intercepts it, the referee allows play to continue. However, an opponent who deliberately prevents a free kick being taken quickly must be cautioned for delaying the restart of play.

If, when a free kick is taken, an attacking team player is less than 1 m (1 yd) from a 'wall' formed by three or more defending team players, an indirect free kick is awarded.

If, when a free kick is taken by the defending team inside its penalty area, any opponents are inside the penalty area because they did not have time to leave, the referee allows play to continue. If an opponent who is in the penalty area when the free kick is taken, or enters the penalty area before the ball is in play, touches or challenges for the ball before it is in play, the free kick is retaken.

If, after the ball is in play, the kicker touches the ball again before it has touched another player an indirect free kick is awarded; if the kicker commits a handball offence:

- a direct free kick is awarded
- a penalty kick is awarded if the offence occurred inside the kicker's penalty area unless the kicker was the goalkeeper in which case an indirect free kick is awarded

3. 违规与处罚

罚任意球时，如果对方队员距离球不足规定的距离，除非可掌握有利，否则应重罚任意球。如果队员快速罚出任意球，随后距球不足9.15米（10码）的对方队员将球截获，裁判员允许比赛继续。然而，故意阻止对方快速发球的队员必须以延误比赛恢复为由予以警告。

当任意球踢出时，一名进攻队员距离防守方3人或3人以上组成的“人墙”不足1米（1码），将被判罚间接任意球。

守方队员在本方罚球区内快速罚出任意球时，如果对方队员未来得及离开罚球区，裁判员允许比赛继续。在踢任意球时，处在罚球区内的对方队员，或在比赛恢复前进入罚球区的对方队员，在比赛恢复前触及球或争抢球，应重踢任意球。

如果比赛已经恢复，罚球队员在其他队员触及球前再次触球，则判罚间接任意球。如果罚球队员手球犯规：

- 判罚直接任意球。
- 如果违规情况发生在罚球队员本方罚球区内，则判罚球点球。除非罚球队员为守门员，这种情况下判罚间接任意球。

14. The Penalty Kick

A penalty kick is awarded if a player commits a direct free kick offence inside their penalty area or off the field as part of play as outlined in Laws 12 and 13.

A goal may be scored directly from a penalty kick.

1. Procedure

The ball must be stationary on the penalty mark and the goalposts, crossbar and goal net must not be moving.

The player taking the penalty kick must be clearly identified.

The defending goalkeeper must remain on the goal line, facing the kicker, between the goalposts, without touching the goalposts, crossbar or goal net, until the ball has been kicked.

The players other than the kicker and goalkeeper must be:

- at least 9.15 m (10 yds) from the penalty mark
- behind the penalty mark
- inside the field of play
- outside the penalty area

After the players have taken positions in accordance with this Law, the referee signals for the penalty kick to be taken.

The player taking the penalty kick must kick the ball forward; backheeling is permitted provided the ball moves forward.

When the ball is kicked, the defending goalkeeper must have at least part of one foot touching, or in line with, the goal line.

第十四章　罚球点球

队员在本方罚球区内，或如第十二章、第十三章已明确的正常比赛移动中离开比赛场地后，犯有可判罚直接任意球的犯规，则判罚球点球。

罚球点球可直接射入球门得分。

1. 程序

球必须放定在罚球点上。球门立柱、横梁和球网不能移动。

必须清晰指定主罚的队员。

守方守门员必须处在球门柱之间的球门线上，面向主罚队员，且不可触碰球门立柱、横梁或球网，直至球被踢出。

主罚队员和守门员以外的其他场上队员必须：

- 距离罚球点至少9.15米（10码）。
- 在罚球点后。
- 在比赛场地内。
- 在罚球区外。

场上队员的位置符合规则规定后，裁判员示意执行罚球点球。

主罚队员必须向前踢球。允许使用脚后跟踢球，只要球向前移动。

在球被踢出时，防守方守门员必须至少有一只脚的一部分接触着球门线，或者与球门线齐平。

The ball is in play when it is kicked and clearly moves.

The kicker must not play the ball again until it has touched another player.

The penalty kick is completed when the ball stops moving, goes out of play or the referee stops play for any offence.

Additional time is allowed for a penalty kick to be taken and completed at the end of each half of the match or extra time. When additional time is allowed, the penalty kick is completed when, after the kick has been taken, the ball stops moving, goes out of play, is played by any player (including the kicker) other than the defending goalkeeper, or the referee stops play for an offence by the kicker or the kicker's team. If a defending team player (including the goalkeeper) commits an offence and the penalty is missed/saved, the penalty is retaken.

2. Offences and sanctions

Once the referee has signalled for a penalty kick to be taken, the kick must be taken; if it is not taken the referee may take disciplinary action before signalling again for the kick to be taken.

If, before the ball is in play, one of the following occurs:

- the player taking the penalty kick or a team-mate offends:
    - if the ball enters the goal, the kick is retaken
    - if the ball does not enter the goal, the referee stops play and restarts with an indirect free kick

    except for the following when play will be stopped and restarted with an indirect free kick, regardless of whether or not a goal is scored:

    - a penalty kick is kicked backwards
    - a team-mate of the identified kicker takes the kick; the referee cautions the player who took the kick
    - feinting to kick the ball once the kicker has completed the run-up (feinting in the run-up is permitted); the referee cautions the kicker

当球被踢且明显移动，即为比赛恢复。

主罚队员在其他队员触及球前不得再次触球。

当球停止移动、离开比赛场地，或因发生任何违反规则的情况而裁判员停止比赛时，即为罚球完成。

在上下半场或加时赛上下半场结束时，允许补足时间以完成罚球点球程序。进行补时时，当球罚出后停止移动、离开比赛场地、除守方守门员外的其他任何队员（包括主罚队员）触球，或因主罚队员、主罚的一方违规而裁判员停止比赛时，视为罚球程序完成。如果防守方队员（包括守门员）违规，且罚球点球未进 / 扑出，应重踢罚球点球。

2. 违规与处罚

一旦裁判员示意执行罚球点球，球必须踢出，如未踢出，裁判员可以在再次示意踢罚球点球之前执行纪律处罚。

如果在比赛恢复前，出现如下任一情况：

- 主罚队员或同队队员违犯规则：
  - 如果球进门，则重踢罚球点球。
  - 如果球未进门，则裁判员停止比赛，以间接任意球恢复比赛。

如下情况，无论进球与否裁判员将停止比赛，以间接任意球恢复比赛：

- 向后踢罚球点球。
- 已确认的主罚队员的同队队员踢罚球点球，裁判员警告该名罚球队员。
- 罚球队员完成助跑后用假动作踢球（在助跑过程中使用假动作是允许的），裁判员警告该名队员。

- the goalkeeper offends:
  - if the ball enters the goal, a goal is awarded
  - if the ball misses the goal or rebounds from the crossbar or goalpost(s), the kick is only retaken if the goalkeeper's offence clearly impacted on the kicker
  - if the ball is prevented from entering the goal by the goalkeeper, the kick is retaken

  If the goalkeeper's offence results in the kick being retaken, the goalkeeper is warned for the first offence in the game and cautioned for any subsequent offence(s) in the game

- a team-mate of the goalkeeper offends:
  - if the ball enters the goal, a goal is awarded
  - if the ball does not enter the goal, the kick is retaken
- a player of both teams offends, the kick is retaken unless a player commits a more serious offence (e.g. 'illegal' feinting)
- both the goalkeeper and the kicker commit an offence at the same time, the kicker is cautioned and play restarts with an indirect free kick to the defending team

If, after the penalty kick has been taken:

- the kicker touches the ball again before it has touched another player:
  - an indirect free kick (or direct free kick for a handball offence) is awarded
- the ball is touched by an outside agent as it moves forward:
  - the kick is retaken unless the ball is going into the goal and the interference does not prevent the goalkeeper or a defending player playing the ball, in which case the goal is awarded if the ball enters the goal (even if contact was made with the ball) unless the interference was by the attacking team
- the ball rebounds into the field of play from the goalkeeper, the crossbar or the goalposts and is then touched by an outside agent:

• 守门员违犯规则：

- 如果球进门，则进球得分有效。

- 如果球未射中球门范围或从门框弹出，则仅当守门员的违规行为明显地影响了主罚队员的情况下，才执行重罚。

- 如果球被守门员扑救而未进球，则重罚。

在一场比赛中，针对守门员的违规行为导致了重踢罚球点球的情况，如果守门员是首次违规，则对其实施劝诫，之后其所有违规均需实施警告。

• 守门员的同队队员违犯规则：

- 如果球进门，进球得分有效。

- 如果球未进门，应重踢罚球点球。

• 如果双方队员违犯规则，应重踢罚球点球。除非某一队员违犯规则的程度更重（如使用不合法的假动作）。

• 如果守门员与主罚队员同时违规，警告主罚队员，以防守方踢间接任意球恢复比赛。

罚球点球被踢出后，如果：

• 主罚队员在其他队员触及球前再次触球：

- 应判罚间接任意球（或因手球犯规而判罚直接任意球）。

• 球在向前移动过程中被场外因素触及：

- 应重踢罚球点球。但如果球将要进门时，干扰因素没有阻止防守队员处理球，随后球进门，则视为进球有效（即使干扰因素与球发生接触），除非干扰因素是来自攻方球队。

• 球从守门员身体、横梁或球门柱弹回比赛场地内，随后被场外因素触及：

- the referee stops play
- play is restarted with a dropped ball at the position where it touched the outside agent

3. Summary table

	Outcome of the penalty kick	
	Goal	**No Goal**
Encroachment by attacking player	Penalty is retaken	Indirect free kick
Encroachment by defending player	Goal	Penalty is retaken
Encroachment by defending and attacking player	Penalty is retaken	Penalty is retaken
Offence by goalkeeper	Goal	Not saved: penalty is not retaken (unless kicker is clearly impacted) Saved: penalty is retaken and warning for goalkeeper; caution for any further offence(s)
Goalkeeper and kicker offend at the same time	Indirect free kick and caution for kicker	Indirect free kick and caution for kicker
Ball kicked backwards	Indirect free kick	Indirect free kick
'Illegal' feinting	Indirect free kick and caution for kicker	Indirect free kick and caution for kicker
Wrong kicker	Indirect free kick and caution for wrong kicker	Indirect free kick and caution for wrong kicker

- 裁判员停止比赛。
- 在被场外因素触及的地点以坠球恢复比赛。

3. 概要

罚球点球的结果

	进球	未进球
攻方队员提前进入	重踢罚球点球	间接任意球
守方队员提前进入	进球有效	重踢罚球点球
双方队员提前进入	重踢罚球点球	重踢罚球点球
守门员违规	进球有效	未扑救：不重罚（除非罚球队员受到影响） 扑救：重踢罚球点球，劝诫守门员；警告守门员后续的违规行为
守门员和主罚队员同时违规	间接任意球并警告罚球队员	间接任意球并警告罚球队员
向后踢罚球点球	间接任意球	间接任意球
不合法的假动作	间接任意球并警告罚球队员	间接任意球并警告罚球队员
非确认主罚的队员罚球	间接任意球并警告该名队员	间接任意球并警告该名队员

23

15. The Throw-in

A throw-in is awarded to the opponents of the player who last touched the ball when the whole of the ball passes over the touchline, on the ground or in the air.

A goal cannot be scored directly from a throw-in:

- if the ball enters the opponents' goal – a goal kick is awarded
- if the ball enters the thrower's goal – a corner kick is awarded

1. Procedure

At the moment of delivering the ball, the thrower must:

- stand facing the field of play
- have part of each foot on the touchline or on the ground outside the touchline
- throw the ball with both hands from behind and over the head from the point where it left the field of play

All opponents must stand at least 2 m (2 yds) from the point on the touchline where the throw-in is to be taken.

The ball is in play when it enters the field of play. If the ball touches the ground before entering, the throw-in is retaken by the same team from the same position. If the throw-in is not taken correctly, it is retaken by the opposing team.

If a player, while correctly taking a throw-in, deliberately throws the ball at an opponent in order to play the ball again but not in a careless or a reckless manner or using excessive force, the referee allows play to continue.

The thrower must not touch the ball again until it has touched another player.

第十五章　掷界外球

当球的整体从地面或空中越过边线时，由最后触球队员的对方掷界外球。

界外球不能直接掷进球门得分：

- 如果球直接掷入对方球门——判踢球门球。
- 如果球直接掷入本方球门——判踢角球。

1. 程序

在掷出球的瞬间，掷球队员必须：

- 站立面向比赛场地。
- 任何一只脚的一部分在边线上或在边线外的地面上。
- 在球离开比赛场地的地点，用双手将球从头后经头顶掷出。

所有对方队员必须站在距离应掷球的地点所对应的边线上的位置至少2米（2码）的位置。

当球掷入比赛场地内，即为比赛恢复。在球进入比赛场地之前，如果球接触地面，则由同一队在相同地点重新掷界外球。如果未依照正确程序掷界外球，则由对方掷界外球。

如果一名队员以正确的方式，故意将球掷向对方队员以再次触球，但并未使用草率的、鲁莽的方式或过分的力量，裁判员允许比赛继续。

掷球队员在其他队员触及球前不得再次触球。

2. Offences and sanctions

If, after the ball is in play, the thrower touches the ball again before it has touched another player, an indirect free kick is awarded; if the thrower commits a handball offence:

- a direct free kick is awarded
- a penalty kick is awarded if the offence occurred inside the thrower's penalty area unless the ball was handled by the defending team's goalkeeper, in which case an indirect free kick is awarded

An opponent who unfairly distracts or impedes the thrower (including moving closer than 2 m (2 yds) to the place where the throw-in is to be taken) is cautioned for unsporting behaviour, and if the throw-in has been taken, an indirect free kick is awarded.

For any other offence, the throw-in is taken by a player of the opposing team.

2. 违规与处罚

如果比赛已经恢复，掷球队员在其他队员触及球前再次触球，则判罚间接任意球。如果掷球队员手球犯规：

- 判罚直接任意球。
- 如果违规情况出现在掷球队员本方罚球区内，则判罚球点球。除非掷球队员为守门员，这种情况下判罚间接任意球。

对方队员通过不正当的方式干扰或阻碍掷球队员（包括移动至距掷球位置少于2米（2码）的地点）应以非体育行为予以警告，如果界外球已被掷出，则判罚间接任意球。

对于其他任何违反本章条文的情况，应由对方队员掷界外球。

FIFA WOMEN'S WORLD CUP FRANCE
VISA
VISA

FIFA WOMEN'S WORLD CUP FRANCE 20
VISA
VISA
4

16. The Goal Kick

A goal kick is awarded when the whole of the ball passes over the goal line, on the ground or in the air, having last touched a player of the attacking team, and a goal is not scored.

A goal may be scored directly from a goal kick, but only against the opposing team; if the ball directly enters the kicker's goal, a corner kick is awarded to the opponents.

1. Procedure

- The ball must be stationary and is kicked from any point within the goal area by a player of the defending team
- The ball is in play when it is kicked and clearly moves
- Opponents must be outside the penalty area until the ball is in play

2. Offences and sanctions

If, after the ball is in play, the kicker touches the ball again before it has touched another player, an indirect free kick is awarded; if the kicker commits a handball offence:

- a direct free kick is awarded
- a penalty kick is awarded if the offence occurred inside the kicker's penalty area, unless the kicker was the goalkeeper, in which case an indirect free kick is awarded

If, when a goal kick is taken, any opponents are inside the penalty area because they did not have time to leave, the referee allows play to continue. If an opponent who is in the penalty area when the goal kick is taken, or enters the penalty area before the ball is in play, touches or challenges for the ball before it is in play, the goal kick is retaken.

第十六章　球门球

当球的整体从地面或空中越过球门线，而最后由攻方队员触及，且并未出现进球，则判为球门球。

球门球可以直接射入对方球门而得分。如果球直接进入踢球队员本方球门，则判给对方角球。

1. 程序

- 球必须放定，由守方球队中的一名场上队员在球门区内任意位置踢球。
- 当球被踢且明显移动，即为比赛恢复。
- 对方队员必须处在罚球区外直到比赛恢复。

2. 违规与处罚

如果比赛已经恢复，踢球队员在其他队员触及球前再次触球，则判罚间接任意球。如果踢球队员手球犯规：

- 判罚直接任意球。
- 如果违规情况出现在踢球队员本方罚球区内，则判罚球点球。除非踢球队员为守门员，这种情况下判罚间接任意球。

如果球门球踢出时，对方队员因没有时间离开而处于罚球区内，裁判员允许比赛继续。在踢球门球时处在罚球区内的对方队员，或在比赛恢复前进入罚球区的对方队员，在比赛恢复前触及球或争抢球，应重踢球门球。

If a player enters the penalty area before the ball is in play and fouls or is fouled by an opponent, the goal kick is retaken and the offender may be cautioned or sent off, depending on the offence.

For any other offence, the kick is retaken.

在比赛恢复前，如果队员进入罚球区内，对对方队员或被对方队员犯规，应重踢球门球。依据犯规情况，犯规队员可被警告或罚令出场。

对于其他任何违反本章条文的情况，应重踢球门球。

FARINEZ
1

FARINEZ
1

17. The Corner Kick

A corner kick is awarded when the whole of the ball passes over the goal line, on the ground or in the air, having last touched a player of the defending team, and a goal is not scored.

A goal may be scored directly from a corner kick, but only against the opposing team; if the ball directly enters the kicker's goal, a corner kick is awarded to the opponents.

1. Procedure

- The ball must be placed in the corner area nearest to the point where the ball passed over the goal line
- The ball must be stationary and is kicked by a player of the attacking team
- The ball is in play when it is kicked and clearly moves; it does not need to leave the corner area
- The corner flagpost must not be moved
- Opponents must remain at least 9.15 m (10 yds) from the corner arc until the ball is in play

2. Offences and sanctions

If, after the ball is in play, the kicker touches the ball again before it has touched another player, an indirect free kick is awarded; if the kicker commits a handball offence:

- a direct free kick is awarded
- a penalty kick is awarded if the offence occurred inside the kicker's penalty area, unless the kicker was the goalkeeper, in which case an indirect free kick is awarded

第十七章　角球

当球的整体从地面或空中越过球门线，而最后由守方队员触及，且并未出现进球，则判为角球。

角球可以直接射入对方球门而得分。如果角球直接射入踢球队员本方球门，则判给对方角球。

1. 程序

- 球必须放在球越过球门线时最接近的角球区内。
- 球必须放定，由攻方球队中的一名场上队员踢球。
- 当球被踢且明显移动时，即为比赛恢复。无须将球踢出角球区。
- 不得移动角旗杆。
- 对方队员必须距角球弧至少9.15米（10码），直到比赛恢复。

2. 违规与处罚

如果比赛已经恢复，踢球队员在其他队员触球前再次触球，则判罚间接任意球。如果踢球队员手球犯规：

- 判罚直接任意球。
- 如果违规情况出现在踢球队员本方罚球区内，则判罚球点球。除非踢球队员为守门员，这种情况下判罚间接任意球。

If a player, while correctly taking a corner kick, deliberately kicks the ball at an opponent in order to play the ball again but not in a careless or reckless manner or using excessive force, the referee allows play to continue.

For any other offence, the kick is retaken.

如果一名队员在以正确方式踢角球的过程中，故意将球踢向对方队员以再次获得球权，但并未使用草率的、鲁莽的方式或过分的力量，裁判员允许比赛继续。

对于其他任何违反本章条文的情况，应重踢角球。

KROOS
8

KROOS
8

Video assistant referee (VAR) protocol

视频助理裁判操作规范

Protocol – principles, practicalities and procedures

The VAR protocol, as far as possible, conforms to the principles and philosophy of the Laws of the Game.

The use of video assistant referees (VARs) is only permitted where the match/competition organiser has fulfilled all the Implementation Assistance and Approval Programme (IAAP) requirements as set out in FIFA's IAAP documents, and has received written permission from FIFA.

1. Principles

The use of VARs in football matches is based on a number of principles, all of which must apply in every match using VARs.

1. A video assistant referee (VAR) is a match official, with independent access to match footage, who may assist the referee only in the event of a '**clear and obvious error**' or '**serious missed incident**' in relation to:

   a. **Goal/no goal**
   b. **Penalty/no penalty**
   c. **Direct red card** (not second yellow card/caution)
   d. **Mistaken identity** (when the referee cautions or sends off the wrong player of the offending team)

2. The referee must always make a decision, i.e. the referee is not permitted to give 'no decision' and then use the VAR to make the decision; a decision to allow play to continue after an alleged offence can be reviewed.
3. The original decision given by the referee will not be changed unless the video review clearly shows that the decision was a 'clear and obvious error'.

操作规范——
原则、实施方法和操作程序

视频助理裁判操作规范最大程度遵循了《足球竞赛规则》的原则和理念。

只有当比赛/竞赛方完全满足了视频助理裁判协助实施和审核项目（IAAP）的要求（国际足联IAAP文件所述内容），且得到国际足联书面许可后，方可使用视频助理裁判。

1. 原则

在足球比赛中使用视频助理裁判应基于若干原则，任何使用视频助理裁判的比赛都必须遵循这些原则。

1. 视频助理裁判员作为比赛官员，可独立调用其所需要的比赛画面，且仅在有关以下各类事件的判罚存在**“清晰而明显的错误”**或**“遗漏的严重事件”**时，方可协助裁判员：

a. **进球/未进球**。
b. **罚球点球/不是罚球点球**。
c. **直接红牌**（不包括第二次警告/黄牌）。
d. **纪律处罚对象错误**（裁判员对违规球队执行警告或罚令出场时错认了受处罚队员）。

2. 裁判员必须先做出决定。不允许裁判员“不做任何决定”，而后利用视频助理裁判员再做决定；对于疑似犯规的情况，裁判员在做出比赛继续的决定后也可以进行回看。

3. 除非回看分析充分表明裁判员做出的最初决定是“清晰而明显的错误”，否则不得更改该决定。

4. Only the referee can initiate a 'review'; the VAR (and other match officials) can only recommend a 'review' to the referee.
5. The final decision is always taken by the referee, either based on information from the VAR or after the referee has undertaken an 'on-field review' (OFR).
6. There is no time limit for the review process as accuracy is more important than speed.
7. The players and team officials must not surround the referee or attempt to influence if a decision is reviewed, the review process or the final decision.
8. The referee must remain 'visible' during the review process to ensure transparency.
9. If play continues after an incident which is then reviewed, any disciplinary action taken/required during the post-incident period is not cancelled, even if the original decision is changed (except a caution/sending-off for stopping or interfering with a promising attack or DOGSO).
10. If play has stopped and been restarted, the referee may not undertake a 'review' except for a case of mistaken identity or for a potential sending-off offence relating to violent conduct, spitting, biting or extremely offensive, insulting and/or abusive action(s).
11. The period of play before and after an incident that can be reviewed is determined by the Laws of the Game and VAR protocol.
12. As the VAR will automatically 'check' every situation/decision, there is no need for coaches or players to request a 'review'.

2. Reviewable match-changing decisions/incidents

The referee may receive assistance from the VAR only in relation to four categories of match-changing decisions/incidents. In all these situations, the VAR is only used *after the referee has made a (first/original) decision* (including allowing play to continue), or if a serious incident is missed/not seen by the match officials.

The referee's original decision will not be changed unless there was a 'clear and obvious error' (this includes any decision made by the referee based on information from another match official e.g. offside).

4. 只有裁判员可发起“回看分析”；视频助理裁判员（以及其他比赛官员）只可向裁判员建议发起“回看分析”。

5. 无论是基于视频助理裁判员提供的信息，还是裁判员进行了“在场回看分析”，最终决定必须由裁判员做出。

6. 回看分析流程没有时间限制，准确性比速度更重要。

7. 在回看分析过程中，队员和球队官员不得围堵裁判员，以试图对回看分析进程以及最终决定施加影响。

8. 在回看分析进程中，裁判员必须保持“可见”状态，以确保该环节的透明度。

9. 如果一事件发生后比赛继续进行，裁判员随后对该事件进行了回看分析。在事件后继续比赛的过程中执行/需要执行的任何纪律处罚不得撤销，即使最初的决定发生了改变（因破坏或干扰了有希望的进攻机会或明显进球得分机会而执行的警告/罚令出场除外）。

10. 如果比赛停止又随之恢复后，除纪律处罚对象错误或涉及到暴力行为、吐口水、咬人或极具攻击性、侮辱性和/或辱骂性的行为的潜在红牌事件外，裁判员不得执行“回看分析”。

11. 在回看分析时，事件前后回看的时段长度，由《足球竞赛规则》和视频助理裁判员操作规范决定。

12. 视频助理裁判员会自行“查看”每个情况/决定，无需教练员或队员要求进行“回看分析”。

2. 可回看分析的改变比赛走势的决定/事件

裁判员只能就涉及四类改变比赛走势的决定/事件，得到视频助理裁判员的协助。无论何种情况，只有*在裁判员已经做出（第一/最初）决定（包括示意比赛继续）后*，或一严重事件被遗漏/未被比赛官员察觉时，方可使用视频助理裁判员。

除非裁判员最初的决定是“清晰而明显的错误”（包括裁判员根据其他比赛官员提供的信息做出的任何决定，如越位），否则不得更改。

The categories of decision/incident which may be reviewed in the event of a potential 'clear and obvious error' or 'serious missed incident' are:

a. Goal/no goal

- attacking team offence in the build-up to or scoring of the goal (handball, foul, offside etc.)
- ball out of play prior to the goal
- goal/no goal decisions
- offence by goalkeeper and/or kicker at the taking of a penalty kick or encroachment by an attacker or defender who becomes directly involved in play if the penalty kick rebounds from the goalpost, crossbar or goalkeeper

b. Penalty kick/no penalty kick

- attacking team offence in the build-up to the penalty incident (handball, foul, offside etc.)
- ball out of play prior to the incident
- location of offence (inside or outside the penalty area)
- penalty kick incorrectly awarded
- penalty kick offence not penalised

c. Direct red cards (not second yellow card/caution)

- DOGSO (especially position of offence and positions of other players)
- serious foul play (or reckless challenge)
- violent conduct, biting or spitting at another person
- using offensive, insulting or abusive action(s)

d. Mistaken identity (red or yellow card)

If the referee penalises an offence and then gives the wrong player from the offending (penalised) team a yellow or red card, the identity of the offender can be reviewed; the actual offence itself cannot be reviewed unless it relates to a goal, penalty incident or direct red card.

若存在潜在的“清晰而明显的错误”或“遗漏的严重事件”，可以进行回看分析的决定/事件类别包括：

a. 进球/未进球

- 攻方球队在进攻发展阶段或形成得分时违规（手球、犯规、越位等）。
- 在进球前球已离开比赛场地。
- 进球与否。
- 在踢罚球点球时，守门员和/或主罚队员违规；或者任何一方的其他队员提前进入（限制区域），并在球从球门柱、横梁或守门员处弹回后，直接卷入比赛。

b. 罚球点球/不是罚球点球

- 攻方球队在进攻发展阶段或形成罚球点球时违规（手球、犯规、越位等）。
- 在事件发生前球已离开比赛场地。
- 犯规的地点（罚球区内或外）。
- 错判罚球点球。
- 漏判罚球点球。

c. 直接红牌（不包括第二次警告/黄牌）

- 破坏明显进球得分机会（尤其要考虑犯规位置和其他队员位置）。
- 严重犯规（或鲁莽的抢截）。
- 暴力行为、咬人或向其他人吐口水。
- 使用攻击性、侮辱性或辱骂性的行为。

d. 纪律处罚（出示红黄牌）对象错误

若裁判员判罚犯规后，出示红黄牌时错认了受处罚队员，可通过回看分析确认；犯规行为本身不得进行回看分析，除非其涉及进球、罚球点球事件或直接红牌。

3. Practicalities

Use of VARs during a match involves the following practical arrangements:

- The VAR watches the match in the video operation room (VOR) assisted by an assistant VAR (AVAR) and replay operator (RO)
- Depending on the number of camera angles (and other considerations) there may be more than one AVAR or RO
- Only authorised persons are allowed to enter the VOR or communicate with the VAR/AVAR/RO during the match
- The VAR has independent access to, and replay control of, TV broadcast footage
- The VAR is connected to the communication system being used by the match officials and can hear everything they say; the VAR can only speak to the referee by pushing a button (to avoid the referee being distracted by conversations in the VOR)
- If the VAR is busy with a 'check' or a 'review', the AVAR may speak to the referee, especially if the game needs to be stopped or to ensure play does not restart
- If the referee decides to view the replay footage, the VAR will select the best angle/replay speed; the referee can request other/additional angles/speeds

4. Procedures

Original decision

- The referee and other match officials must always make an initial decision (including any disciplinary action) as if there was no VAR (except for a 'missed' incident)
- The referee and other match officials are not permitted to give 'no decision' as this will lead to 'weak/indecisive' officiating, too many 'reviews' and significant problems if there is a technology failure
- The referee is the only person who can make the final decision; the VAR has the same status as the other match officials and can only assist the referee

3. 实施方法

在比赛中使用视频助理裁判涉及以下操作内容：

- 视频助理裁判员在视频操作室中观看比赛，并由助理视频助理裁判员和回放操作员提供协助。
- 根据摄像机位数量（及其他因素），可增加助理视频助理裁判员或回放操作员人数。
- 只有经授权的人员可在比赛过程中进入视频操作室或与视频助理裁判员、助理视频助理裁判员、回放操作员联络。
- 视频助理裁判员可独立使用、控制回放电视转播画面。
- 视频助理裁判员和比赛官员所使用的通信系统是对接的，其可以听到比赛官员的所有对话；视频助理裁判员只有按下按钮（以避免视频操作室内的对话干扰到裁判员）时方可与裁判员对话。
- 视频助理裁判员忙于进行“查看”或“回看分析”时，助理视频助理裁判员可与裁判员对话，尤其是需要停止比赛或阻止比赛恢复时。
- 裁判员决定自行观看回放画面时，视频助理裁判员负责提供最佳的摄像机位画面/回放速度；裁判员也可要求提供其他摄像机位画面/回放速度。

4. 操作程序

最初的决定

- 裁判员和其他比赛官员必须先做出初始决定（包括任何纪律处罚），就像没有视频助理裁判员一样（“遗漏”的事件除外）。
- 不允许裁判员和其他比赛官员先“不做任何决定”，这会让执法工作显得“不坚决/不果断”，并造成过多的“回看分析”事件，若出现技术故障时，还会导致重大问题。
- 裁判员是唯一做出最终决定的人；视频助理裁判员和其他比赛官员一样，只可协助裁判员。

- Delaying the flag/whistle for an offence is only permissible in *a very clear attacking situation* when a player is about to score a goal or has a clear run into/towards the opponents' penalty area
- If an assistant referee delays a flag for an offence, the assistant referee must raise the flag if the attacking team scores a goal, is awarded a penalty kick, free kick, corner kick or throw-in, or retains possession of the ball after the initial attack has ended; in all other situations, the assistant referee should decide whether or not to raise the flag, depending on the requirements of the game

Check

- The VAR automatically 'checks' the TV camera footage for every potential or actual goal, penalty or direct red card decision/incident, or a case of mistaken identity, using different camera angles and replay speeds
- The VAR can 'check' the footage in normal speed and/or in slow motion but, in general, slow-motion replays should only be used for facts, e.g. position of offence/player, point of contact for physical offences and handball, ball out of play (including goal/no goal); normal speed should be used for the 'intensity' of an offence or to decide if it was a handball offence
- If the 'check' does not indicate a 'clear and obvious error' or 'serious missed incident', there is usually no need for the VAR to communicate with the referee – this is a 'silent check'; however, it sometimes helps the referee/assistant referee to manage the players/match if the VAR confirms that no 'clear and obvious error' or 'serious missed incident' occurred
- If the restart of play needs to be delayed for a 'check', the referee will signal this by clearly holding a finger to the earpiece/headset and extending the other hand/arm; this signal must be maintained until the 'check' is complete as it announces that the referee is receiving information (which may be from the VAR or another match official)
- If the 'check' indicates a probable 'clear and obvious error' or 'serious missed incident', the VAR will communicate this information to the referee, who will then decide whether or not to initiate a 'review'

- 在犯规发生后延迟举旗/鸣哨的情况，仅适用于队员即将完成射门得分或已经清晰地向对方罚球区内/方向跑动这样*非常明显的进攻发展情景*。
- 若助理裁判员在犯规发生后延迟举旗，其必须在随后攻方球队进球得分、获得罚球点球、任意球、角球、界外球，或在该次进攻结束后仍握有控球权时举旗示意；除上述以外的情况，助理裁判员应根据当时比赛的需要决定是否举旗。

查看

- 视频助理裁判员利用不同的摄像机位和回放速度，通过电视镜头画面自行“查看”每一潜在或实际的进球、罚球点球或直接红牌的决定/事件，或纪律处罚对象错误情况。
- 视频助理裁判员可“查看”常速和/或慢速画面，但一般来说，只在判定客观性事实时使用慢速画面，如犯规/队员的位置、有身体接触的犯规，以及手球的接触部位、球出界（包括进球与否）等；而在判定犯规“强度”或是否手球犯规等情形时，应使用常速画面。
- 若“查看”表明未出现“清晰、明显的错漏判”或“遗漏的严重事件”，通常视频助理裁判员无需与裁判员联络——此流程为“静默查看”；但有时视频助理裁判员向裁判员确认未发生“清晰、明显的错漏判”或“遗漏的严重事件”，可帮助裁判员/助理裁判员管理好队员/比赛。
- 若需进行“查看”并延迟恢复比赛，裁判员需以手指指向耳麦/耳机，另一手掌/手臂外展的方式明确示意；该示意信号需要保持到“查看”完成后，以表明裁判员在此阶段正在接收信息（可能来自视频助理裁判员或其他比赛官员）。
- 若查看表明有可能出现“清晰、明显的错漏判”或“遗漏的严重事件”，视频助理裁判员将此信息告知裁判员，由裁判员决定是否发起“回看分析”。

Review

- The referee can initiate a 'review' for a potential 'clear and obvious error' or 'serious missed incident' when:
  - the VAR (or another match official) recommends a 'review'
  - the referee suspects that something serious has been 'missed'
- If play has already stopped, the referee delays the restart
- If play has not already stopped, the referee stops play when the ball is next in a neutral zone/situation (usually when neither team is in an attacking move) and shows the 'TV signal'
- The VAR describes to the referee what can be seen on the TV replay(s) and the referee then:
  - shows the 'TV signal' (if not already shown) and goes to the referee review area to view replay footage – 'on-field review' (OFR) – before making a final decision. The other match officials will not review the footage unless, in exceptional circumstances, asked to do so by the referee
    or
  - makes a final decision based on the referee's own perception and the information from the VAR, and, where appropriate, input from other match officials – VAR-only review
- At the end of both review processes, the referee must show the 'TV signal' immediately followed by the final decision
- For subjective decisions, e.g. intensity of a foul challenge, interference at offside, handball considerations, an 'on-field review' (OFR) is appropriate
- For factual decisions, e.g. position of an offence or player (offside), point of contact (handball/foul), location (inside or outside the penalty area), ball out of play etc. a VAR-only review is usually appropriate but an 'on-field review' (OFR) can be used for a factual decision if it will help manage the players/ match or 'sell' the decision (e.g. a crucial match-deciding decision late in the game)
- The referee can request different cameras angles/replay speeds but, in general, slow-motion replays should only be used for facts, e.g. position of offence/player, point of contact for physical offences and handball, ball out of

回看分析

- 裁判员可在下列情况下，针对可能的“清晰、明显的错漏判”或“遗漏的严重事件”发起回看分析：

  - 当视频助理裁判员（或其他比赛官员）建议“回看分析”时。
  - 当裁判员怀疑“遗漏”了某一严重事件时。

- 若比赛已经停止，则裁判员需延迟恢复比赛。
- 若比赛还未停止，则裁判员在比赛发展至中立区域/情景（通常是双方均无进攻机会）时停止比赛，并比划“电视示意信号”。
- 视频助理裁判员向裁判员描述回放所显示的情况，随后裁判员：

  - 比划“电视示意信号”（如果之前未示意），并在做出最终决定前，自行前往裁判员回看分析区域观看比赛回放——此为“在场回看分析”。其他比赛官员仅在特殊情况下，在裁判员的要求下，方可观看比赛画面。

  或

  - 凭借个人认知、视频助理裁判员提供的信息、其他比赛官员适时的介入，做出最终决定——此为由视频助理裁判方完成的回看分析。

- 在上述两类回看分析流程完成后，裁判员必须再次比划“电视示意信号”，随后立即做出最终决定。
- 在场回看分析适用于主观性决定，如犯规动作的强度、是否构成越位犯规、手球的考量（位置、意图等）。
- 由视频助理裁判方完成的回看分析，通常适用于客观性决定，如犯规或队员位置（越位）、身体接触位置（手球/犯规）、地点（罚球区内外）、球出界等。若能够帮助裁判员管理好队员/比赛，或使判罚（如在比赛末段出现的改变比赛走势的关键性决定）更具说服力，也可对客观性决定进行在场回看分析。
- 裁判员可要求调取不同的摄像机位画面/回放速度，但一般来说，只在判定客观性事实时使用慢速画面，如犯规/队员的位置、有身体接触的犯规，以及手球的接触部位、球出界（包括进球与否）等。而在判

play (including goal/no goal); normal speed should be used for the 'intensity' of an offence or to decide if it was a handball offence

- For decisions/incidents relating to goals, penalty/no penalty and red cards for denying an obvious goal-scoring opportunity (DOGSO), it may be necessary to review the attacking phase of play which led directly to the decision/incident; this may include how the attacking team gained possession of the ball in open play
- The Laws of the Game do not allow restart decisions (corner kicks, throw-ins etc.) to be changed once play has restarted, so they cannot be reviewed
- If play has stopped and restarted, the referee may only undertake a 'review', and take the appropriate disciplinary sanction, for a case of mistaken identity or for a potential sending-off offence relating to violent conduct, spitting, biting or extremely offensive, insulting and/or abusive action(s)
- The review process should be completed as efficiently as possible, but the accuracy of the final decision is more important than speed. For this reason, and because some situations are complex with several reviewable decisions/ incidents, there is no maximum time limit for the review process

Final decision

- When the review process is completed, the referee must show the 'TV signal' and communicate the final decision
- The referee will then take/change/rescind any disciplinary action (where appropriate) and restart play in accordance with the Laws of the Game

Players, substitutes and team officials

- As the VAR will automatically 'check' every situation/incident, there is no need for coaches or players to request a '**check**' or '**review**'
- Players, substitutes and team officials must not attempt to influence or interfere with the review process, including when the final decision is communicated
- During the review process, players should remain on the field of play; substitutes and team officials should remain off the field of play

定犯规“强度”或是否手球犯规等情形时，应使用常速画面。

- 对于涉及进球、罚球点球和破坏明显进球得分机会的红牌的决定/事件，必要时应回看分析直接导致决定/事件出现的进攻发展阶段，这可能包括进攻方是如何在运动战中获得控球权的。
- 《足球竞赛规则》不允许在比赛已经恢复后更改比赛恢复方式的决定（角球、界外球等），因此不得对此前发生的事件进行回看分析。
- 若比赛停止又随之恢复后，裁判员只可针对纪律处罚对象错误或潜在的涉及暴力行为、咬人或极具攻击性、侮辱性和/或辱骂性的行为的罚令出场犯规进行回看分析，并执行相应的纪律处罚。
- 回看分析流程应尽可能高效完成，但最终决定的准确性比操作速度更重要。由于此原因，也因为某些复杂情况涉及到多个需回看分析的决定/事件，对回看分析流程没有时长的限制。

最终决定

- 当回看分析流程完成后，裁判员必须比划“电视示意信号”，并传达最终决定。
- 裁判员随即执行/更改/撤销任何纪律处罚（恰当时），依据《足球竞赛规则》恢复比赛。

场上队员、替补队员和球队官员

- 视频助理裁判员会自行“查看”每一情况/事件，无需教练员或队员申请“**查看**”或“**回看分析**”。
- 场上队员、替补队员和球队官员不得试图影响或干扰回看分析流程，包括传达最终决定后。
- 回看分析过程中，场上队员应留在比赛场地内，替补队员和球队官员应留在比赛场地外。

- A player/substitute/substituted player/team official who excessively shows the "TV signal" or enters the RRA will be cautioned
- A player/substitute/substituted player/team official who enters the VOR will be sent off

Match validity

In principle, a match is not invalidated because of:

- malfunction(s) of the VAR technology (as for goal line technology (GLT))
- wrong decision(s) involving the VAR (as the VAR is a match official)
- decision(s) not to review an incident
- review(s) of a non-reviewable situation/decision

Incapacitated VAR, AVAR or replay operator

Law 6 – The Other Match Officials stipulates: "Competition rules must state clearly who replaces a match official who is unable to start or continue and any associated changes." In matches using VARs, this also applies to replay operators.

As special training and qualifications are needed to be a video match official (VMO)/replay operator, the following principles must be included in competition rules:

- A VAR, AVAR or replay operator who is unable to start or continue may only be replaced by someone who is qualified for that role
- If no qualified replacement can be found for the VAR or replay operator,* the match must be played/continue without the use of VARs
- If no qualified replacement can be found for the AVAR,* the match must be played/continue without the use of VARs unless, in exceptional circumstances, both teams agree in writing that the match may be played/continue with only the VAR and replay operator

*This does not apply where there is more than one AVAR/replay operator.

- 过分比划电视示意信号或进入裁判员回看分析区域的场上队员、替补队员、已替换下场队员或球队官员将被警告。
- 进入视频操作室的场上队员、替补队员、已替换下场队员或球队官员将被罚令出场。

比赛有效性

原则上，以下情况出现后，比赛结果仍然有效：

- 视频助理裁判技术出现故障（类同于球门线技术）。
- 视频助理裁判员参与做出了错误决定（视频助理裁判员也是比赛官员）。
- 做出了不予回看分析某一事件的决定。
- 对不可回看的事件进行了回看分析。

无法比赛的视频助理裁判员、助理视频助理裁判员及回放操作员

第六章——其他比赛官员中规定：竞赛规程必须明确由谁替换不能开始或继续执法的比赛官员，以及任何相应产生的更替。而在使用视频助理裁判的比赛中，此条款同样适用于回放操作员。

鉴于视频比赛官员及回放操作员需经过专门的训练和认证，竞赛规程中必须包含以下原则：

- 不能开始或继续比赛的视频助理裁判员、助理视频助理裁判员或回放操作员，只能由具备相应资质的人员替换。
- 无具备资质的视频助理裁判员或回放操作员*可供替换，则比赛必须在不使用视频助理裁判的情况下开始/继续。
- 如无具备资质的助理视频助理裁判员*可供替换，则比赛必须在不使用视频助理裁判的情况下开始/继续。除非比赛双方书面同意，方可在只有视频助理裁判员和回放操作员的情况下，仍然使用视频助理裁判开始/继续进行比赛。

*不适用于使用多名助理视频助理裁判员/回放操作员的比赛。

FIFA Quality Programme

国际足联品质计划

FIFA Quality Programme

The FIFA Quality Programme sets criteria, based on well-founded research, for products, playing surfaces and technologies used in the game of football. In addition to mandatory quality requirements in some fields of application, uniform recommendations are offered in other areas, on the basis of which competition organisers can further specify their own regulations.

Independent testing institutes verify the functionality of the products, playing surfaces and technologies in accordance with the respective standard. The institutes conducting these tests are subject to the approval of FIFA. The following quality marks identify those products, playing surfaces and technologies tested and certified to the prevailing requirements:

FIFA® BASIC | FIFA® QUALITY | FIFA® QUALITY PRO

FIFA Basic*
The test requirements for this standard are designed to identify products that fulfil basic performance, accuracy, safety and durability criteria for football. The focus is on setting minimum standards while ensuring affordability for use at all levels of the game.

FIFA Quality
The test requirements emphasise the durability and safety of these products, playing surfaces and technologies more than for the FIFA Basic standard. Basic performance and accuracy criteria are tested, but the main focus is on ensuring extensive use.

国际足联品质计划

基于充分研究而制订的国际足联品质计划，规定了足球比赛中所使用的各类产品、场地表面及技术设备的品质标准。竞赛组织方可以在其竞赛规程中，添加一些实施方面的强制要求，以及其他领域的统一建议。

独立检测机构依照各项分类标准，对各类产品、场地表面及技术设备的功能进行检验认证。这些检测机构须得到国际足联的许可。下列品质标志代表该产品、场地表面及技术设备已经过了检测并满足了相应的标准。

国际足联基础标准（FIFA Basic）*

针对此标准所进行的测试，用于证明该产品满足了足球运动所要求的基本的表现力、精准度、安全性及耐用性。此级别重在限定保障各个层面足球比赛的最低可用标准。

国际足联优质标准（FIFA Quality）

与基础标准相比，该测试在产品、场地表面及技术设备的耐用性和安全性方面有着更高要求，在表现力和精准度上也需要通过基本测试，但重点放在更广泛的适用方面。

FIFA Quality Pro

The emphasis of the test requirements is on first-class performance, accuracy and safety. Products, playing surfaces and technologies with this quality mark are designed for optimal performance and use at the highest level.

For more information on the FIFA Quality Programme, the individual standards and the certified products, playing surfaces and technologies, visit **https://football-technology.fifa.com**.

*FIFA Basic is replacing the International Match Standard (IMS). Footballs and playing surfaces tested to this previous standard remain eligible for use until their certification expires.

国际足联专业标准（FIFA Quality Pro）

该测试强调顶级的表现力、精准度和安全性。拥有此品质标志的产品、场地表面及技术设备，是为最高级别比赛和最佳的表现而设计。

如需获得关于国际足联品质计划的更多信息、各项单独标准、已获得认证的产品、场地表面及技术设备列表等，可访问https://football-technology.fifa.com。

*国际足联基础标准取代了之前的国际比赛标准（IMS）。通过了IMS测试的足球和比赛场地，在其认证期满之前，仍可视为合格。

Law changes 2021/22

竞赛规则变更内容
2021/2022

Outline summary of Law changes

Herewith an outline of the main changes/clarifications.

Changes affecting more than one Law

Notes on the Laws of the Game (all Laws) – metric units

- Clarification that, if there is any divergence between metric and imperial units, the metric units are authoritative

Laws 4, 5, 12 and VAR protocol – non-violent inappropriate behaviour

- To allow some non-violent inappropriate behaviour to be considered 'offensive, insulting or abusive' and result in a sending-off, 'action(s)/acting' replace 'gesture(s)/gesturing' in the relevant descriptions

Laws 1, 2 and 4 – FIFA Quality Programme

- Information about the FIFA Quality Programme is now included after the VAR protocol – details have been removed from the Law text

Individual Law changes (in Law order)

Law 1 – The Field of Play

- The goalposts and crossbar (and goals) must be the same shape
- The GLT signal can be sent to the video operation room (VOR)

Law 6 – The Other Match Officials

- There is now a FIFA list of international video match officials (VMOs)

Law 7 – The Duration of the Match

- Stoppage time relates to 'lost' playing time

规则变更概要

本部分简要列出本版规则变更或明确的主要内容。

涉及若干章节的变更

竞赛规则注解（全部章节）——公制单位

- 明确了：如果在公制单位和英制单位之间存在任何计量误差，一律以公制单位为准。

第四章、第五章、第十二章及视频助理裁判操作规范——非暴力行为的不当行为

- 将一些形式的非暴力行为的不当行为（如带有攻击性地触碰对方队员）纳入“攻击性、侮辱性或辱骂性”的范畴，在与之相关章节的罚令出场条款中用“行为/行动”代替“语言/动作”。

第一章、第二章、第四章——国际足联品质计划

- 已将国际足联品质计划的有关信息列于视频助理裁判操作规范之后——其细节内容已从规则相关章节中移除。

涉及单一章节的变更（按章节顺序排序）

第一章　比赛场地

- 球门柱和横梁必须是相同的形状，两个球门也必须相同。
- 球门线技术信号可以发送至视频操作室。

第六章　其他比赛官员

- 现已有国际级视频比赛官员名单。

第七章　比赛时间

- 补时时间取决于“损耗”的比赛时间。

Law 11 – Offside

- Inclusion of the Law 12 definition of where the arm ends (bottom of the armpit) for the purposes of determining an offside/onside position

Law 12 – Fouls and Misconduct

- Handball:
  - Not every contact of the ball with the hand/arm is an offence
  - A player's hand/arm position should be judged in relation to their body movement in that particular situation
  - Removal from the accidental attacking handball offence of the references to a 'team-mate' and 'creating a goal-scoring opportunity'
- The offence of using a 'trick' to circumvent the Law against the goalkeeper handling the ball from a deliberate kick from a team-mate applies at goal kicks; the instigator is to be cautioned (YC)
- A free kick/penalty kick can only be awarded for an offence against someone on the team lists or a match official

VAR protocol

- Written permission to use VARs is only required from FIFA
- Principles have been established covering scenarios when a video match official or replay operator is unable to start or continue a match

第十一章 越位

- 在判定越位/越位位置时，采用第十二章对臂部的上端边界的定义（与腋窝底部齐平）。

第十二章 犯规与不正当行为

- 手球：
  - 队员的手/臂部触球，并非每次都是犯规。
  - 应结合队员身体动作的具体情形来评判其手/臂部的位置。
  - 删除了意外手球后有关“同队队员得分”及“创造进球得分机会”的犯规条款。
- 对于施诡计以逃避规则有关守门员用手接同队队员故意踢来的球的违规行为的认定，同样适用于踢球门球时出现此行为的情况。发起该行为者将被警告（黄牌）。
- 任意球/罚球点球的判罚，只能针对犯规对象为在比赛名单上的人员以及比赛官员的犯规行为。

视频助理裁判操作规范

- 使用视频助理裁判的书面许可仅需自国际足联处获得。
- 确立了当视频比赛官员无法开始或继续执法比赛时的处理原则。

Details of all Law changes

The following are the changes to the Laws of the Game for the 2021/22 edition. For each change, the new/amended/additional wording is given, together with the old wording, where appropriate – followed by an explanation of the change.

Changes affecting more than one Law

Notes on the Laws of the Game (all Laws) – metric units (p.7)

Other languages

(...)

Measurements

If there is any divergence between metric and imperial units, the metric units are authoritative.

Laws 4, 5, 12 and VAR protocol – non-violent inappropriate behaviour

To allow some forms of non-violent inappropriate behaviour (e.g. offensively touching another person) to be considered 'offensive, insulting or abusive' and thus a sending-off offence, 'action(s)/acting' replace ~~'gesture(s)/gesturing'~~ in the following Laws:

Law 4 – The Players' Equipment

- 5. Slogans, statements, images and advertising – Interpreting the Law

Law 5 – The Referee

- 4. Video assistant referee (VAR) – Reviews after play has restarted

Law 12 – Fouls and Misconduct

- 2. Indirect free kick

规则变更详解

以下是竞赛规则2021/2022版本的变更内容。针对每处变更，新的/修订的/增加的条文与旧条文对照列出，并有相应的解析。

涉及若干章节的变更

竞赛规则注解（全部章节）——公制单位（第7页）

其他语言

（……）

计量单位

如果在公制单位和英制单位之间存在任何计量误差，一律以公制单位为准。

第四章、第五章、第十二章及视频助理裁判操作规范——非暴力行为的不当行为

将一些形式的非暴力行为的不当行为（如带有攻击性地触碰对方队员）纳入“攻击性、侮辱性或辱骂性”的范畴，在罚令出场的条款中用“行为/行动”代替“~~语言/动作~~”。涉及下列章节：

第四章——队员装备

- 5. 标语、言论、图像及广告——规则解读

第五章——裁判员

- 4. 视频助理裁判员（VAR）

第十二章——犯规与不正当行为

- 2. 间接任意球

- 3. Disciplinary action – Celebration of a goal
- 3. Disciplinary action – Sending-off offences
- 3. Disciplinary action – Team officials

Video assistant referee (VAR) protocol
- 1. Principles
- 2. Reviewable match-changing decisions/incidents
- 4. Procedures

Laws 1, 2 and 4 – FIFA Quality Programme

There is a new section outlining the FIFA Quality Programme (FQP). Certain details regarding the FQP and the related standards have been removed from the Laws so that future FQP changes will not require Law changes. The resulting text changes are as follows:

Law 1 – The Field of Play (p.18)

1. Field surface

Amended text

Where artificial surfaces are used in competition matches between representative teams of national football associations affiliated to FIFA or international club competition matches, the surface must meet the requirements of the FIFA Quality Programme for Football Turf ~~or the International Match Standard~~, unless special dispensation is given by The IFAB.

- 3. 纪律措施——庆祝进球
- 3. 纪律措施——罚令出场的犯规
- 3. 纪律措施——球队官员

视频助理裁判操作规范

- 1. 原则
- 2. 可回看分析的改变比赛走势的决定/事件
- 4. 操作程序

第一章、第二章、第四章——国际足联品质计划

新增国际足联品质计划（FQP）章节。涉及该计划及其相关标准的细节文字，已经从相关规则章节正文中移除，未来针对该计划的调整更新，将无需对规则进行改动。由此带来的本次文字改动如下：

第一章 比赛场地（第18页）

1. 场地表面

修订的条文

除国际足球理事会特许外，在国际足联所属的国家协会代表队之间、国际俱乐部之间比赛中使用的人造草皮场地，必须达到《国际足联品质计划——足球场地》~~或《国际比赛标准》~~的要求。

Law 1 – The Field of Play (pp.23 and 25)

11. Goal line technology (GLT)

Amended text

GLT systems may be used to verify whether a goal has been scored to support the referee's decision.
~~Where GLT is used, modifications to the goal frame may be permitted in accordance with the specifications stipulated in the FIFA Quality Programme for GLT and with the Laws of the Game.~~ The use of GLT must be stipulated in the competition rules.
(...)

Requirements and specifications of GLT
If GLT is used in competition matches, the competition organisers must ensure that the system (including any potentially permitted modifications to the goal frame or technology in the ball) ~~is certified according to one of the following standards:~~ meets the requirements of the FIFA Quality Programme for GLT.

- ~~FIFA Quality PRO~~
- ~~FIFA Quality~~
- ~~IMS – INTERNATIONAL MATCH STANDARD~~

~~An independent testing institute must verify the accuracy and functionality of the different technology providers' systems in accordance with the FIFA Quality Programme for GLT Testing Manual.~~ Where GLT is used, the referee must test the technology's functionality before the match as set out in the Testing Manual. If the technology does not function in accordance with the Testing Manual, the referee must not use the GLT system and must report this to the appropriate authorities.

~~Where GLT is used, the referee must test the technology's functionality before the match as set out in the Testing Manual.~~

11. 球门线技术（GLT）

修订的条文

球门线技术系统可以用于帮助裁判员判定进球与否。

若比赛中使用球门线技术，则允许对球门框架进行改造，但需遵循《国际足联球门线技术质量项目》和《足球竞赛规则》的具体要求。如果使用球门线技术，必须在竞赛规程中注明。

（……）

球门线技术规定及要求

如果在比赛中使用球门线技术，竞赛组织方必须确保该系统（包括有可能对球门框架进行的任何改造、比赛用球的任何科技成分等）符合如下任一标准：《国际足联品质计划——球门线技术》的相关要求。

- 国际足联专业品质。
- 国际足联品质。
- 国际比赛标准。

独立测试机构必须按照国际足联球门线技术品质测试手册的要求，检测不同技术提供方系统的准确性和功能性。若要使用球门线技术，裁判员必须在比赛前依照测试手册对其功能性进行测试。如果该技术未能达到测试手册要求的功能，则裁判员不得使用该球门线技术系统，且必须向相关机构报告。

使用球门线技术时，裁判员必须在赛前按照《国际足联质量项目—球门线技术测试手册》的要求，对该技术的功能进行测试。

Law 2 – The Ball (p.27)

1. Qualities and measurements

Amended text

All balls used in matches played in an official competition organised under the auspices of FIFA or confederations must ~~bear one of the following~~ meet the requirements and bear one of the marks of the FIFA Quality Programme for Footballs.

Each mark indicates (...) and must be approved by The IFAB. ~~The institutes conducting the tests are subject to the approval of FIFA.~~

~~Where goal-line technology (GLT) is used, balls with integrated technology must carry one of the above-listed marks.~~

Law 4 – The Players' Equipment (p.38)

4. Other equipment
Electronic performance and tracking systems (EPTS)

Amended text

Where wearable technology (...) the competition organiser must ensure that the technology attached to the players' equipment is not dangerous and meets ~~one of the following standards: IMS (International Match Standard) or FIFA Quality~~ the requirements for wearable EPTS under the FIFA Quality Programme for EPTS.

~~The institutes conducting these tests are subject to the approval of FIFA.~~
(...)
~~A professional standard was developed by FIFA and approved by The IFAB in order to~~ The FIFA Quality Programme for EPTS supports ~~the~~ competition organisers (...)

~~The following mark indicates that an EPTS (wearable or optical) has been officially tested to the requirements in terms of reliability and accuracy of positional data in football.~~

第二章　球（第27页）

1. 质量与测量

修订的条文

由国际足联、洲际联合会主办的正式赛事中，使用的所有比赛用球必须~~印有如下标志之一：~~达到符合《国际足联品质计划——足球》的要求，并印有相关标志。

印有这些标志即表明（……）也必须得到国际足球理事会批准。~~相关的检测机构也要得到国际足联的认证。~~

~~在使用球门线技术（GLT）时，含有集成技术的比赛用球必须印有上述三种标志之一。~~

第四章　队员装备（第38页）

4. 其他装备

表现跟踪电子系统（EPTS）

修订的条文

在由国际足联、洲际联合会（……）竞赛组织方必须确保队员所装备的技术设备不具有危险性，且满足~~以下标准之一：国际比赛标准（IMS）或国际足联品质认证（FIFA Quality）。~~《国际足联品质计划——EPTS》中对于可穿戴EPTS的要求。

~~相关检测机构需得到国际足联认可。~~

（……）

《国际足联品质计划——EPTS》可以为竞赛组织方（……）提供支持~~，国际足联开发了一项行业标准，并已由国际足球理事会批准。~~

~~如下标志表示该表现跟踪电子系统（可穿戴设备或数码设备）已通过足球比赛数据可靠性和准确性要求的官方测试。~~

Law 1 – The Field of Play (p.23)

10. Goals

Amended text

A goal consists of (...) The goalposts and crossbar must be made of approved material ~~They must be square, rectangular, round, elliptical or a combination of these shapes~~ and must not be dangerous. The goalposts and crossbar of both goals must be the same shape, which must be square, rectangular, round, elliptical or a hybrid of these options.

It is recommended that all goals used in an official competition organised under the auspices of FIFA or confederations meet the requirements of the FIFA Quality Programme for Football Goals.

Explanation

- The goalposts and crossbar must be the same shape; both goals must be the same.
- A reference to the FIFA Quality Programme for Football Goals has been added.

Law 1 – The Field of Play (p.25)

11. Goal line technology (GLT)

Amended text

Principles of GLT

The indication of whether a goal has been scored must be immediate and automatically confirmed within one second by the GLT system only to the match officials (via the referee's watch, by vibration and visual signal); it may also be sent to the video operation room (VOR).

Explanation

Where VARs are in use, the GLT signal may be sent to the video operation room (VOR).

涉及单一章节的变更（按章节顺序排序）

第一章　比赛场地（第23页）

10. 球门

修订的条文

球门由（……）球门柱和横梁必须由经批准的材料制成~~。其形状必须为正方形、矩形、圆形、椭圆形或上述形状组合构成~~，且不具危险性。两个球门的球门柱、横梁必须均为相同形状，即正方形、矩形、圆形、椭圆形或上述形状结合而成的一种形状。

建议国际足联或洲际联合会举办的正式赛事中的所有球门均符合《国际足联品质计划——足球球门》的要求。

解析

- 球门柱和横梁必须为相同形状；比赛场地的两个球门也必须相同。
- 添加了有关《国际足联品质计划——足球球门》的说明。

第一章　比赛场地（第25页）

11. 球门线技术（GLT）

修订的条文

球门线技术原则

有关进球与否的提示信号，必须在1秒钟内由球门线技术系统即时自动确认，该信息仅可传送给比赛官员（通过裁判员手表的振动和可视信号）；同时也可以发送至视频操作室。

解析

- 在使用视频助理裁判的比赛中，球门线技术信号可以被发送至视频操作室。

Law 6 – The Other Match Officials (p.50)

Amended text

The VAR and AVAR are the 'video' match officials (VMOs) and assist the referee in accordance with the Laws of the Game and the VAR protocol ~~as determined by The IFAB~~.

Explanation

There is now a FIFA list of international video match officials (VMOs).

Law 7 – The Duration of the Match (p.57)

3. Allowance for time lost

Amended text

Allowance is made by the referee in each half for all playing time lost in that half through (...)

Explanation

Clarification that if, for example, there is a stoppage towards the end of the game that is longer than the remaining playing time, the 'additional time' played (and shown by the fourth official) is the remaining playing time, not the length of the stoppage.

第六章　其他比赛官员（第50页）

修订的条文

视频助理裁判员和助理视频助理裁判员统称为 视频比赛官员（VMOs），并~~按照国际足球理事会的规定，~~依照竞赛规则及视频助理裁判操作规范协助裁判员。

解析

- 国际足联现已新增国际级视频比赛官员。

第七章　比赛时间（第57页）

3. 对损耗时间的补足

修订的条文

裁判员对每半场所有因如下情况而损耗的比赛时间予以补足：

（……）

解析

说明了如下情况：如果在比赛结束前出现的一次比赛停止的时长超过了剩余的比赛时间，则“补时”时长（如第四官员所展示的）是将要补足的剩余比赛时长，而非本次比赛停止的时长。

Law 11 – Offside (p.69)

1. Offside position

Additional text

The hands and arms of all players, including the goalkeepers, are not considered. For the purposes of determining offside, the upper boundary of the arm is in line with the bottom of the armpit.

Explanation

The shoulder is not part of the arm for handball. It is therefore a part of the body with which a goal can be legitimately scored and so must be considered when judging offside.

Law 12 – Fouls and Misconduct (p.73)

1. Direct free kick

Additional text

A direct free kick is awarded if a player commits any of the following offences:

- (...)
- bites or spits at someone on the team lists or a match official

Explanation

A free kick/penalty kick can only be awarded for an offence committed against someone on the team lists (players, substitutes, substituted players, sent-off players and team officials) or a match official.

第十一章　越位（第69页）

1. 越位位置

新增的条文

所有队员包括守门员的手和臂部不在越位位置判定范围内。在判定越位位置时，臂部的上端边界定义为与腋窝底部齐平。

解析

在判定手球时，肩部不属于手臂的一部分。因此，肩部属于身体躯干的一部分，并且属于可以合理地用来射门得分的部位，从而也必须被纳入判定越位位置的范围。

第十二章　犯规与不正当行为（第73页）

1. 直接任意球

新增的条文

如果场上队员实施如下犯规时，判罚直接任意球：

- （……）
- 对在比赛名单上的人员或比赛官员实施咬人或吐口水。

解析

任意球/罚球点球的判罚，只能针对犯规对象为在比赛名单上的人员（场上队员、替补队员、已替换下场或已罚令出场的队员、球队官员）以及比赛官员的犯规。

Law 12 – Fouls and Misconduct (p.73)

1. Direct free kick – Handling the ball

Old text (showing deletions)

(...)

It is an offence if a player:

- deliberately touches the ball with their hand/arm, ~~including~~ moving the hand/arm towards the ball
- scores in the opponents' goal directly from their hand/arm, even if accidental, including by the goalkeeper
- after the ball has touched their ~~or a team-mate's~~ hand/arm, even if accidental, immediately:
  - scores in the opponents' goal
  - ~~creates a goal-scoring opportunity~~
- ~~touches the ball with their hand/arm when:~~
  - ~~the hand/arm has made their body unnaturally bigger~~
  - ~~the hand/arm is above/beyond their shoulder level (unless the player deliberately plays the ball which then touches their hand/arm)~~

~~The above offences apply even if the ball touches a player's hand/arm directly from the head or body (including the foot) of another player who is close.~~

~~Except for the above offences, it is not an offence if the ball touches a player's hand/arm:~~

- ~~directly from the player's own head or body (including the foot)~~
- ~~directly from the head or body (including the foot) of another player who is close~~
- ~~if the hand/arm is close to the body and does not make the body unnaturally bigger~~
- ~~when a player falls and the hand/arm is between the body and the ground to support the body, but not extended laterally or vertically away from the body~~

第十二章　犯规与不正当行为（第73页）

1. 直接任意球——手球

旧条文（删除部分已标出）

（……）

以下情况视为手球犯规：

- 故意用手/臂部触球，~~包含~~手/臂部向球移动的动作。
- 队员（包括守门员）手/臂部触球后，球直接进入了对方球门，即使是意外手球。
- 队员~~或其同队队员~~手/臂部触球后（即使是意外手球），立即：
  - 进球得分。
  - ~~创造了进球得分的机会。~~
- ~~当手/臂部触球时：~~
  - ~~手/臂部的位置使身体不自然地扩大。~~
  - ~~手/臂部处于肩部以上/以外（除队员主动处理球后球接触了自己手臂的情形外）。~~

~~以上对手球犯规的认定同样适用于球接触距离很近的其他队员的头或身体（包括脚）后直接接触手球队员的手/臂部的情况。~~

~~除上述犯规情况外，球接触手/臂部不视为犯规：~~

- ~~球接触队员自己的头或身体（包括脚）后直接接触了手/臂部。~~
- ~~球接触距离很近的其他队员的头或身体（包括脚）后直接接触手球队员的手/臂部。~~
- ~~手球队员的手/臂部距离身体很近，且没有不自然地扩大身体范围。~~
- ~~队员倒地时，手或臂部处于身体与地面之间以支撑身体，且手臂没有向横向或纵向伸展离开身体。~~

New text

(...)
Not every touch of a player's hand/arm with the ball is an offence.

It is an offence if a player:

- deliberately touches the ball with their hand/arm, for example moving the hand/arm towards the ball
- touches the ball with their hand/arm when it has made their body unnaturally bigger. A player is considered to have made their body unnaturally bigger when the position of their hand/arm is not a consequence of, or justifiable by, the player's body movement for that specific situation. By having their hand/arm in such a position, the player takes a risk of their hand/arm being hit by the ball and being penalised
- scores in the opponents' goal:
  - directly from their hand/arm, even if accidental, including by the goalkeeper
  - immediately after the ball has touched their hand/arm, even if accidental

Explanation

- Not every contact between the hand/arm and the ball is a handball offence.
- Referees must judge the 'validity' of the hand/arm's position in relation to what the player is doing in that particular situation.
- Accidental handball by a team-mate before a goal is scored and accidental handball creating a goal-scoring opportunity have been removed as offences.

新条文

（……）

队员的手/臂部触球，并非每次都是犯规。

以下行为属于手球犯规：

- 故意用手/臂部触球，例如手/臂部向球移动。
- 当手/臂部触球时，其位置使身体不自然地扩大。使身体不自然扩大，是指队员的手/臂部的位置并非此情形下其身体的动作形成的正当结果或合理位置。队员将手/臂部置于此位置，是冒了被球击中并被判罚犯规的风险。
- 球进入对方球门：
  - 队员（包括守门员）手/臂部触球后，球直接进入了对方球门，即使是意外手球。
  - 队员手/臂部触球后（即使是意外手球），立即进球得分。

解析

- 并非每一次球与队员手/臂部的接触，都是手球犯规。
- 裁判员必须结合具体情形下队员的行为，去判断其手/臂部位置的“合理性”。
- 队员意外手球，之后其同队队员立即进球得分或立即获得进球得分机会，不再被视为犯规。

Law 12 – Fouls and Misconduct (pp. 75 and 79)

2. Indirect free kick

Additional text

An indirect free kick is awarded if a player:

- (...)
- initiates a deliberate trick for the ball to be passed (including from a free kick or goal kick) to the goalkeeper with the head, chest, knee etc. to circumvent the Law, whether or not the goalkeeper touches the ball with the hands; the goalkeeper is penalised if responsible for initiating the deliberate trick
- commits any other offence (...)

(...)

3. Disciplinary action – Cautions for unsporting behaviour

Amended text

There are different circumstances when a player must be cautioned for unsporting behaviour, including if a player:

- (...)
- ~~uses~~ initiates a deliberate trick for the ball to be passed ~~to pass the ball~~ (including from a free kick or goal kick) to the goalkeeper with the head, chest, knee etc. to circumvent the Law, whether or not the goalkeeper touches the ball with the hands; the goalkeeper is cautioned if responsible for initiating the deliberate trick

Explanation

The offence of using a 'trick' to circumvent the Law that prevents the goalkeeper from handling a deliberate kick from a team-mate will now apply at goal kicks. The goalkeeper is cautioned if responsible for initiating the 'trick'.

2. 间接任意球

新增的条文

如果一名场上队员犯有如下行为时，则判罚间接任意球：

- （……）
- 故意发起施诡计用头、胸、膝等部位将球传递给守门员以逃避规则相关条款处罚的行为（包括在踢任意球或球门球时），无论守门员是否用手触球。如果该行为由守门员发起，则处罚守门员。
- 犯有规则中没有提及的（……）。

（……）

3. 纪律措施——对非体育行为的警告

修订的条文

在一些情况下必须以非体育行为警告相关队员，例如：

- （……）

故意发起施诡计用头、胸、膝等部位将球传递给守门员以逃避规则相关条款处罚（包括在踢任意球或球门球时），无论守门员是否用手触球。如果该行为由守门员发起，则警告守门员。

解析

对于施诡计以逃避规则有关守门员用手接同队队员故意踢来的球的违规行为的认定，现同样适用于踢球门球时出现此行为的情况。如果该违规行为是由守门员发起，则警告守门员。

Law 12 – Fouls and Misconduct (pp.84–85)

4. Restart of play after fouls and misconduct

Amended text

If the ball is in play and a player commits a physical offence inside the field of play against:

- an opponent – an indirect or direct free kick or penalty kick
- a team-mate, substitute, substituted or sent-off player, team official or a match official – a direct free kick or penalty kick
- ~~any other person – a dropped ball~~

All verbal offences are penalised with an indirect free kick.

If the referee stops play for an offence committed by a player, inside or outside the field of play, against an outside agent, play is restarted with a dropped ball, unless a free kick is awarded for leaving the field of play without the referee's permission.

Explanation

A free kick/penalty kick can only be awarded for an offence committed against someone on the team lists (players, substitutes, substituted players, sent-off players and team officials) or a match official. If play is stopped because of an incident involving any other person, animal, object etc. (outside agent), play restarts with a dropped ball, except where a free kick is awarded for leaving the field of play without the referee's permission.

Video assistant referee (VAR) protocol (p.105)

Amended text

The use of video assistant referees (VARs) is only permitted where the match/competition organiser has fulfilled all the Implementation Assistance and Approval Programme (IAAP) ~~VAR protocol and implementation~~ requirements, as set out in ~~the VAR Handbook~~ FIFA's IAAP documents, and has received written permission from ~~The IFAB and~~ FIFA.

第十二章　犯规与不正当行为（第84–85页）

4. 犯规与不正当行为出现后的比赛恢复方式

修订的条文

如果比赛进行中，场上队员在比赛场地内，以身体行为对如下人员实施犯规：

- 对方场上队员——以间接或直接任意球、罚球点球恢复比赛。
- 同队队员、替补队员、已替换下场或已罚令出场的队员、球队官员或比赛官员——以直接任意球或罚球点球恢复比赛。
- ~~任何其他人—以坠球恢复比赛。~~

所有口头的违规行为，均判罚间接任意球。

如果一名场上队员，在比赛场地内或场地外，对场外因素实施犯规，裁判员停止了比赛，则以坠球恢复比赛，除非裁判员以队员未经允许离开比赛场地为由判罚任意球。

解析

任意球/罚球点球的判罚，只能针对犯规对象为在比赛名单上的人员（场上队员、替补队员、已替换下场或已罚令出场的队员、球队官员）以及比赛官员的犯规。如果比赛因包含其他人员、动物、物品等等（场外因素）的事件而停止，则以坠球恢复比赛，除非因未经裁判员允许离开比赛场地而判罚任意球。

视频助理裁判操作规范（第105页）

修订的条文

只有当比赛/竞赛方完全满足了视频助理裁判协助实施和审核项目（IAAP）~~视频助理裁判操作规范与实施~~的要求（~~《视频助理裁判手册》~~国际足联IAAP文件所述内容），且得到~~国际足球理事会与~~国际足联书面许可后，方可使用视频助理裁判。

Explanation

Written permission to use VARs is only required from FIFA (see also Law 5.4).

Video assistant referee (VAR) protocol (p.112)

4. Procedures

Additional text

Incapacitated VAR, AVAR or replay operator

Law 6 – The Other Match Officials stipulates: "Competition rules must state clearly who replaces a match official who is unable to start or continue and any associated changes." In matches using VARs, this also applies to replay operators.

As special training and qualifications are needed to be a video match official (VMO)/replay operator, the following principles must be included in competition rules:

- A VAR, AVAR or replay operator who is unable to start or continue may only be replaced by someone who is qualified for that role
- If no qualified replacement can be found for the VAR or replay operator,* the match must be played/continue without the use of VARs
- If no qualified replacement can be found for the AVAR,* the match must be played/continue without the use of VARs unless, in exceptional circumstances, both teams agree in writing that the match may be played/continue with only the VAR and replay operator

*This does not apply where there is more than one AVAR/replay operator.

Explanation

Competitions must include in their rules the principles to be followed if a video match official (VMO) or replay operator (RO) becomes incapacitated before or during a match.

解析

使用视频助理裁判的书面许可仅需自国际足联处获得（另见第五章第4节）。

视频助理裁判操作规范（第112页）

4. 操作程序

新增的条文

无法比赛的视频助理裁判员、助理视频助理裁判员及回放操作员

第六章——其他比赛官员中规定：竞赛规程必须明确由谁替换不能开始或继续执法的比赛官员，以及任何相应产生的更替。而在使用视频助理裁判的比赛中，此条款同样适用于回放操作员。

鉴于视频比赛官员及回放操作员需经过专门的训练和认证，竞赛规程中必须包含以下原则：

- 不能开始或继续比赛的视频助理裁判员、助理视频助理裁判员或回放操作员，只能由具备相应资质的人员替换。
- 无具备资质的视频助理裁判员或回放操作员* 可供替换，则比赛必须在不使用视频助理裁判的情况下开始/继续。
- 如无具备资质的助理视频助理裁判员* 可供替换，则比赛必须在不使用视频助理裁判的情况下开始/继续。除非比赛双方书面同意，方可在只有视频助理裁判员和回放操作员的情况下，仍然使用视频助理裁判开始/继续进行比赛。

* 不适用于使用多名助理视频助理裁判员/回放操作员的比赛。

解析

竞赛方必须在其规程中明确当视频比赛官员或回放操作员不能比赛或不能继续比赛时的替换原则。

Glossary – Football terms (p.141)
Offensive, insulting or abusive language/action(s)
Verbal or physical behaviour which is rude, hurtful, disrespectful; punishable by a sending-off (red card)

Glossary – Referee terms (p.147)
'Video' match officials (VMOs)
These are the VAR and AVAR who assist the referee in accordance with the Laws of the Game and the VAR protocol

术语汇编——足球术语（第141页）

攻击性、侮辱性或辱骂性的语言/行为

粗鲁的、伤害性的、无礼的语言或肢体行为，应罚令出场（红牌）。

术语汇编——裁判术语（第147页）

“视频”比赛官员(VMOs)

包括视频助理裁判员和助理视频助理裁判员。他们按照竞赛规则和视频助理裁判员操作手册的要求协助裁判员。

FIFA WOMEN'S WORLD CUP FRANC

FIFA WOMEN'S WORLD CUP FRANC

Glossary

术语汇编

The Glossary contains words/phrases which need clarification or explanation beyond the detail in the Laws and/or which are not always easily translated into other languages.

Football bodies

The IFAB – The International Football Association Board
Body composed of the four British FAs and FIFA which is responsible for the Laws of the Game worldwide. In principle, changes to the Laws may only be approved at the Annual General Meeting usually held in February or March

FIFA – Fédération Internationale de Football Association
The governing body responsible for football throughout the world

Confederation
Body responsible for football in a continent. The six confederations are AFC (Asia), CAF (Africa), Concacaf (North, Central America and Caribbean), CONMEBOL (South America), OFC (Oceania) and UEFA (Europe)

National football association
Body responsible for football in a country

术语汇编收纳了在规则正文中需要详细说明或解释的词语 / 词组，以及较难准确地翻译成其他语言的术语。

足球机构

IFAB——国际足球理事会

国际足球理事会由4个英联邦足球协会和国际足球联合会组成，是负责《足球竞赛规则》的全球机构。原则上，竞赛规则的修订只能由年度大会批准，该会议通常在每年二三月举行。

FIFA——国际足球联合会

国际足球联合会是世界足球运动的主管机构。

洲际联合会

洲际联合会负责本大洲足球运动，6个洲际联合会分别是亚洲足球联合会（AFC）、非洲足球联合会（CAF）、中北美洲及加勒比海足球联合会（CONCACAF）、南美洲足球联合会（CONMEBOL）、大洋洲足球联合会（OFC）和欧洲足球协会联盟（UEFA）。

国家足球协会

负责本国足球运动。

Football terms

A

Abandon
To end/terminate a match before the scheduled finish

Additional time
Time allowed at the end of each half for time 'lost' because of substitutions, injuries, disciplinary action, goal celebrations etc.

Advantage
The referee allows play to continue when an offence has occurred if this benefits the non-offending team

Assessment of injured player
Quick examination of an injury, usually by a medical person, to see if the player requires treatment

Away goals rule
Method of deciding a match/tie when both teams have scored the same number of goals; goals scored away from home count double

足球术语

A

中止

在比赛程序尚未完成前，终止 / 取消该场比赛。

补时

因队员替换、受伤、纪律处罚、庆祝进球等“损耗”的时间，在各半场结束时予以补足。

有利

当犯规发生，未犯规的一方能从中获得利益时，裁判员允许比赛继续进行。

对受伤队员的伤情评估

通常由医护人员对场上受伤队员伤势进行的快速诊断，用以确定是否需要治疗。

客场进球规则

当两队进球数相同时，用来判定比赛胜负的方法。此时客场球队的进球将被双倍计算。

B

Brutality
An act which is savage, ruthless or deliberately violent

C

Caution
Disciplinary sanction which results in a report to a disciplinary authority; indicated by showing a yellow card; two cautions in a match result in a player or team official being sent off

Challenge
An action when a player competes/contests with an opponent for the ball

Charge (an opponent)
Physical challenge against an opponent, usually using the shoulder and upper arm (which is kept close to the body)

'Cooling' break
In the interests of player welfare and safety, competition rules may allow, in certain weather conditions (high humidity and temperatures), 'cooling' breaks (usually ninety seconds to three minutes) to allow the body's temperature to fall; these are different from 'drinks' breaks

B

野蛮行为

野蛮、粗暴的行为或故意使用暴力的行径。

C

警告

一种被记录和报告的纪律处罚，以出示黄牌作为表示。一名队员或球队官员在一场比赛中得到两次警告将被罚令出场。

争抢

一名队员与对方对抗/争夺控球权的行为。

冲撞（对方队员）

用身体对对方队员使用的争抢动作，通常使用肩部或上臂（紧贴身体）。

“降温”暂停

为保障队员的权益与安全，竞赛规程可以允许在特定的天气条件下（高温高湿），在比赛中实施“降温”暂停（时长通常为90秒至3分钟），以使队员身体降温。“降温”暂停不同于“补水”暂停。

D

Deceive

Act to mislead/trick the referee into giving an incorrect decision/disciplinary sanction which benefits the deceiver and/or their team

Deliberate

An action which the player intended/meant to make; it is not a 'reflex' or unintended reaction

Direct free kick

A free kick from which a goal can be scored by kicking the ball directly into the opponents' goal without having to touch another player

Discretion

Judgment used by a referee or other match official when making a decision

Dissent

Public protest or disagreement (verbal and/or physical) with a match official's decision; punishable by a caution (yellow card)

Distract

Disturb, confuse or draw attention (usually unfairly)

'Drinks' break

Competition rules may allow 'drinks' breaks (of no more than one minute) for players to rehydrate; these are different from 'cooling' breaks

Dropped ball

A method of restarting play – the referee drops the ball for one player of the team that last touched the ball (except in the penalty area where the ball is dropped for the goalkeeper); the ball is in play when it touches the ground

D

欺骗

误导 / 使用诡计使裁判员做出错误的判罚 / 纪律处罚，以使该名队员自身和 / 或其球队获利。

故意

队员有意/有目的而做出的行为，而非“本能的”或无意识的反应。

直接任意球

可以将球直接射入对方球门，无需触碰其他队员，即可得分的任意球。

酌情考虑

裁判员或其他比赛官员在做出判罚时的判断。

异议

对裁判员的判罚以公开方式表示异议或抗议（用语言和/或肢体动作），需在公众视野下给予警告（黄牌）。

干扰

扰乱、迷惑或吸引注意力（通常是以不公平的方式）。

“补水”暂停

竞赛规程可以允许“补水”暂停（不超过1分钟），使队员得以补充水分。“补水”暂停不同于“降温”暂停。

坠球

恢复比赛的方式之一——裁判员坠球给最后触球的球队的一名队员（除非是在罚球区内，需坠球给守方守门员），当球接触地面时比赛即为恢复。

E

Electronic performance and tracking system (EPTS)
System which records and analyses data about the physical and physiological performance of a player

Endanger the safety of an opponent
Put an opponent at danger or risk (of injury)

Excessive force
Using more force/energy than is necessary

Extra time
A method of trying to decide the outcome of a match involving two equal additional periods of play not exceeding 15 minutes each

F

Feinting
An action which attempts to confuse an opponent. The Laws define permitted and 'illegal' feinting

Field of play (pitch)
The playing area confined by the touchlines and goal lines and goal nets where used

E

表现跟踪电子系统(EPTS)

记录、分析队员体能和生理活动数据的系统。

危及对方安全

使对方队员处在(受伤的)危险或风险中。

过分力量

使用超出必要的力量或力气。

加时赛

一种决定比赛结果的方式，分为两个不超过15分钟且相等时长的半场。

F

假动作

试图迷惑对方队员的行为。规则中已经定义了允许的和不合规的假动作。

比赛场地

由边线、球门线和球门网围成的比赛区域。

G

Goal line technology (GLT)
Electronic system which immediately informs the referee when a goal has been scored i.e. the ball has wholly passed over the goal line in the goal (see Law 1 for details)

H

Holding offence
A holding offence occurs only when a player's contact with an opponent's body or equipment impedes the opponent's movement

Hybrid system
A combination of artificial and natural materials to create a playing surface which requires sunlight, water, air circulation and mowing

I

Impede
To delay, block or prevent an opponent's action or movement

Indirect free kick
A free kick from which a goal can only be scored if another player (of any team) touches the ball after it has been kicked

Intercept
To prevent a ball reaching its intended destination

G

球门线技术（GLT）

可立即向裁判员传递进球与否，即球的整体是否越过球门线信息的电子系统（细节详见第一章）。

H

拉扯犯规

仅指队员通过接触对方队员身体或者装备的方式，阻止对方队员移动的违规行为。

混和系统

人造和天然结合材料制成的草皮，同样需要阳光、水分、空气循环和剪草处理。

I

阻碍

延缓 / 阻挡或阻止对方队员的行动或移动。

间接任意球

在踢出后，由其他场上队员（任意一方）触球后才可进球得分的任意球。

阻截

阻止球到达预定的地点。

K

Kick
The ball is kicked when a player makes contact with it the foot and/or the ankle

Kicks from the penalty mark
Method of deciding the result of a match by each team alternately taking kicks until one team has scored one more goal and both teams have taken the same number of kicks (unless during the first 5 kicks for each team, one team could not equal the other team's score even if they scored from all their remaining kicks)

N

Negligible
Insignificant, minimal

O

Offence
An action which breaks/violates the Laws of the Game

Offensive, insulting or abusive language/action(s)
Verbal or physical behaviour which is rude, hurtful, disrespectful; punishable by a sending-off (red card)

Outside agent
Any animal, object or structure, etc., as well as any person who is not a match official or on the team list (players, substitutes and team officials)

K

踢

队员使用脚和/或脚踝接触球，则视为踢球。

罚球点球决胜

决定比赛胜负的方式。由双方球队轮流踢罚球点球，直至当双方罚球次数相同时，一队进球数比另一队多一球（除非在前5轮罚球时，一队罚完剩余所有轮次可能的进球数都无法追平另一队）。

N

微不足道

不明显地、轻微地。

O

犯规违规

违背 / 破坏 / 违反规则的行为。有些情况下指对人，特别是对对方队员的不合规行为。

攻击性、侮辱性或辱骂性的语言/行为

粗鲁的、伤害性的、无礼的语言或肢体行为，应罚令出场（红牌）。

场外因素

任何动物、物体或建筑结构体，以及除比赛官员和球队名单（场上队员、替补队员、球队官员）以外的任何人。

P

Penalise
To punish, usually by stopping play and awarding a free kick or penalty kick to the opposing team (see also Advantage)

Play
Action by a player which makes contact with the ball

Playing distance
Distance to the ball which allows a player to touch the ball by extending the foot/leg or jumping or, for goalkeepers, jumping with arms extended. Distance depends on the physical size of the player

Q

Quick free kick
A free kick taken (with the referee's permission) very quickly after play was stopped

R

Reckless
Any action (usually a tackle or challenge) by a player which disregards (ignores) the danger to, or consequences for, the opponent

Restart
Any method of resuming play after it has been stopped

P

判罚

一种惩罚。通常是以停止比赛并判给对方任意球或罚球点球的方式（同时可参考有利）。

处理球

队员做出的用身体接触球的动作。

合理争抢范围

队员可以通过伸脚 / 伸腿或起跳，以及守门员跳起后手臂展开而接触到球的距离范围。此距离取决于队员的体型。

Q

快发任意球

在比赛停止后快速发出的任意球（经裁判员允许）。

R

鲁莽的

队员的行为动作（通常是在抢截或争抢时）不顾及（忽视）可能对对方造成的危险或后果。

比赛恢复

比赛停止后，以任何方式继续比赛。

Restart position
A player's position at a restart is determined by the position of their feet or any part of their body which is touching the ground, except as outlined in Law 11 – Offside

S

Sanction
Disciplinary action taken by the referee

Save
An action by a player to stop or attempt to stop the ball when it is going into or very close to the goal using any part of the body except the hands/arms (unless a goalkeeper within their own penalty area)

Sending-off
Disciplinary action when a player is required to leave the field for the remainder of the match having committed a sending-off offence (indicated by a red card); if the match has started the player cannot be replaced.
A team official may also be sent off.

Serious foul play
A tackle or challenge for the ball that endangers the safety of an opponent or uses excessive force or brutality; punishable by a sending-off (red card)

Signal
Physical indication from the referee or any match official; usually involves movement of the hand or arm or flag, or use of the whistle (referee only)

比赛恢复时的位置

比赛恢复时，场上队员所处的位置以其双脚或身体任何接触地面的部分为准（第十一章涉及的情况除外）。

S

纪律处罚

裁判员实施的纪律措施。

救球

是指队员用除手之外（守门员在本方罚球区内除外）的任何身体部位阻止或试图阻止即将进门或非常接近球门的球。

罚令出场

当队员犯有可被罚令出场的犯规（出示红牌作为表示），不得参加剩余时间的比赛，并要求离开比赛场地时实施的纪律处罚。如果比赛已经开始，则该名队员不得被替换。

球队官员也可以被罚令出场。

严重犯规

当抢截或争抢球时，采用危及对方队员安全，使用过分的力量、野蛮的方式，应罚令出场（红牌）。

信号

裁判员或其他比赛官员使用的肢体示意，通常以手臂、手旗的动作或使用哨音（仅裁判员）的方式。

Simulation
An action which creates a wrong/false impression that something has occurred when it has not (see also Deceive); committed by a player to gain an unfair advantage

Spirit of the game
The main/essential principles/ethos of football as a sport but also within a particular match (see Law 5)

Suspend
To stop a match for a period of time with the intention of eventually restarting play e.g. due to fog, heavy rain, thunderstorm, serious injury

T

Tackle
A challenge for the ball with the foot (on the ground or in the air)

Team list
Official team document usually listing the players, substitutes and team officials

Team official
Any non-player listed on the official team list e.g. coach, physiotherapist, doctor (see Technical staff)

Technical area
Defined area (in stadiums) for the team officials which includes seating (see Law 1 for details)

Technical staff
Official non-playing team members listed on the official team list e.g. coach, physiotherapist, doctor (see Team official)

Temporary dismissal
A temporary suspension from the next part of the match for a player guilty of some/all cautionable offences (depending on competition rules)

佯装

队员制造出错误 / 虚假表象的动作行为，好像有情况发生而其实并没有，企图借此获得不正当的利益（参考欺骗）。

足球比赛精神

足球作为一项体育运动，一种受欢迎的比赛，其主要/核心的原则/精神（详见第五章）。

中断

将比赛暂停一段时间，试图最终能恢复继续比赛。例如，由于大雾、大雨、雷电、严重受伤等情况而造成的中断。

T

抢截

使用脚争抢球（在地面或空中）。

球队名单

列出上场队员、替补队员和球队官员信息的正式文件。

球队官员

任何列入球队正式名单中的非参赛人员，如教练员、理疗师、医生（见技术人员）。

技术区域

（体育场馆内）供球队官员和替补队员使用的有坐席的区域（详见第一章具体内容）。

技术官员

列入球队正式名单中的非参赛人员，如教练员、理疗师、医生（见球队官员）。

暂时罚离

对于受到所有 / 部分类型的警告（取决于竞赛规程）的队员，暂时停止其参与接下来一部分时长比赛的处罚。

U

Undue interference
Action/influence which is unnecessary

Unsporting behaviour
Unfair action/behaviour; punishable by a caution

V

Violent conduct
An action, which is not a challenge for the ball, which uses or attempts to use excessive force or brutality against an opponent or when a player deliberately strikes someone on the head or face unless the force used is negligible

U

不当干涉

不必要的举动 / 干扰。

非体育行为

有失公平的不当举动 / 行为，应予警告。

V

暴力行为

队员不以争抢球为目的，而对对方使用或企图使用过分力量或野蛮动作，或故意击打其他人的头部或面部的行为，除非使用的力量微不足道。

Referee terms

Match official(s)
General term for person or persons responsible for controlling a football match on behalf of a football association and/or competition under whose jurisdiction the match is played

Referee
The main match official for a match who operates on the field of play. Other match officials operate under the referee's control and direction. The referee is the final/ultimate decision-maker

Other match officials
'On-field' match officials
Competitions may appoint other match officials to assist the referee:

- **Assistant referee**
  A match official with a flag positioned on one half of each touchline to assist the referee particularly with offside situations and goal kick/corner kick/throw-in decisions

- **Fourth official**
  A match official with responsibility for assisting the referee with both on-field and off-field matters, including overseeing the technical area, controlling substitutes etc.

- **Additional assistant referee (AAR)**
  A match official positioned on the goal line to assist the referee particularly with situations in/around the penalty area and goal/no-goal decisions

- **Reserve assistant referee**
  Assistant referee who will replace an assistant (and, if competition rules permit, a fourth official and/or AAR) who is unable to continue

裁判术语

比赛官员
指在足球协会和 / 或竞赛主办方管辖下进行的比赛中，代表足球协会和 / 或竞赛方履行执法比赛职责的个人或团队。

裁判员
在比赛场地内执法的主要比赛官员，其他比赛官员在裁判员的管理和领导下履行职责。裁判员的判罚决定为最终决定。

其他比赛官员
“在场”比赛官员
竞赛方可委派其他比赛官员协助裁判员：

• 助理裁判员
持旗的比赛官员，处在两个半场的边线位置协助裁判员做出判罚决定，尤其是涉及越位、球门球、角球、界外球的判罚。

• 第四官员
负责协助裁判员管理场上、场下事务的比赛官员，包括监管技术区域及替补队员等。

• 附加助理裁判员（AAR）
该比赛官员处在球门线位置协助裁判员做出判罚决定，尤其是涉及罚球区内 / 附近的情况，以及进球 / 未进球的判罚。

• 候补助理裁判员
应为一名助理裁判员。用于替换无法继续执法的助理裁判员（如果赛事规程许可，也可替换第四官员和 / 或附加助理裁判员）。

'Video' match officials (VMOs)

These are the VAR and AVAR who assist the referee in accordance with the Laws of the Game and the VAR protocol

- **Video assistant referee (VAR)**

  A current or former referee appointed to assist the referee by communicating information from replay footage only in relation to a 'clear and obvious error' or 'serious missed incident' in one of the reviewable categories

- **Assistant video assistant referee (AVAR)**

  A current or former referee/assistant referee appointed to assist the video assistant referee (VAR)

“视频”比赛官员（VMOs）

包括视频助理裁判员和助理视频助理裁判员。他们按照竞赛规则和视频助理裁判员操作手册的要求协助裁判员。

- 视频助理裁判员

被指派根据视频回放画面与裁判员沟通信息并协助裁判员的现役或已退役的裁判员。视频助理裁判员仅在视频回放画面显示出现了“清晰而明显的错误”或“严重的遗漏事件”时协助裁判员。

- 助理视频助理裁判员

被指派协助视频助理裁判员的现役或已退役的裁判员/助理裁判员。

Practical guidelines for match officials

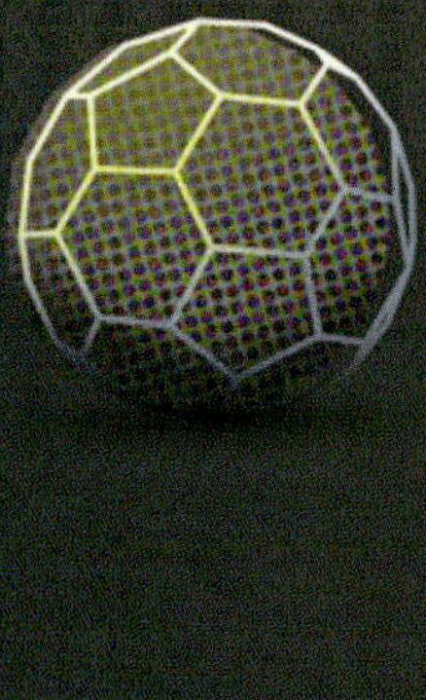

比赛官员
实践指南

Introduction

These guidelines contain practical advice for match officials which supplements the information in the Laws of the Game section.

Reference is made in Law 5 to referees operating within the framework of the Laws of the Game and the 'spirit of the game'. Referees are expected to use common sense and to apply the 'spirit of the game' when applying the Laws of the Game, especially when making decisions relating to whether a match takes place and/or continues.

This is especially true for the lower levels of football where it may not always be possible for the Law to be strictly applied. For example, unless there are safety issues, the referee should allow a game to start/continue if:

- one or more corner flags is missing
- there is a minor inaccuracy with the markings on the field of play such as the corner area, centre circle etc.
- the goalposts/crossbar are not white

In such cases, the referee should, with the agreement of the teams, play/continue the match and must submit a report to the appropriate authorities.

Key:

- AR = assistant referee
- AAR = additional assistant referee

引言

比赛官员实践指南包含的建议是对《足球竞赛规则》内容的补充。

在第五章中已提及，裁判员依据《足球竞赛规则》和“足球运动精神”尽自身最大能力，做出自己认为最合适的决定。希望裁判员在执行《足球竞赛规则》时，结合常识、领会“足球比赛精神”，尤其是在做是否开始和/或继续比赛的相关决定时。

这在低级别的足球比赛中尤为重要。因为在这些级别的比赛中，完全按照规则执行是有难度的。如果在如下情况中，只要不存在安全隐患，裁判员应该开始/继续比赛：

- 缺少一面或多面角旗。
- 比赛场地个别标线不够精确，例如角球区、中圈弧等。
- 球门柱/横梁颜色不是白色的。

在这些情况下，经由双方球队同意，裁判员应该开始/继续比赛，并向相关机构提交报告。

关键词：

- AR=助理裁判员
- AAR=附加助理裁判员

Positioning, movement and teamwork

1. **General positioning and movement**

   The best position is one from which the referee can make the correct decision. All recommendations about positioning must be adjusted using specific information about the teams, the players and events in the match.

   The positions recommended in the graphics are basic guidelines. The reference to a "zone" emphasises that a recommended position is an area within which the referee is likely to be most effective. The zone may be larger, smaller or differently shaped depending on the exact match circumstances.

   Recommendations:

   - The play should be between the referee and the lead AR
   - The lead AR should be in the referee's field of vision so the referee should usually use a wide diagonal system
   - Staying towards the outside of the play makes it easier to keep play and the lead AR in the referee's field of vision
   - The referee should be close enough to see play without interfering with play
   - "What needs to be seen" is not always in the vicinity of the ball. The referee should also pay attention to:
     - player confrontations off the ball
     - possible offences in the area towards which play is moving
     - offences occurring after the ball is played away

选位、移动与团队配合

1. 常规选位与移动

裁判员能够做出准确判断的位置就是最佳的位置。所有有关位置的建议，在比赛中都应根据双方球队、队员，以及场上发生的各种情况进行调整。

插图中所建议的裁判员位置是常规建议，是能够帮助裁判员作出最佳判断的区域。这些区域可大可小，也可有不同形状，全部由比赛的实际情况而定。

建议：

- 比赛应在裁判员和视线较好的助理裁判员注视下进行。
- 视线较好的助理裁判员应在裁判员的视线范围之内，因此裁判员应按对角线方法选位。
- 在比赛发展的区域外进行选位，便于观察比赛进程，同时也能将视线较好的助理裁判员纳入自己的视野范围内。
- 在不影响比赛进程的情况下，裁判员应尽量靠近比赛发展的区域。
- “需要留意的”区域并不总在球的附近。裁判员也应该注意：
    - 无球状态下队员之间的争端。
    - 比赛发展方向的区域内可能发生的犯规。
    - 球离开后的区域内发生的犯规。

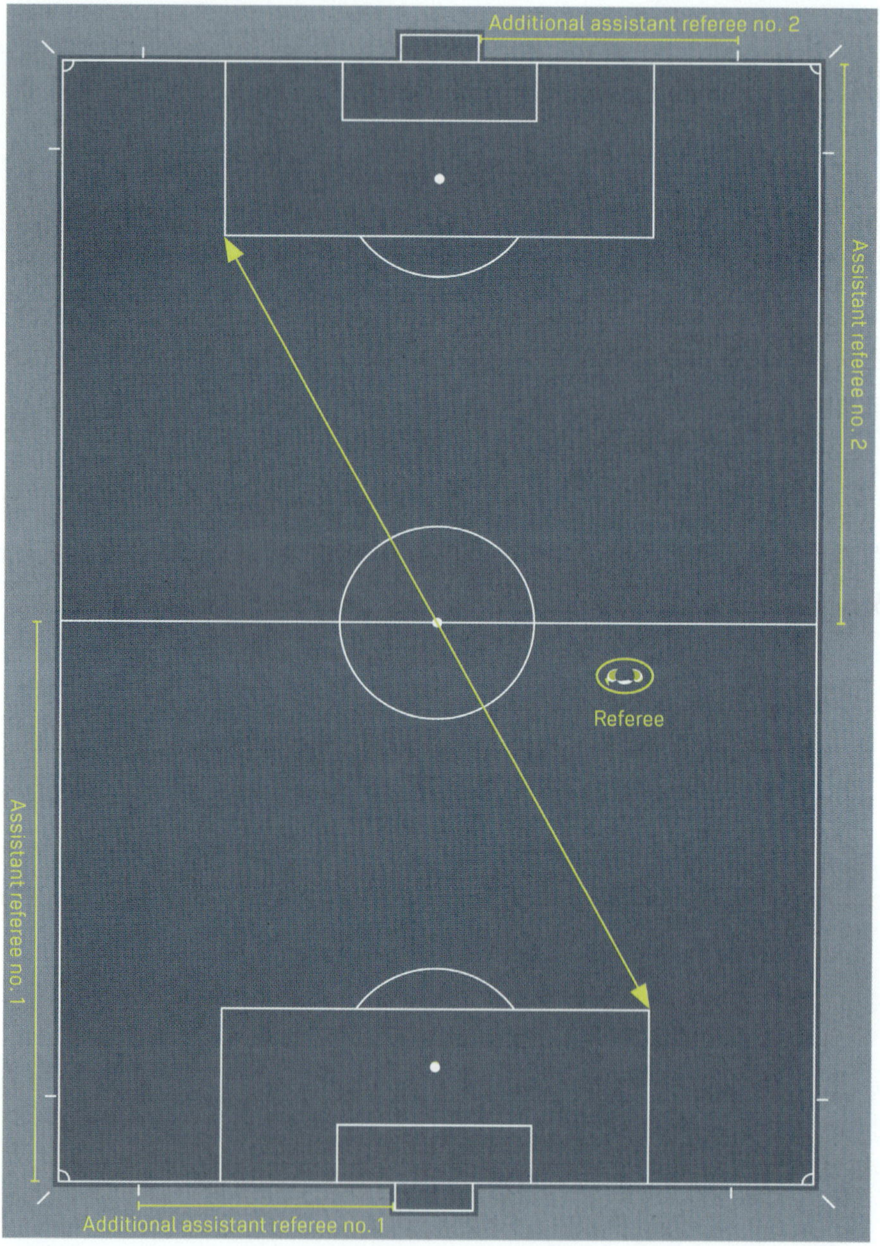

Additional assistant referee no. 2
Assistant referee no. 2
Referee
Assistant referee no. 1
Additional assistant referee no. 1

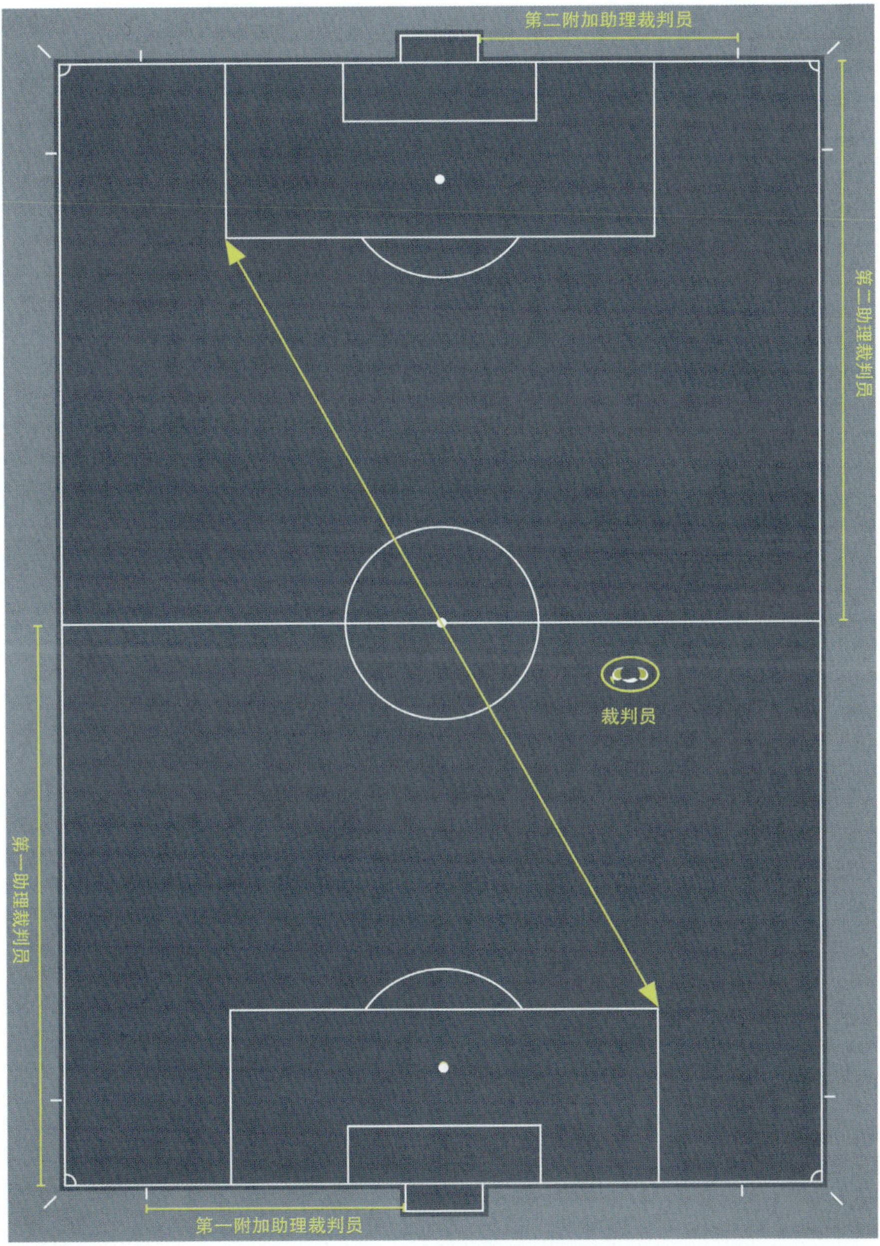
第二附加助理裁判员
第二助理裁判员
裁判员
第一助理裁判员
第一附加助理裁判员

Positioning of assistant referees and additional assistant referees
The AR must be in line with the second-last defender or the ball if it is nearer to the goal line than the second-last defender. The AR must always face the field of play, even when running. Side-to-side movement should be used for short distances. This is especially important when judging offside as it gives the AR a better line of vision.

The AAR position is behind the goal line except where it is necessary to move onto the goal line to judge a goal/no goal situation. The AAR is not allowed to enter the field of play unless there are exceptional circumstances.

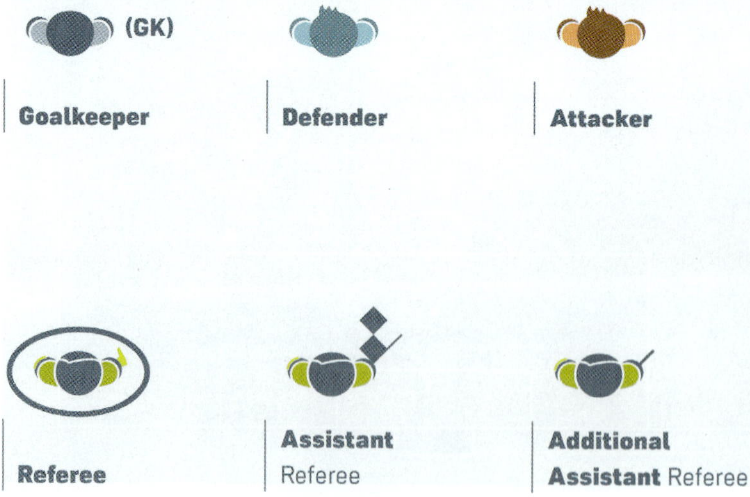

助理裁判员与附加助理裁判员的选位

助理裁判员的位置必须与守方倒数第二名队员齐平，或当球较守方倒数第二名队员更接近于球门线时与球齐平。助理裁判员必须时刻面向比赛场地内，即使是在跑动中。侧滑步应用于短距离移动。这种移动对助理裁判员判断越位尤为重要，因为可以得到更好的观察角度。

附加助理裁判员的位置在球门线后，除非需要进行移动来判断球是否进门。除特殊情况外，不允许附加助理裁判员进入比赛场地内。

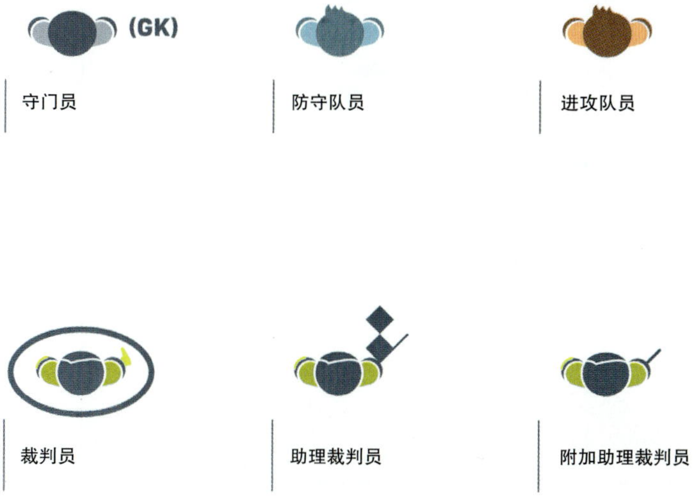

2. Positioning and teamwork

Consultation

When dealing with disciplinary issues, eye contact and a basic discreet hand signal from the AR to the referee may be sufficient. When direct consultation is required, the AR may advance 2–3 metres onto the field of play if necessary. When talking, the referee and AR should both face the field of play to avoid being heard by others and to observe the players and field of play.

Corner kick

The AR's position for a corner kick is behind the corner flag in line with the goal line but the AR must not interfere with the player taking the corner kick and must check that the ball is properly placed in the corner area.

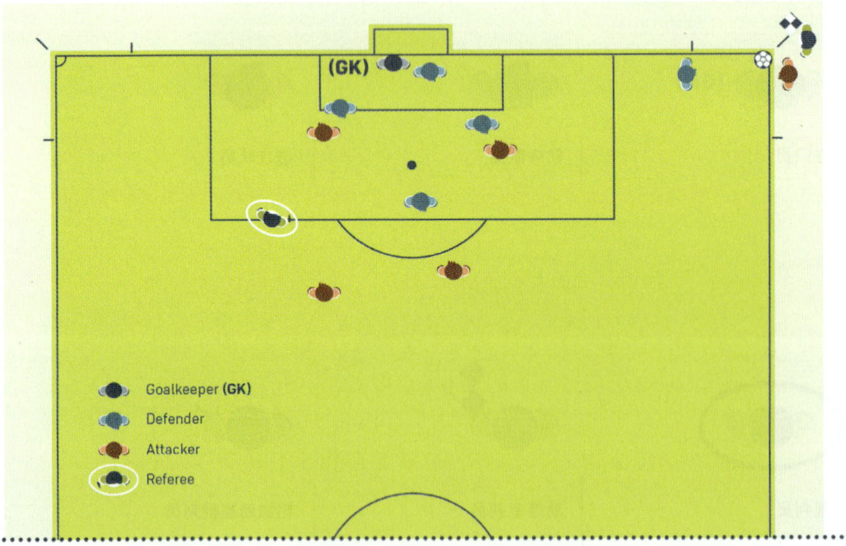

2. 选位与团队配合

（征询）商议

当涉及纪律处罚事宜时，在某些情况下用目光或赛前协商的手势信号与裁判员沟通即可。当需要直接商议时，助理裁判员可以进入场内2～3米。商议时裁判员和助理裁判员都要面向场内，以避免其他人听到商议内容，并利于观察场内的队员。

角球

助理裁判员在队员踢角球时应站在角旗后、球门线的延长线位置，不能影响踢角球的队员，且必须查看球是否正确摆放在角球区内。

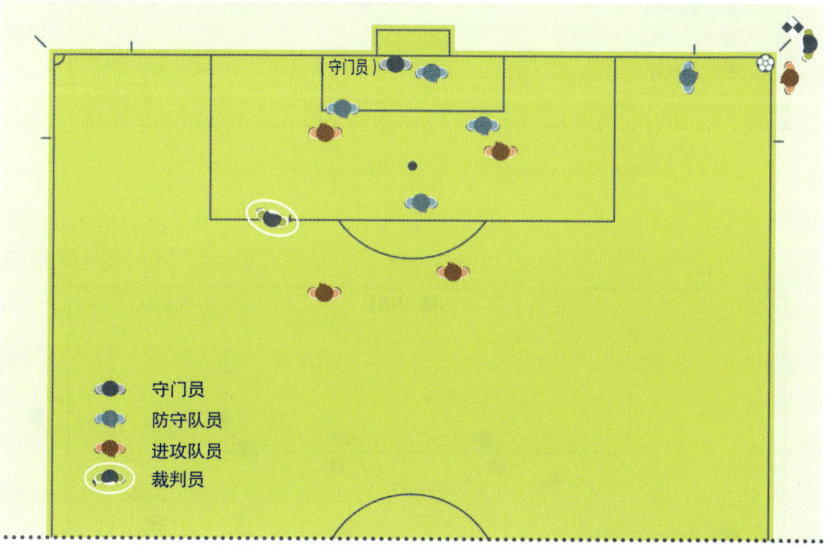

Free kick

The AR's position for a free kick must be in line with the second-last defender to check the offside line. However, the AR must be ready to follow the ball by moving down the touchline towards the corner flag if there is a direct shot on goal.

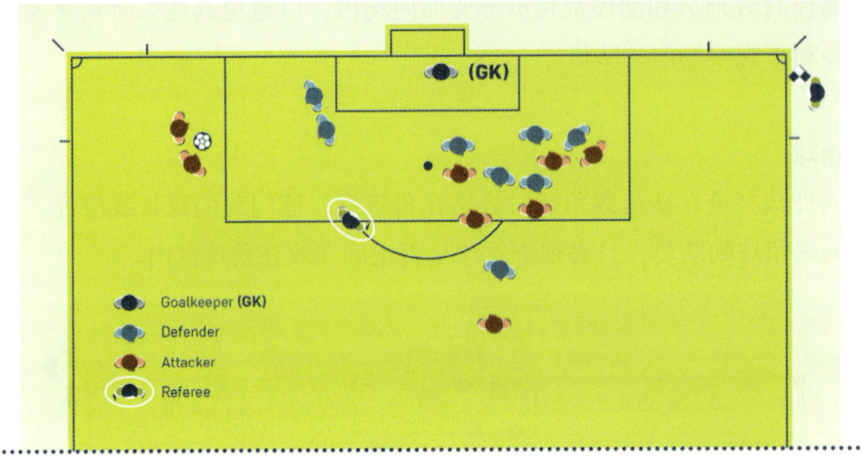

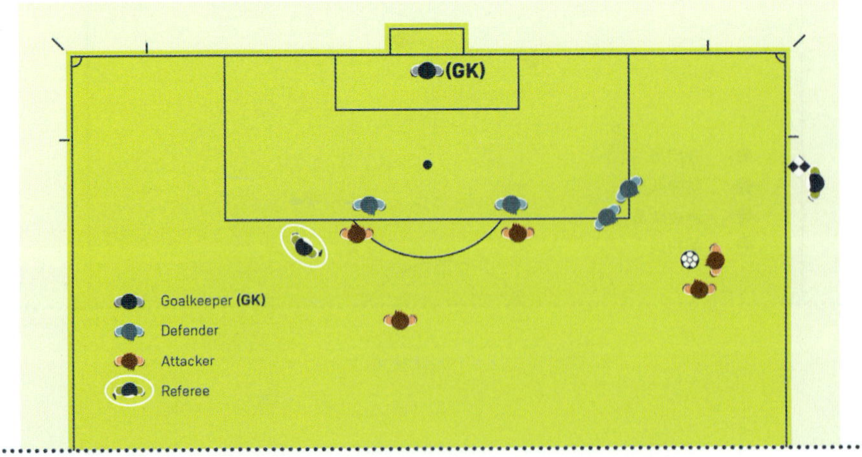

任意球

在踢任意球时，助理裁判员必须处在与守方倒数第二名队员齐平的位置以观察越位情况。无论如何，助理裁判员还必须有所准备，即发生直接射门时要沿边线快速冲向角旗方向以跟随球。

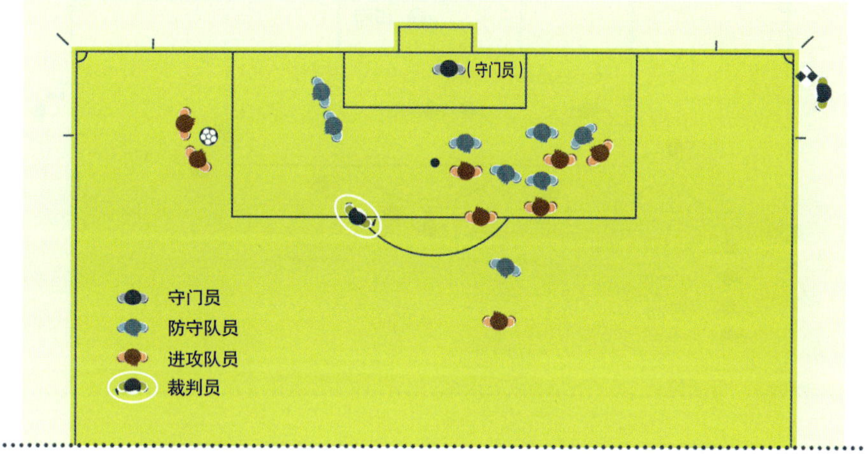

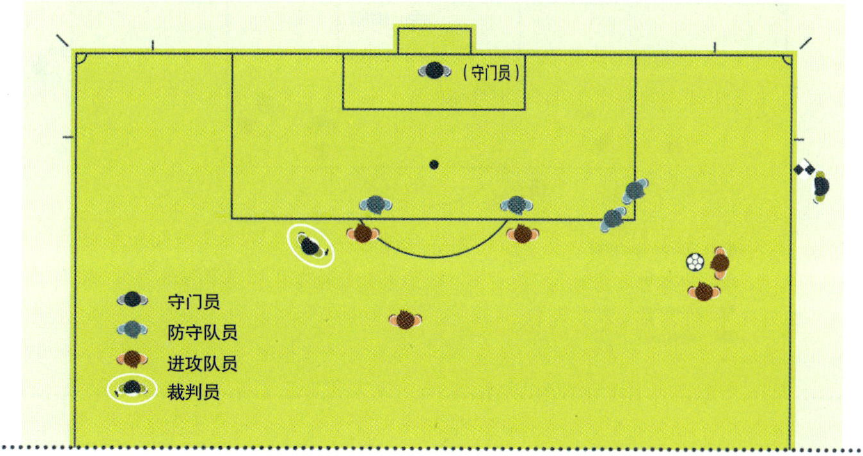

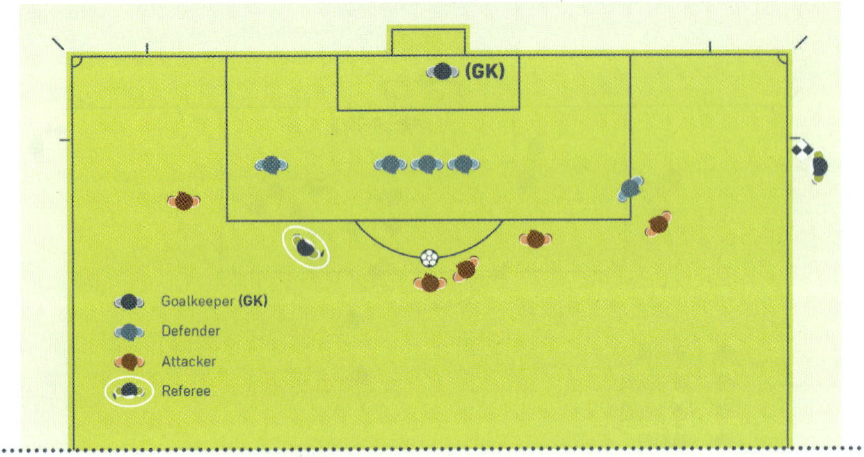
(GK)
Goalkeeper (GK)
Defender
Attacker
Referee

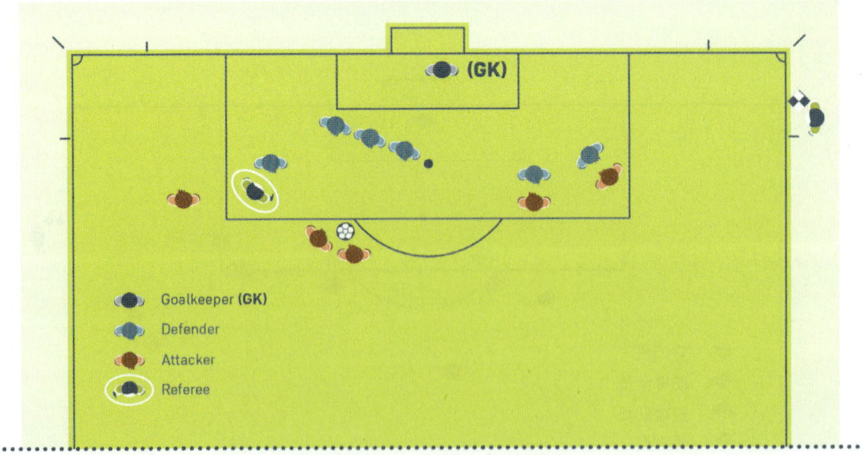
(GK)
Goalkeeper (GK)
Defender
Attacker
Referee

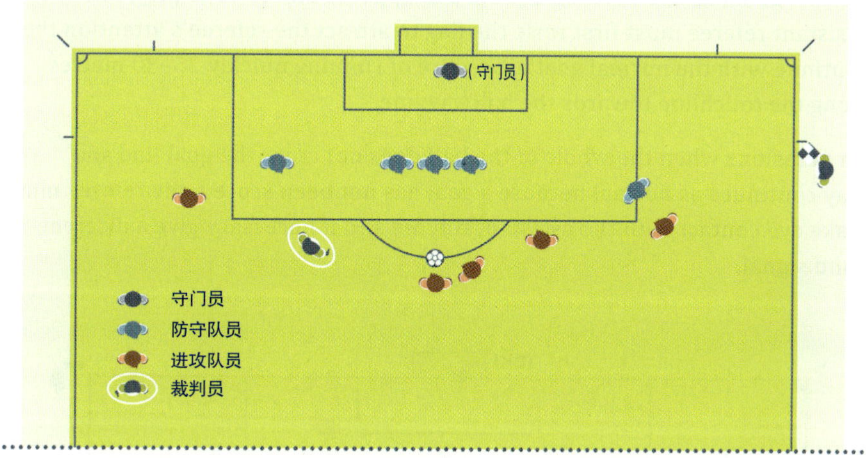
（守门员）
守门员
防守队员
进攻队员
裁判员

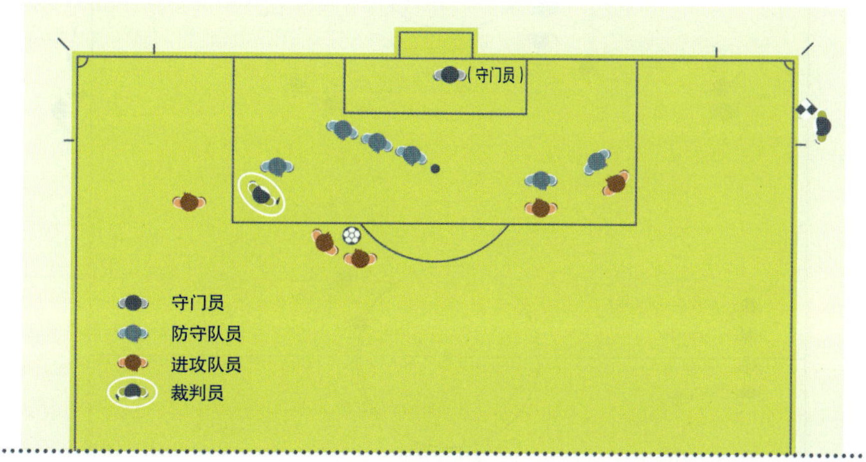
（守门员）
守门员
防守队员
进攻队员
裁判员

Goal/no goal

When a goal has been scored and there is no doubt about the decision, the referee and assistant referee must make eye contact and the assistant referee must then move quickly 25–30 metres along the touchline towards the halfway line without raising the flag.

When a goal has been scored but the ball appears still to be in play, the assistant referee must first raise the flag to attract the referee's attention then continue with the normal goal procedure of running quickly 25–30 metres along the touchline towards the halfway line.

On occasions when the whole of the ball does not cross the goal line and play continues as normal because a goal has not been scored, the referee must make eye contact with the assistant referee and if necessary give a discreet hand signal.

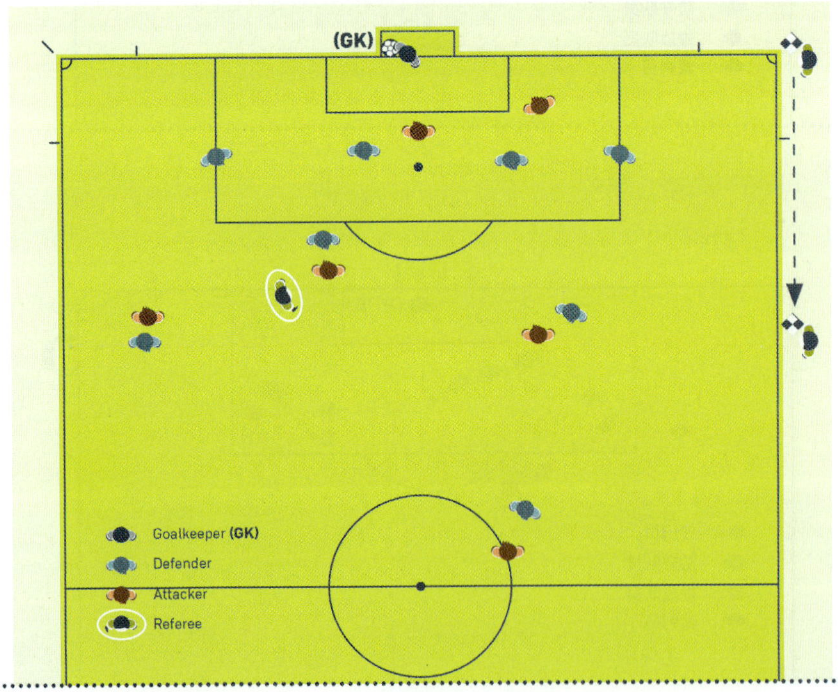

“进球 / 未进球”

当球已进球门并且没有任何疑问时，裁判员和助理裁判员必须用目光相互交流，然后助理裁判员不举旗沿边线快速向中线方向移动25～30米以表示进球。

当球已进球门而比赛仍在继续时，助理裁判员必须首先举旗向裁判员示意球已经进门，然后像正常的进球程序一样沿边线快速向中线方向跑25～30米以表示进球。

有时，球的整体没有越过球门线，比赛正常进行。此时，裁判员必须和助理裁判员进行目光交流，如果需要则用赛前准备好的手势信号相互配合。

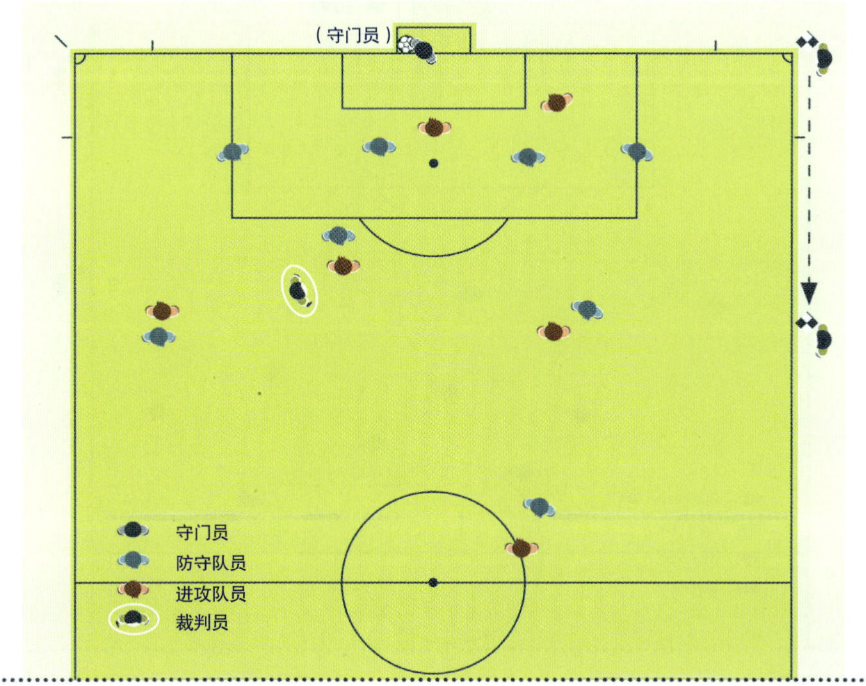

Goal kick

The AR must first check if the ball is inside the goal area. If the ball is not placed correctly, the AR must not move from the position and must make eye contact with the referee and raise the flag. Once the ball is placed correctly inside the goal area, the AR must take a position to check the offside line.

However, if there is an AAR, the AR should take up a position in line with the offside line and the AAR must be positioned at the intersection of the goal line and the goal area, and check if the ball is placed inside the goal area. If the ball is not placed correctly, the AAR must communicate this to the referee.

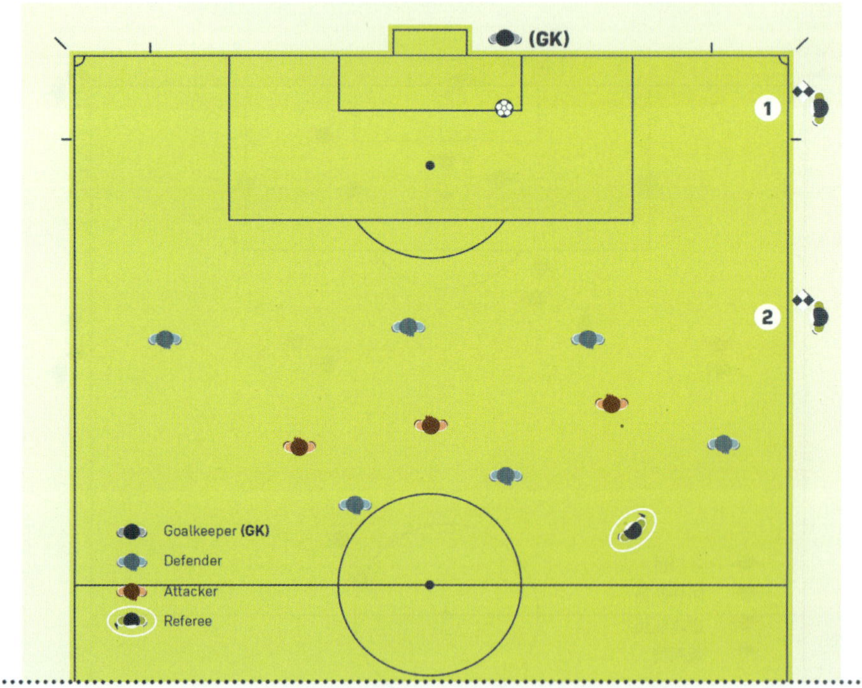

球门球

助理裁判员必须确认球是否放在球门区内。如果球没有放在正确的位置上，助理裁判员不得移动位置，必须用目光与裁判员交流并举旗示意。一旦球被正确地放在球门区内，助理裁判员必须选择观察越位线的位置。

如果有附加助理裁判员，则助理裁判员应选择观察越位线的位置。而附加助理裁判员选择球门线与球门区线相交的位置，检查球是否放在球门区内。如果球没有放在正确的位置上，附加助理裁判员必须与裁判员沟通。

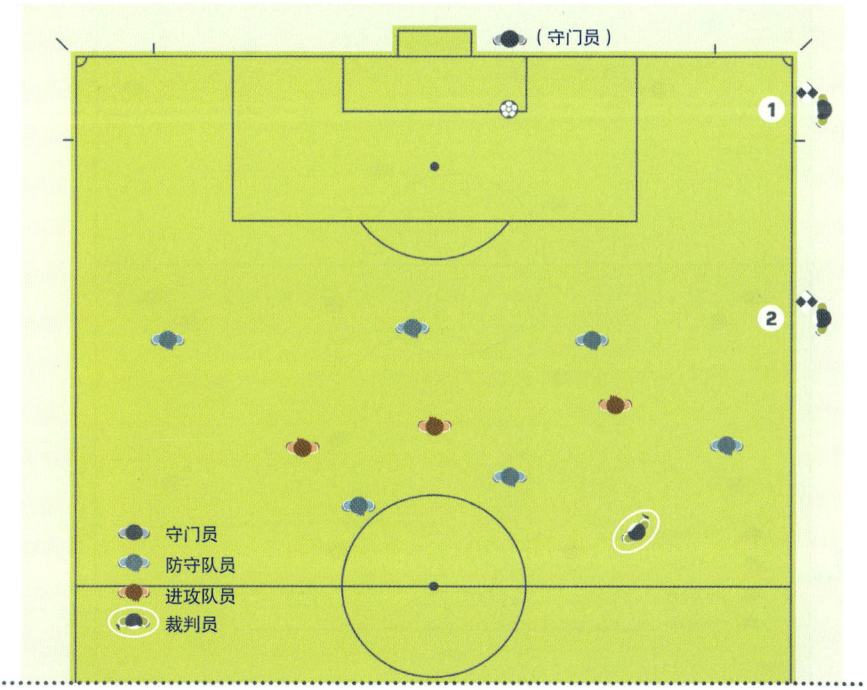

Goalkeeper releasing the ball

The AR must take a position in line with the edge of the penalty area and check that the goalkeeper does not handle the ball outside the penalty area. Once the goalkeeper has released the ball, the AR must take a position to check the offside line.

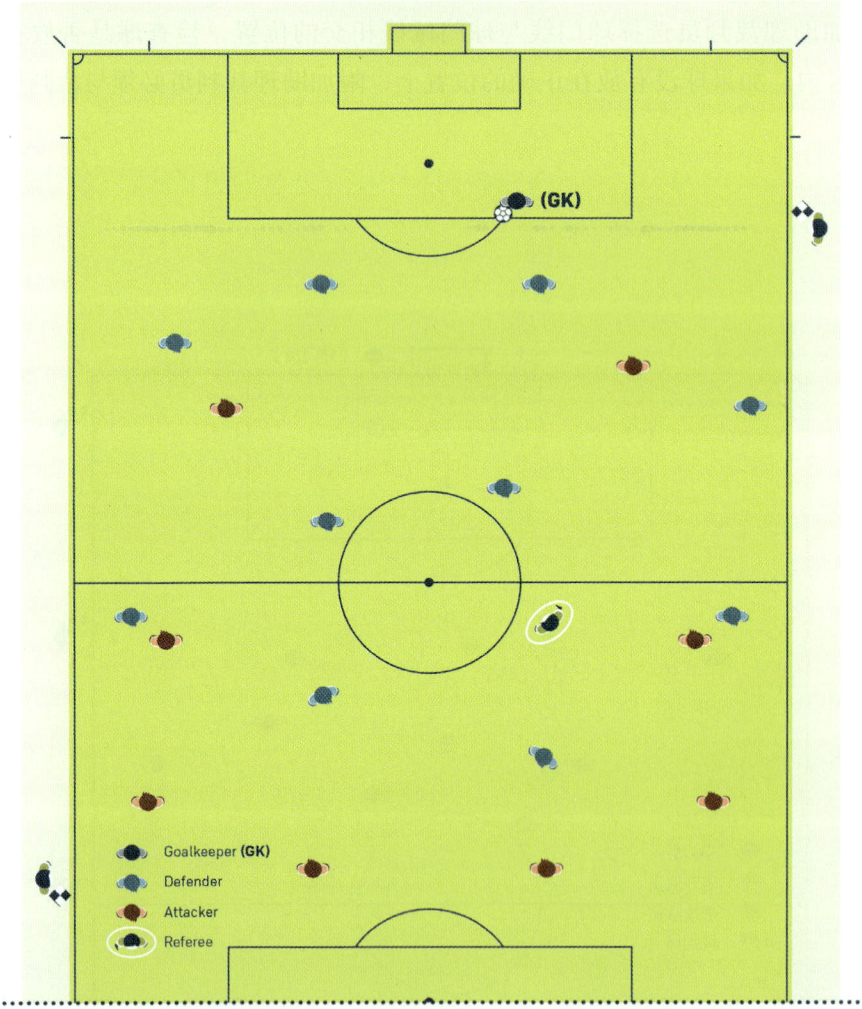

守门员发球

助理裁判员必须选择罚球区线的延长位置查看守门员是否在罚球区外手球。一旦守门员发出球后，助理裁判员必须选择观察越位线的位置。

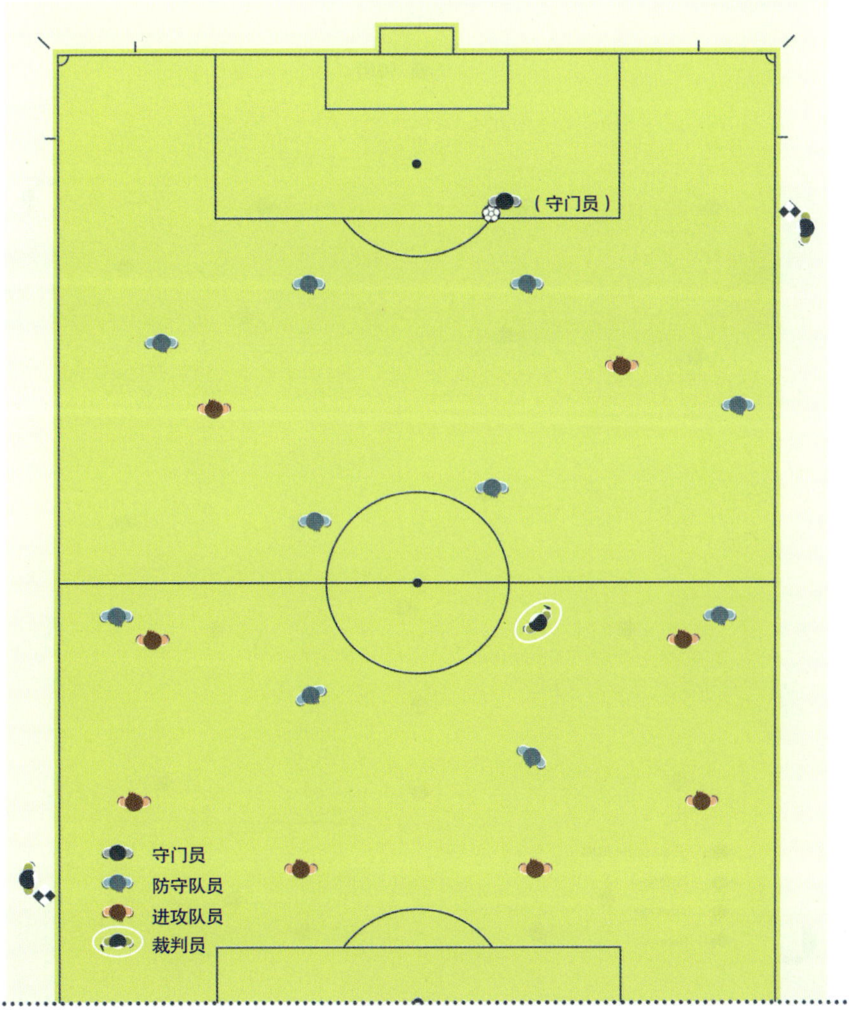

Kick-off

The ARs must be in line with the second-last defender.

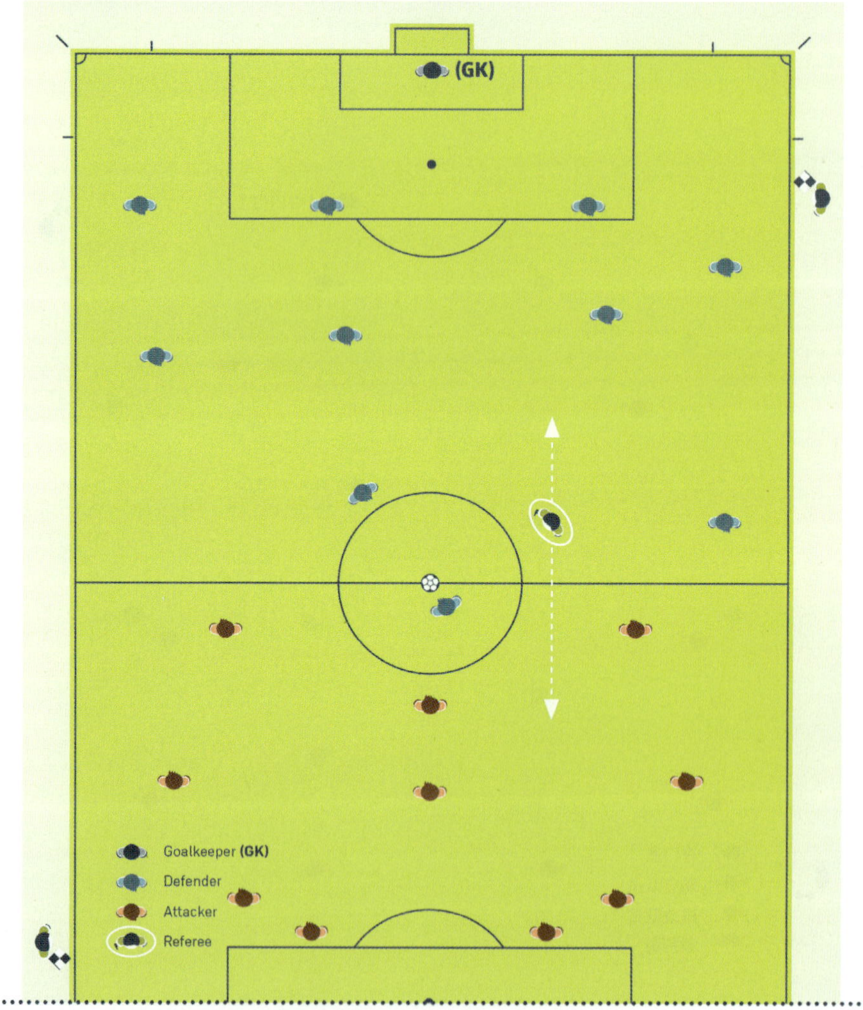

开球

助理裁判员必须与倒数第二名防守队员齐平。

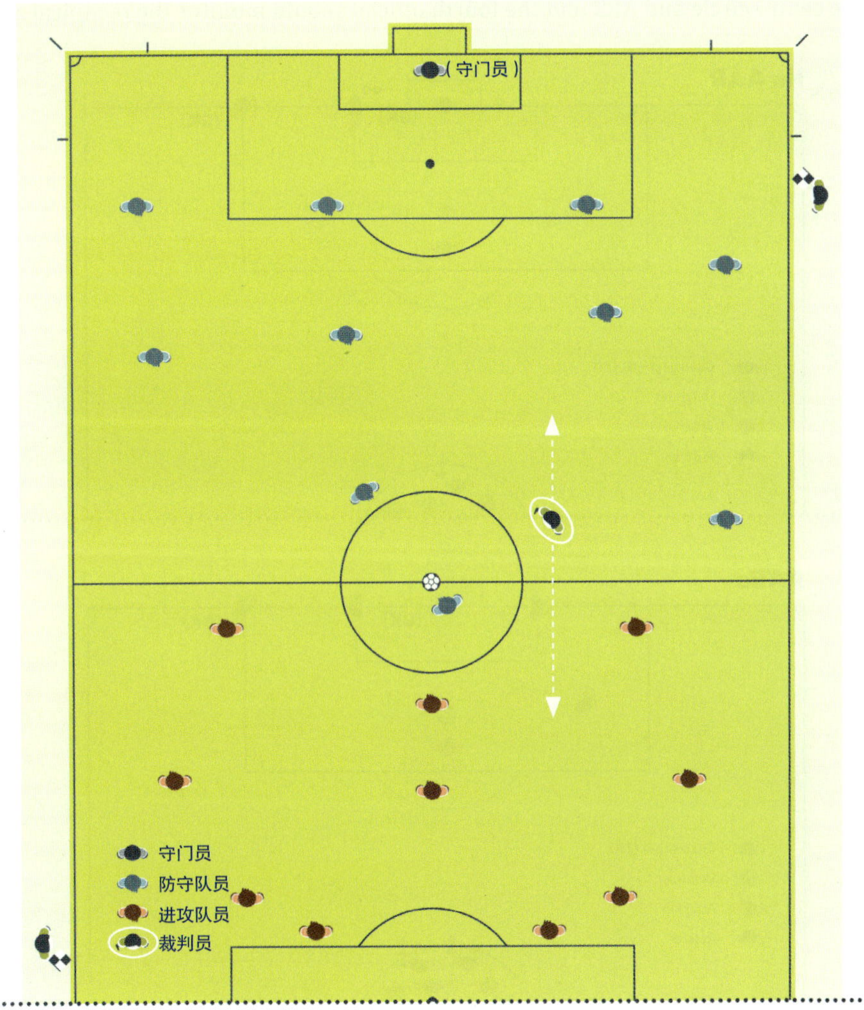

Kicks from the penalty mark

One AR must be positioned at the intersection of the goal line and the goal area. The other AR must be situated in the centre circle to control the players. If there are AARs, they must be positioned at each intersection of the goal line and the goal area, to the right and left of the goal respectively, except where GLT is in use when only one AAR is required. In this case AAR2 and AR1 should monitor the players in the centre circle and AR2 and the fourth official should monitor the technical areas.

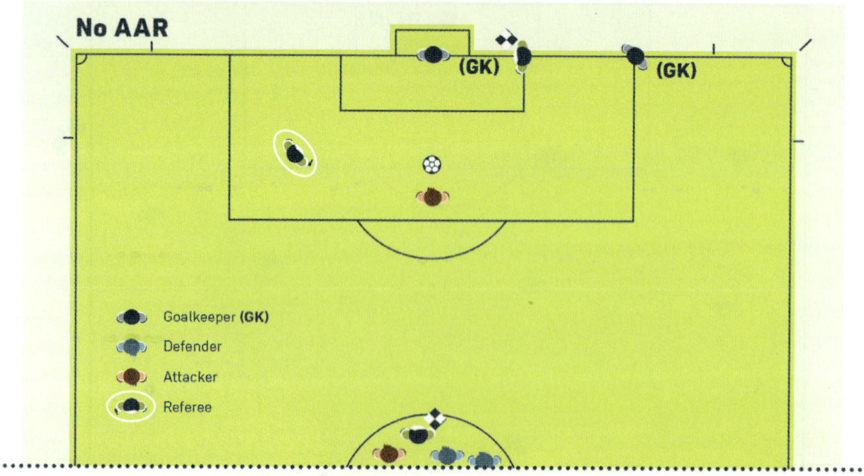

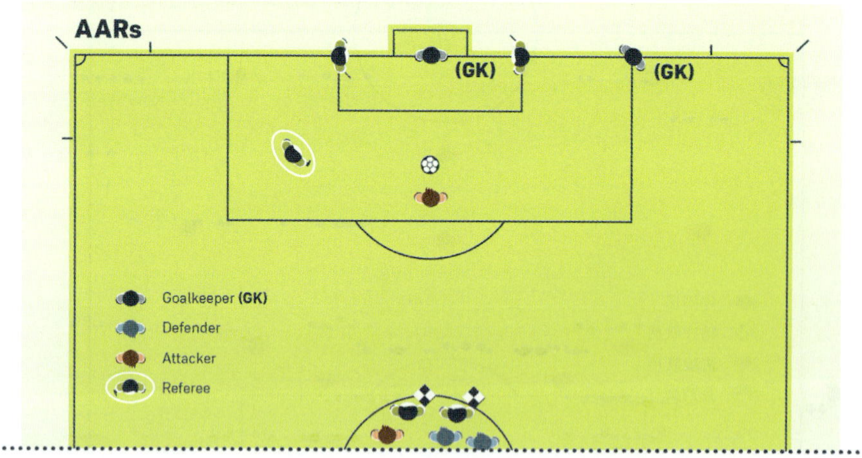

罚球点球决胜

一名助理裁判员必须站在球门线与球门区线相交的位置，另一名助理裁判员必须站在中圈控制队员。如果有附加助理裁判员，则两名附加助理裁判员处于球门线与球门区线的两个交点位置，分别位于球门两侧。如使用球门线技术，则此处只需要一名附加助理裁判员。此时，第二附加助理裁判员与第一助理裁判员应监控中圈内的队员，而第二助理裁判员和第四官员应监控技术区域。

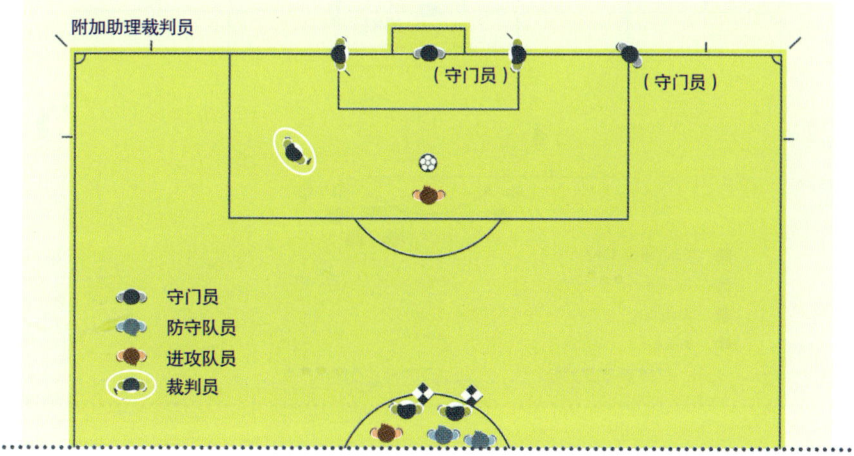

Penalty kick

The AR must be positioned at the intersection of the goal line and the penalty area.

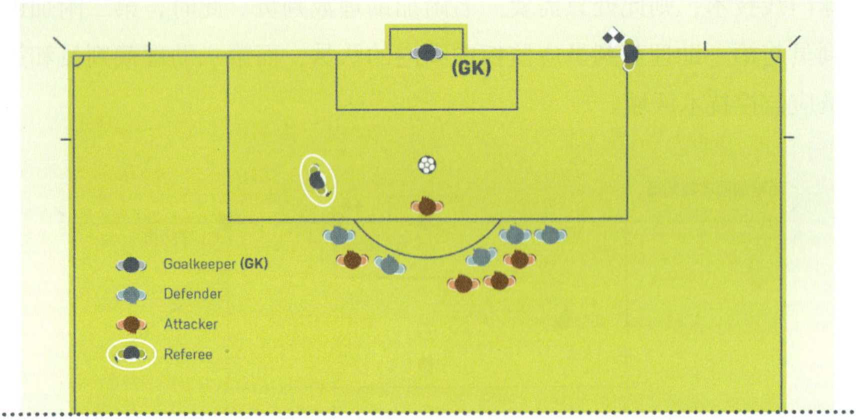

Where there are AARs the AAR must be positioned at the intersection of the goal line and the goal area and the AR is positioned in line with the penalty mark (which is the offside line).

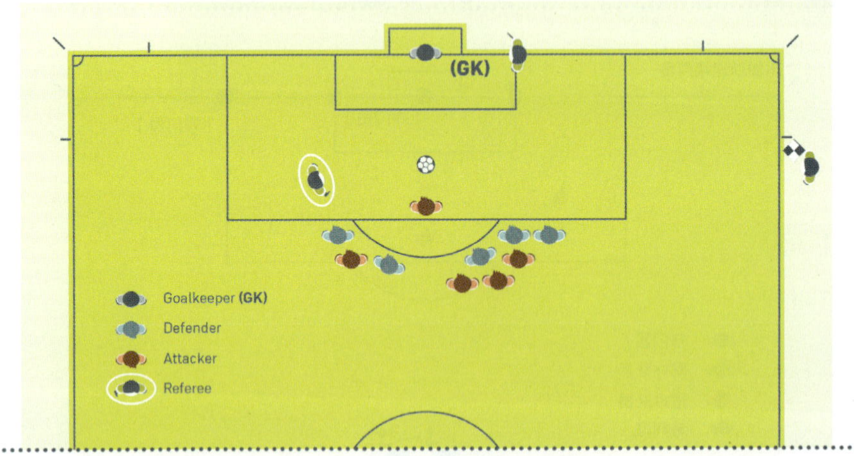

罚球点球

助理裁判员必须站在球门线与罚球区线交点的位置。

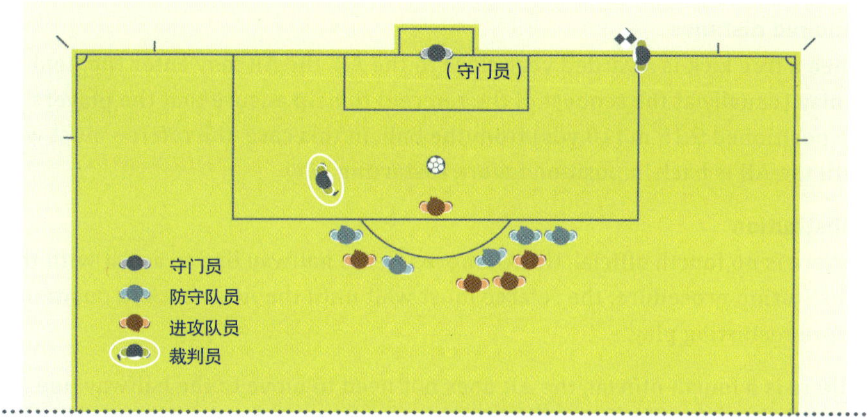

如果设有附加助理裁判员，则附加助理裁判员必须处于球门线与球门区线交点的位置，而助理裁判员处于与罚球点齐平的边线位置（此时这里是越位线位置）。

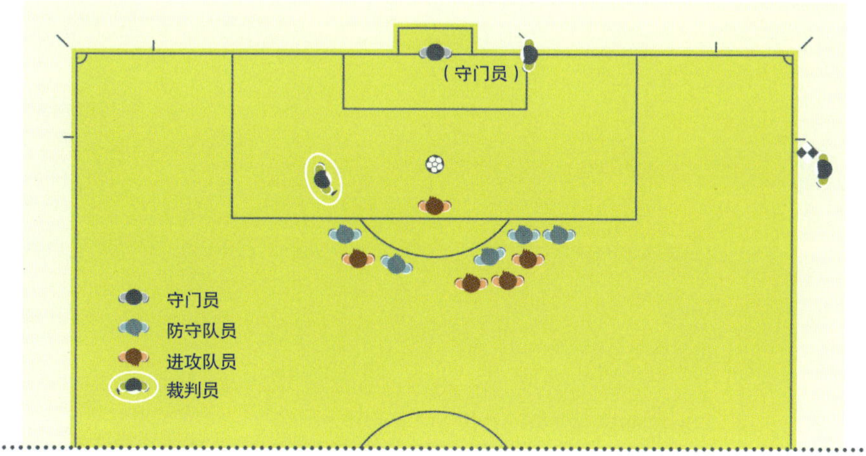

Mass confrontation

In situations of mass confrontation, the nearest AR may enter the field of play to assist the referee. The other AR must observe and record details of the incident. The fourth official should remain in the vicinity of the technical areas.

Required distance

When a free kick is awarded very close to the AR, the AR may enter the field of play (usually at the request of the referee) to help ensure that the players are positioned 9.15 m (10 yds) from the ball. In this case, the referee must wait until the AR is back in position before restarting play.

Substitution

If there is no fourth official, the AR moves to the halfway line to assist with the substitution procedure; the referee must wait until the AR is back in position before restarting play.

If there is a fourth official, the AR does not need to move to the halfway line as the fourth official carries out the substitution procedure unless there are several substitutions at the same time, in which case the AR moves to the halfway line to assist the fourth official.

群体冲突

此类情况下，距事发地较近的助理裁判员可以进入比赛场地内协助裁判员；另一名助理裁判员必须观察和记录事件的细节；第四官员应留在技术区域附近。

规定距离

当罚任意球的地点距助理裁判员很近时，助理裁判员可以进入比赛场地内（通常是在裁判员的要求下）协助确保对方队员距离球至少9.15米（10码）。这种情况下，裁判员必须等助理裁判员回到常规位置后再恢复比赛。

队员替换

在没有第四官员的情况下，助理裁判员移动至中线处协助完成替换程序。裁判员必须等助理裁判员回到位置后再恢复比赛。

在有第四官员的情况下，助理裁判员不必移动至中线处，由第四官员执行替换程序。除非同一时间有多名队员进行替换时，助理裁判员可移动至中线处协助第四官员。

FIFA

FIFA

Body language, communication and whistle

1. Referees

Body language

Body language is a tool that the referee uses to:

- help control the match
- show authority and self-control

Body language is not an explanation of a decision.

Signals

See Law 5 for diagrams of signals

Whistle

The whistle is needed to:

- start play (first and second half of normal play and extra time), after a goal
- stop play:
  - for a free kick or penalty kick
  - if the match is suspended or abandoned
  - at the end of each half
- restart play for:
  - free kicks when the appropriate distance is required
  - penalty kicks
- restart play after it has been stopped for a:
  - caution or sending-off

肢体语言、沟通与哨音

1. 裁判员

肢体语言

裁判员将肢体语言作为工具运用，以：

- 协助其管理比赛。
- 显示其权威和控制力。

肢体语言不是对判罚的解释。

示意信号

详见第五章图例

哨音的使用

需要鸣哨的情况：

- 开始比赛（常规时间的上下半场和加时赛）、进球后恢复比赛。
- 停止比赛：
  - 判罚任意球或罚球点球。
  - 比赛需中断或中止。
  - 各半场结束。

- 恢复比赛：
  - 在需要退出规定距离的任意球罚球时。
  - 罚球点球。

- 因如下情况暂停比赛，后恢复比赛时：
  - 警告或罚令出场。

- injury
- substitution

The whistle is NOT needed to:

- stop play for a clear:
  - goal kick, corner kick, throw-in or goal
- restart play from:
  - most free kicks, and a goal kick, corner kick, throw-in or dropped ball

A whistle which is used too frequently/unnecessarily will have less impact when it is needed.

If the referee wants the player(s) to wait for the whistle before restarting play (e.g. when ensuring that defending players are 9.15m (10 yd) from the ball at a free kick) the referee must clearly inform the attacking player(s) to wait for the whistle.

If the referee blows the whistle in error and play stops, play is restarted with a dropped ball.

2. Assistant referees

Beep signal

The beep signal system is an additional signal which is only used to gain the referee's attention. Situations when the signal beep may be useful include:

- offside
- offences (outside the view of the referee)
- throw-in, corner kick, goal kick or goal (tight decisions)

Electronic communication system

Where an electronic communication system is used, the referee will advise the ARs as to when it may be appropriate to use the communication system with, or instead of, a physical signal.

- 受伤。
- 替换队员。

不需要鸣哨的情况：

- 停止比赛是为了示意：
  - 球权归属明确的球门球、角球、界外球或明显的进球。
- 以下列方式恢复比赛时：
  - 多数情况下的任意球、球门球、角球、界外球或坠球。

过于频繁或不必要的鸣哨，会在需要鸣哨时削弱哨音的作用。

如果裁判员在恢复比赛前，要求队员在其鸣哨后才可以罚球〔如需要确保防守队员距离球不少于9.15米（10码）〕时，必须以明确的信号告知进攻队员等待哨音。

如果裁判员错误地吹停了比赛，则以坠球恢复比赛。

2. 助理裁判员

蜂鸣信号

蜂鸣信号作为附加信号，仅用于引起裁判员注意。该信号在如下情况时能起到一定作用：

- 越位。
- 犯规（裁判员视线范围外）。
- 掷界外球、角球、球门球或进球（难以判断的情形）。

电子通信设备

在使用电子通信设备的情况下，裁判员可以建议助理裁判员在适当的时候使用电子通信设备进行沟通，以取代肢体信号。

Flag technique
The AR's flag must always be unfurled and visible to the referee. This usually means the flag is carried in the hand closest to the referee. When making a signal, the AR stops running, faces the field of play, makes eye contact with the referee and raises the flag with a deliberate (not hasty or exaggerated) motion. The flag should be like an extension of the arm. The ARs must raise the flag using the hand that will be used for the next signal. If circumstances change and the other hand must be used, the AR should move the flag to the opposite hand below the waist. If the AR signals that the ball is out of play, the signal must be maintained until the referee acknowledges it.

If the AR signals for a sending-off offence and the signal is not seen immediately:

- if play has been stopped, the restart may be changed in accordance with the Laws (free kick, penalty kick, etc.)
- if play has restarted, the referee may still take disciplinary action but not penalise the offence with a free kick or penalty kick

Gestures
As a general rule, the AR should not use obvious hand signals. However, in some instances, a discreet hand signal may assist the referee. The hand signal should have a clear meaning which should have been agreed in the pre-match discussion.

Signals
See Law 6 for diagrams of signals

Corner kick/goal kick
When the ball wholly passes over the goal line the AR raises the flag with the right hand (better line of vision) to inform the referee that the ball is out of play and then if it is:

- near to the AR – indicate whether it is a goal kick or a corner kick
- far from the AR – make eye contact and follow the referee's decision

When the ball clearly passes over the goal line the AR does not need to raise the flag to indicate that the ball has left the field of play. If the goal kick or

旗示技巧

助理裁判员必须始终将手旗展开，并将其保持在裁判员可见的范围内，这就意味着助理裁判员需将手旗握在最靠近裁判员的那只手中。在给出示意信号时，助理裁判员停止跑动，面向场内，与裁判员进行目光交流，随后举旗给出明确的（而非仓促、夸张的）示意信号。手旗应像手臂的延伸。助理裁判员必须用准备做出下一个信号的手举旗。如果情况发生变化而需要用另一只手，则应在腰部以下换手。如果助理裁判员示意球已离开比赛场地，则必须保持这个示意信号，直至裁判员做出反应。

如果助理裁判员示意可罚令出场的犯规，而该信号没有立即被裁判员注意：

- 如果比赛已经停止，则可以根据规则的相关规定，更改比赛恢复方式（如任意球、罚球点球）。
- 如果比赛已经恢复，裁判员仍可执行纪律处罚，但不得对此次犯规重新判罚任意球或罚球点球。

示意动作

一般情况下，助理裁判员不应使用明显的手势信号，但在某些情况下，谨慎的手势信号可以起到协助裁判员的作用。手势信号应有明确含义，并应在赛前准备时达成一致。

旗示信号

详见第六章图例。

角球 / 球门球

当球的整体完全越过球门线时，助理裁判员使用右手举旗（以便拥有更好的视角），示意裁判员球已经离开比赛场地，随后：

- 如果从靠近助理裁判员的一侧离开比赛场地——示意球门球或角球。
- 如果从远离助理裁判员的一侧离开比赛场地——与裁判员进行目光交流，遵从裁判员的决定。

如果球明显越过球门线，助理裁判员不必举旗示意球已经离开比赛场地。如果球门球或角球的球权归属明确时，助理裁判员也不必给出信号，尤其是裁判员已经给出信号的情况下。

corner kick decision is obvious, it is not necessary to give a signal, especially when the referee gives a signal.

Fouls

The AR must raise the flag when a foul or misconduct is committed in the immediate vicinity or out of the referee's vision. In all other situations, the AR must wait and offer an opinion if it is required and then inform the referee what was seen and heard, and which players were involved.

Before signalling for an offence, the AR must determine that:

- the offence was out of the referee's view or the referee's view was obstructed
- the referee would not have applied the advantage

When an offence occurs which requires a signal from the AR,
the AR must:

- raise the flag with the same hand that will also be used for the remainder of the signal – this gives the referee a clear indication as to who will be awarded the free kick
- make eye contact with the referee
- give the flag a slight wave back and forth (avoiding any excessive or aggressive movement)

The AR must use the "wait and see technique" to allow play to continue and not raise the flag when the team against which an offence has been committed will benefit from the advantage; it is therefore very important for the AR to make eye contact with the referee.

Fouls inside the penalty area

When a foul is committed by a defender inside the penalty area out of the vision of the referee, especially if near to the AR's position, the AR must first make eye contact with the referee to see where the referee is positioned and what action has been taken. If the referee has not taken any action, the AR must signal with the flag, use the electronic beep signal and then visibly move down the touchline towards the corner flag.

犯规

当犯规或不正当行为发生在距离助理裁判员很近的区域，或裁判员视线范围外时，助理裁判员应举旗示意。对于所有其他情况，助理裁判员必须等候并在裁判员需要时给出自己的意见，告知裁判员自己所看到和听到的情况，以及涉及到的队员。

在示意犯规前，助理裁判员必须确定：

- 犯规发生在裁判员视野范围外，或裁判员视线受到阻挡。
- 裁判员不会对此犯规掌握有利。

当发生犯规或违规，需要助理裁判员示意时，助理裁判员必须：

- 用同一只手举旗和做接下来的示意——这样能够向裁判员明确显示任意球的归属。
- 与裁判员进行目光交流。
- 来回轻微摇动手旗（避免任何过度或夸张的示意）。

当被犯规队可以从掌握有利中获益时，助理裁判员必须掌握“等和看的技巧”，允许比赛继续，不用举旗示意犯规。此时，助理裁判员和裁判员的目光交流很重要。

罚球区内的犯规

当防守方在其罚球区内犯规，且犯规处于裁判员视线外，尤其是靠近助理裁判员时，助理裁判员必须首先与裁判员进行目光交流，观察裁判员的位置和采取的行动。如果裁判员没有做出任何判罚，助理裁判员必须使用手旗蜂鸣信号，随后明确地沿边线向角旗移动。

Fouls outside the penalty area

When a foul is committed by a defender outside the penalty area (near the boundary of the penalty area), the AR should make eye contact with the referee, to see the referee's position and what action has been taken, and signal with the flag if necessary. In counter-attack situations, the AR should be able to give information such as whether or not a foul has been committed and whether a foul was committed inside or outside the penalty area, and what disciplinary action should be taken. The AR should make a clear movement along the touchline towards the halfway line to indicate when the offence took place outside the penalty area.

Goal – no goal

When it is clear that the ball has wholly passed over the goal line in the goal, the AR must make eye contact with the referee without giving any additional signal.

When a goal has been scored but it is not clear whether the ball has passed over the line, the AR must first raise the flag to attract the referee's attention and then confirm the goal.

Offside

The first action of the AR for an offside decision is to raise the flag (using the right hand, giving the AR a better line of vision) and then, if the referee stops play, use the flag to indicate the area of the field of play in which the offence occurred. If the flag is not immediately seen by the referee, the AR must maintain the signal until it has been acknowledged or the ball is clearly in the control of the defending team.

Penalty kick

If the goalkeeper blatantly moves off the goal line before the ball is kicked and prevents a goal from being scored, the AR should indicate the encroachment according to the pre-match instructions from the referee.

Substitution

Once the AR has been informed (by the fourth official or team official) that a substitution is requested, the AR must signal this to the referee at the next stoppage.

罚球区外的犯规

当防守方在其罚球区外（靠近罚球区的边界线）犯规时，助理裁判员应与裁判员目光交流，观察裁判员的位置和采取的行动，并在必要时给出旗示信号。在某队打反击的情形下，助理裁判员应能够提供是否犯规、犯规发生在罚球区内还是罚球区外、应给予什么纪律处罚等相关信息。当出现罚球区外的犯规时，助理裁判员应明确地做出沿边线向中线移动的动作。

进球–未进球

当球的整体已经清晰地从球门范围内越过球门线时，助理裁判员必须与裁判员目光交流，无须给出任何附加信号。

当进球得分已经形成，但球的整体越过球门线并不明显时，助理裁判员必须举旗引起裁判员注意，然后确认进球有效。

越位

助理裁判员示意越位时的第一步骤是举旗（使用右手，以便有更好的观察视角），随后如果裁判员停止比赛，则使用手旗示意越位发生的区域。如果旗示信号没有立即被裁判员看到，则助理裁判员必须坚持举旗示意越位，直至裁判员做出反应或球已明显被防守方控制。

罚球点球

如果守门员在球被踢前，非常明显地离开了球门线，且阻止了球进门，助理裁判员应按照裁判员在赛前沟通指定的方式向裁判员示意。

队员替换

一旦助理裁判员接到队员替换的信号（由第四官员或球队官员给出），必须在随后比赛停止时示意裁判员。

Throw-in

When the ball wholly passes over the touchline:

- near to the AR – a direct signal should be made to indicate the direction of the throw-in
- far from the AR and the throw-in decision is an obvious one – the AR must make a direct signal to indicate the direction of the throw-in
- far from the AR and the AR is in doubt about the direction of the throw-in – the AR must raise the flag to inform the referee that the ball is out of play, make eye contact with the referee and follow the referee's signal

3. Additional assistant referees

The AARs use a radio communication system (not flags) to communicate with the referee. If the radio communication system fails to work, the AARs will use an electronic signal beep flagstick. AARs do not usually use obvious hand signals but, in some instances, a discreet hand signal may give valuable support to the referee. The hand signal should have a clear meaning and such signals should be agreed in the pre-match discussion.

The AAR, having assessed that the ball has wholly passed over the goal line within the goal, must:

- immediately inform the referee via the communication system that a goal should be awarded
- make a clear signal with the left arm perpendicular to the goal line pointing towards the centre of the field (flagstick in the left hand is also required). This signal is not required when the ball has very clearly passed over the goal line.

The referee will make the final decision.

掷界外球

当球的整体越过边线时：

- 如果是在靠近助理裁判员的一侧——直接示意掷界外球的球权归属。
- 如果是在助理裁判员远端，且球权归属明确——直接示意掷界外球的球权归属。
- 如果是在助理裁判员远端，且球权归属不明确——助理裁判员必须举旗示意裁判员球已离开比赛场地，并与裁判员目光交流，跟随裁判员的示意信号。

3. 附加助理裁判员

附加助理裁判员使用无线通信系统（非手旗）与裁判员进行交流。如果无线通信系统失灵，则附加助理裁判员使用电子感应信号棒。附加助理裁判员通常不使用明显的手势信号，但在某些情况下，谨慎的手势信号可以为裁判员提供有价值的帮助。手势信号应有明确含义，并应在赛前准备时达成一致。

附加助理裁判员在确认球已经整体越过球门内的球门线时，必须：

- 立即通过无线通信系统告知裁判员进球有效。
- 做出左臂垂直于球门线、左手持信号棒指向场地中央的明确信号。当球非常明显地越过球门线时不必做出该信号。

由裁判员做最终决定。

Other advice

1. **Advantage**

   The referee may play advantage whenever an offence occurs but should consider the following in deciding whether to apply the advantage or stop play:

   - the severity of the offence – if the offence warrants a sending-off, the referee must stop play and send off the player unless there is a clear opportunity to score a goal
   - the position where the offence was committed - the closer to the opponent's goal, the more effective the advantage can be
   - the chances of an immediate, promising attack
   - the atmosphere of the match

2. **Allowance for time lost**

   Many stoppages in play are entirely natural (e.g. throw-ins, goal kicks). An allowance is made only when delays are excessive.

3. **Holding an opponent**

   Referees are reminded to make an early intervention and to deal firmly with holding offences, especially inside the penalty area at corner kicks and free kicks. To deal with these situations:

   - the referee must warn any player holding an opponent before the ball is in play
   - caution the player if the holding continues before the ball is in play
   - award a direct free kick or penalty kick and caution the player if it happens once the ball is in play

其他建议

1. 有利

无论是犯规还是违规违例，裁判员均可掌握有利，但应考虑如下情况决定掌握有利还是停止比赛：

- 犯规的严重程度——如果是可被罚令出场的犯规，裁判员必须停止比赛，将相关队员罚令出场，除非有明显的进球得分机会。
- 犯规发生的位置——离对方球门越近，掌握有利的效果越好。
- 能够即刻发起有效进攻的可能性。
- 当时比赛的气氛。

2. 对损耗时间的补足

比赛中的许多中断极为正常（如掷界外球、球门球等），当这些停顿延误的时间较长时才允许（针对这些停顿）补时。

3. 拉扯对方队员

裁判员应提早干预并严格处理拉扯犯规，尤其是在踢角球和任意球时，出现在罚球区内的此类行为。为了处理这些情况：

- 裁判员必须在比赛恢复前劝诫有拉扯行为的队员。
- 对比赛恢复前仍然继续此类行为的队员予以警告。
- 一旦比赛恢复，仍出现类似行为的队员，判罚直接任意球或罚球点球。

4. Offside

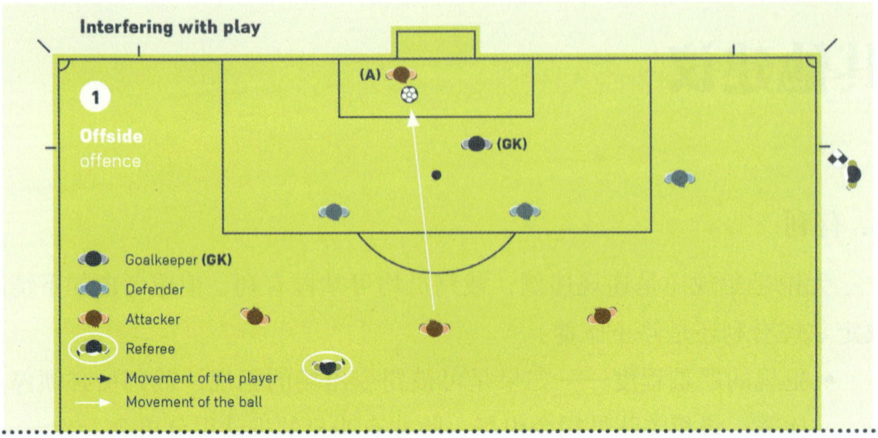

An attacker **in an offside position** (A), not interfering with an opponent, **touches the ball**. The assistant referee must raise the flag when the player **touches the ball**.

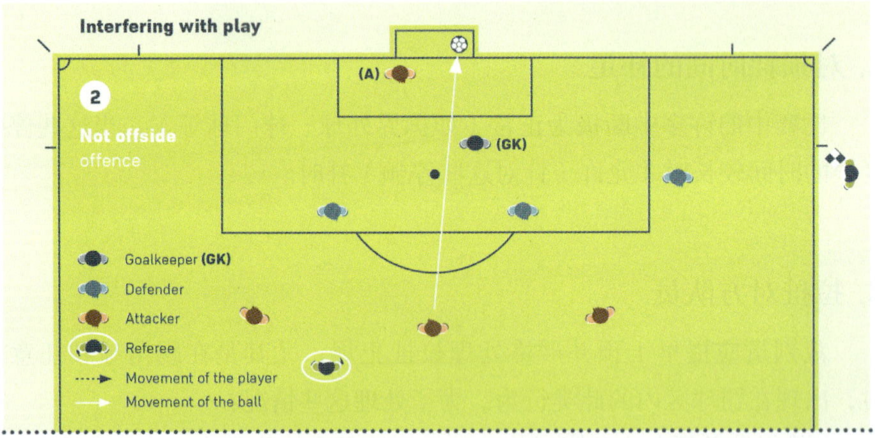

An attacker **in an offside position** (A), not interfering with an opponent, **does not touch the ball**. The player did not touch the ball, so cannot be penalised.

4. 越位

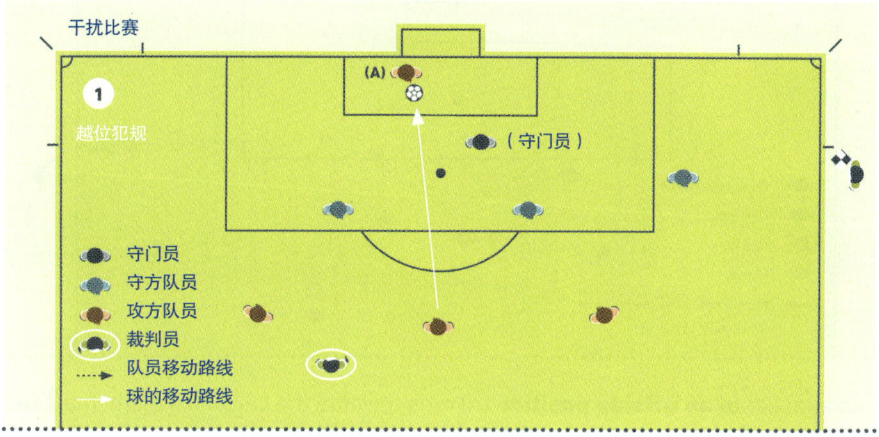

攻方队员（A）**处在越位位置**，并未干扰对方队员，但**触到了球**。助理裁判员必须在其**触球**时举旗示意其越位犯规。

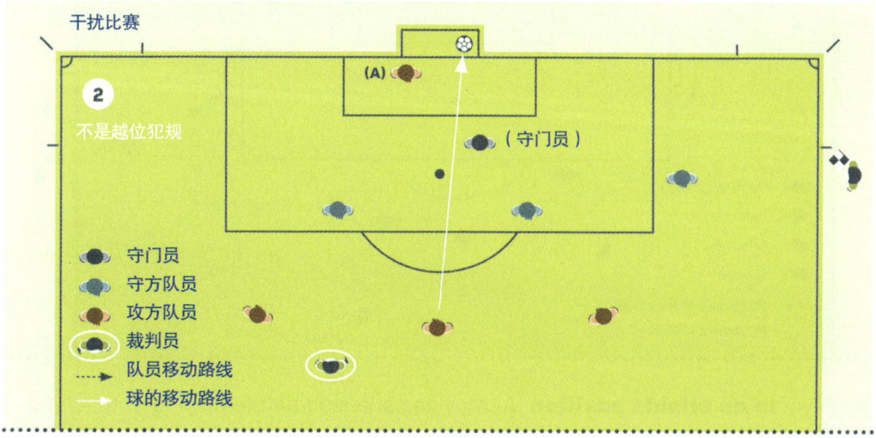

攻方队员（A）**处在越位位置**，未干扰对方队员，也**未触球**。不能判罚其越位犯规。

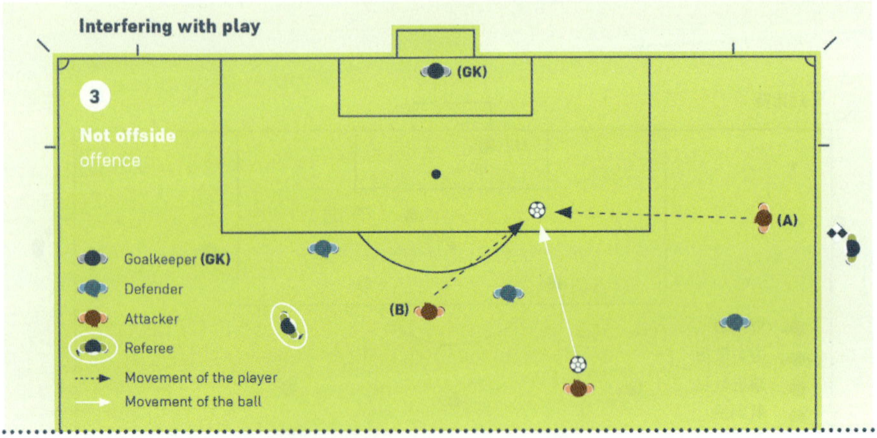

An attacker **in an offside position** (A) runs towards the ball and a team-mate **in an onside position** (B) also runs towards the ball and plays it. (A) did not touch the ball, so cannot be penalised.

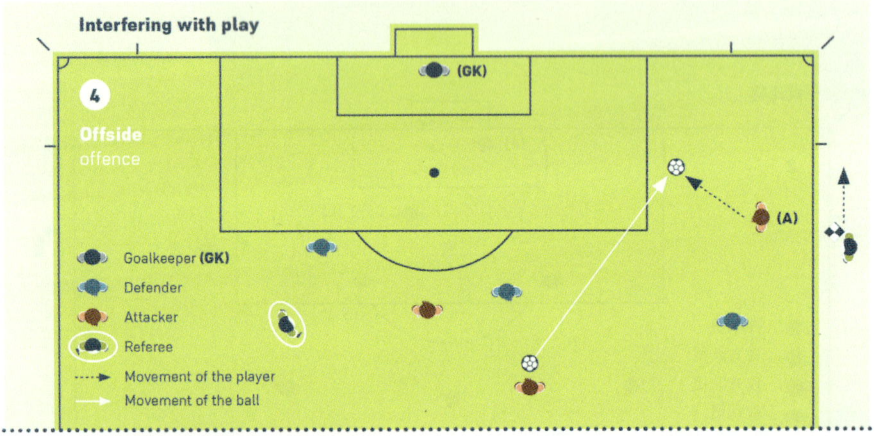

A player **in an offside position** (A) may be penalised before playing or touching the ball, if, in the opinion of the referee, no other team-mate in an onside position has the opportunity to play the ball.

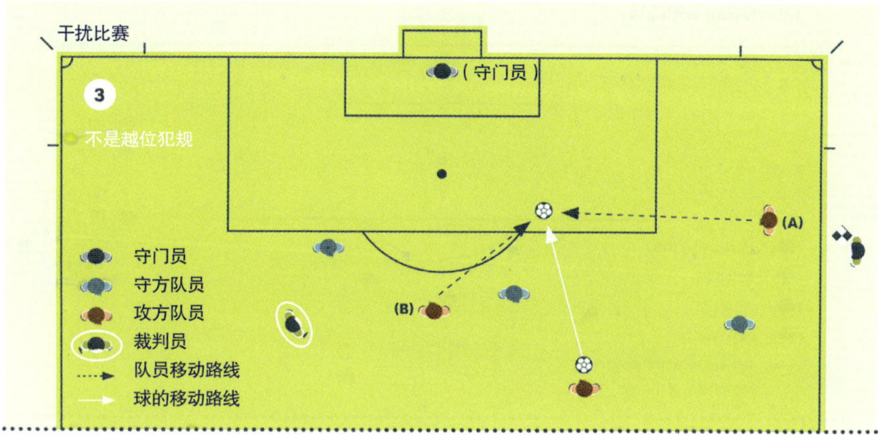

攻方队员（A）**处在越位位置**并跑向球，其队友（B）从**不越位的位置**跑向球。队员（A）未触球，则不能被判罚越位犯规。

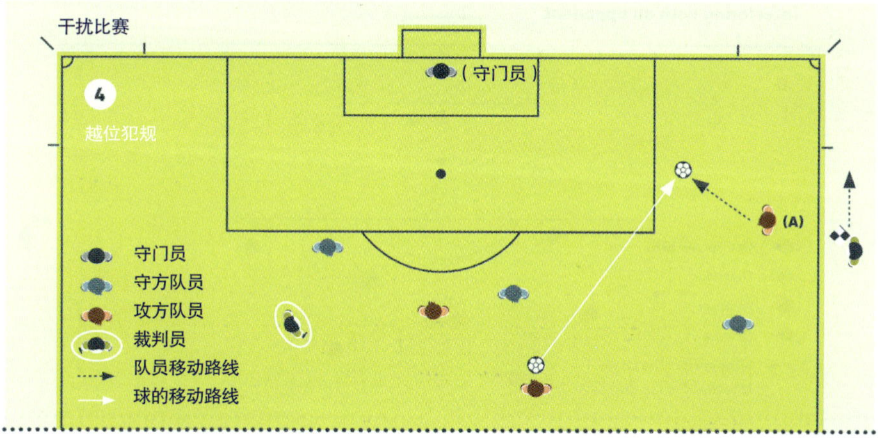

攻方队员（A）**处在越位位置**，如果裁判员认为不在越位位置的同队其他队员没有触球的机会，则在队员（A）触球前即可判罚其越位犯规。

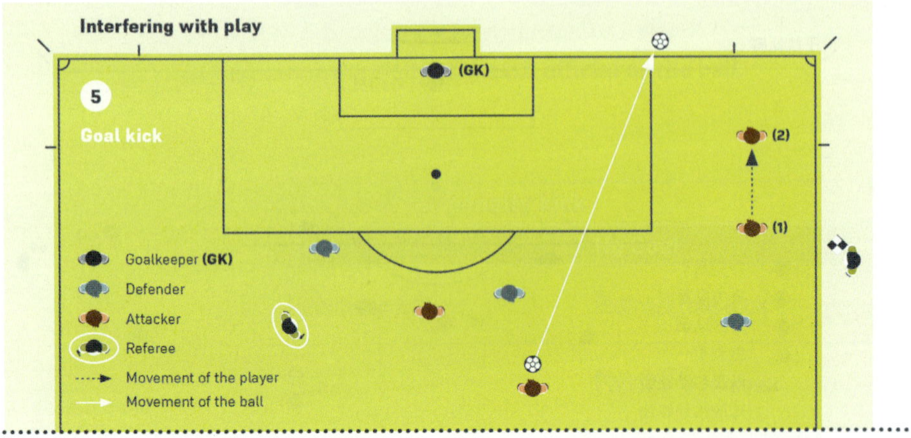

An attacker **in an offside position** (1) runs towards the ball and **does not touch** the ball. The assistant referee must signal **"goal kick"**.

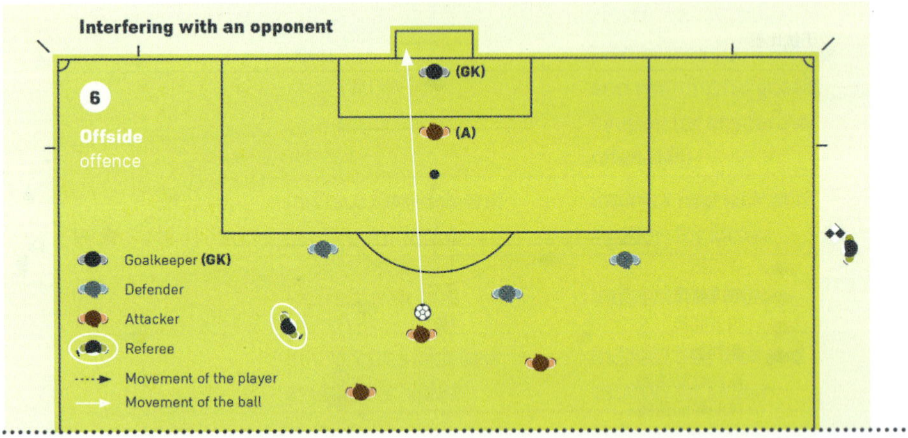

An attacker **in an offside position** (A) is clearly obstructing the goalkeeper's line of vision. The player must be penalised for preventing an opponent from playing or being able to play the ball.

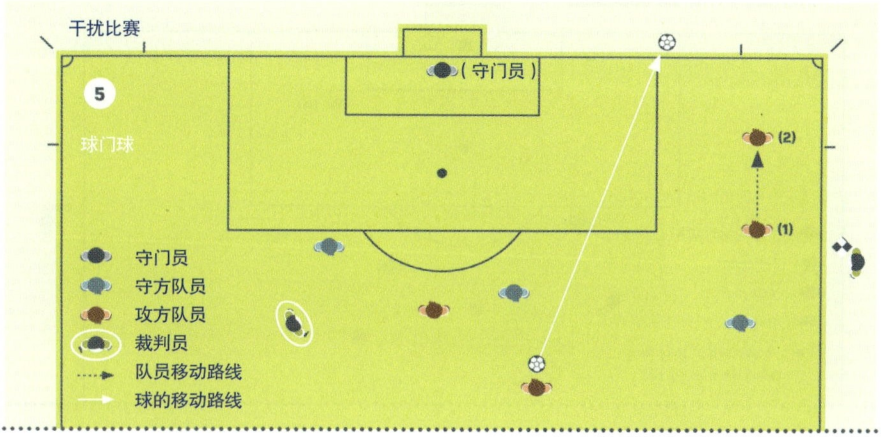

攻方队员**处于越位位置**（1）并跑向球，但**并未触球**。助理裁判员必须示意**“球门球”**。

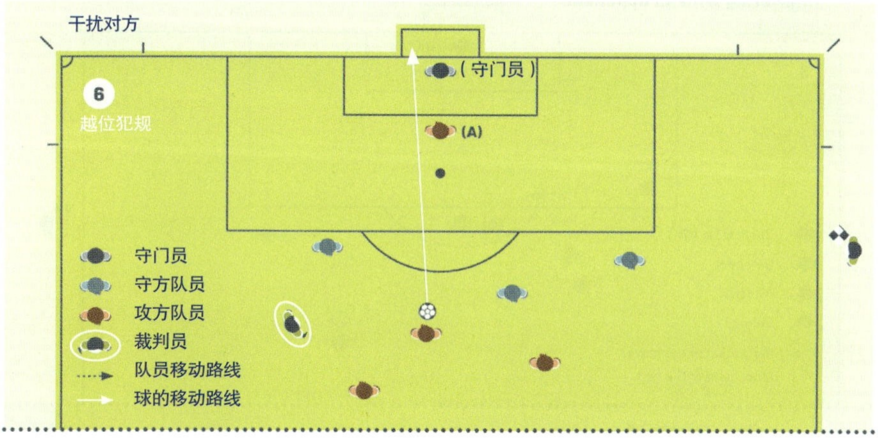

处于越位位置的攻方队员（A）明显地阻碍了守门员的视线。必须以妨碍对方队员处理球或处理球的能力为由判罚其越位犯规。

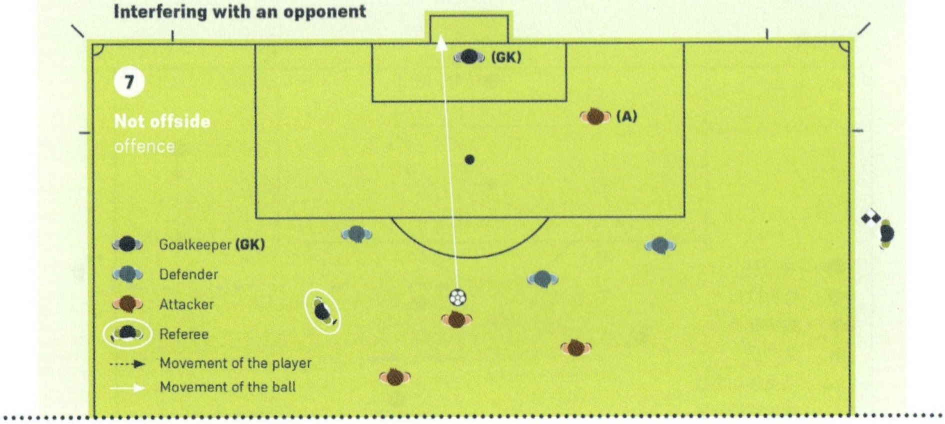

An attacker **in an offside position** (A) is **not** clearly obstructing the goalkeeper's line of vision or challenging an opponent for the ball.

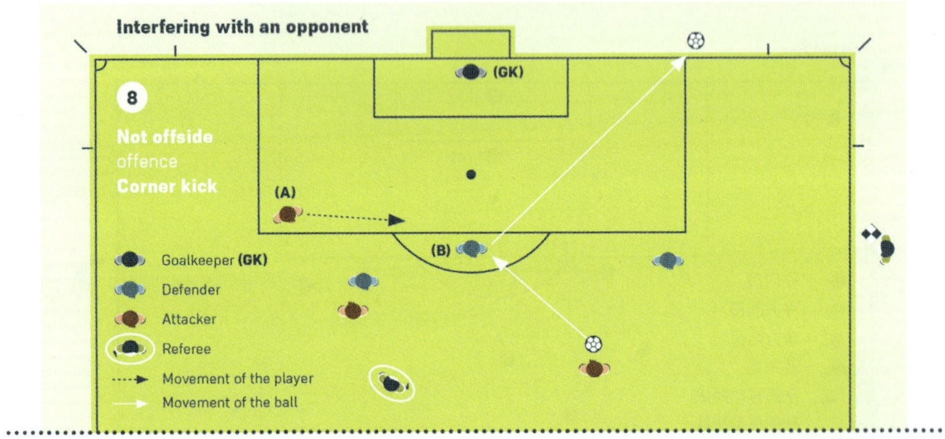

An attacker **in an offside position** (A) runs towards the ball but does not prevent the opponent from playing or being able to play the ball.
(A) is **not** challenging an opponent (B) for the ball.

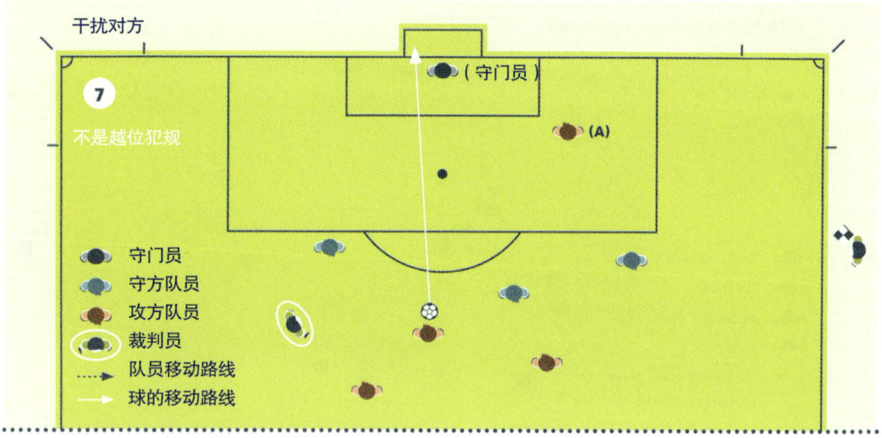

处于越位位置的攻方队员（A）**没有**明显地阻挡守门员的视线，也没有与对方队员争抢球。

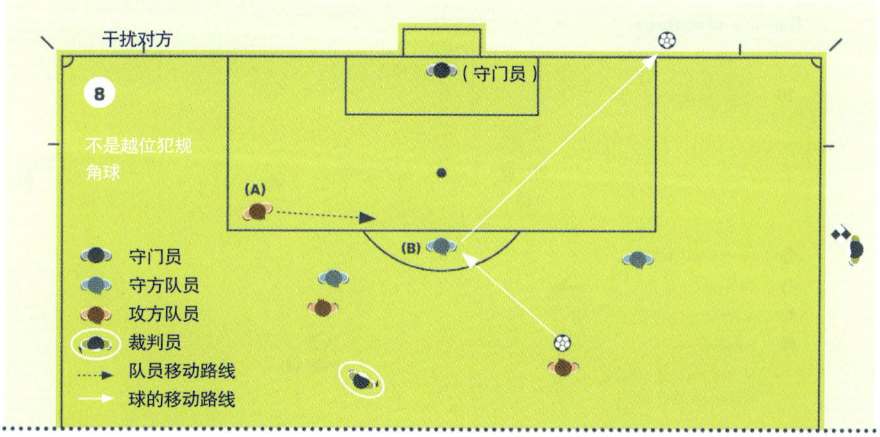

处于越位位置的攻方队员（A）跑向球，但**并未**妨碍对方队员处理球或处理球的能力。队员（A）未与对方队员（B）争抢球。

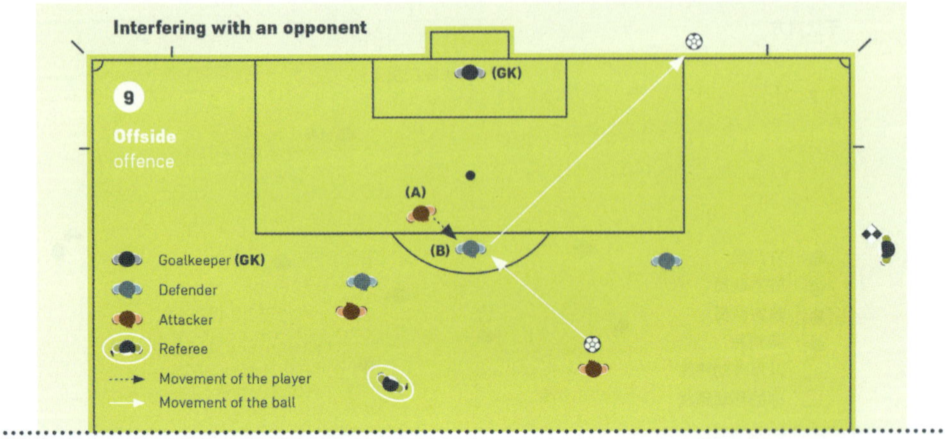

An attacker **in an offside position** (A) runs towards the ball preventing the opponent (B) from playing or being able to play the ball by challenging the opponent for the ball. (A) is challenging an opponent (B) for the ball.

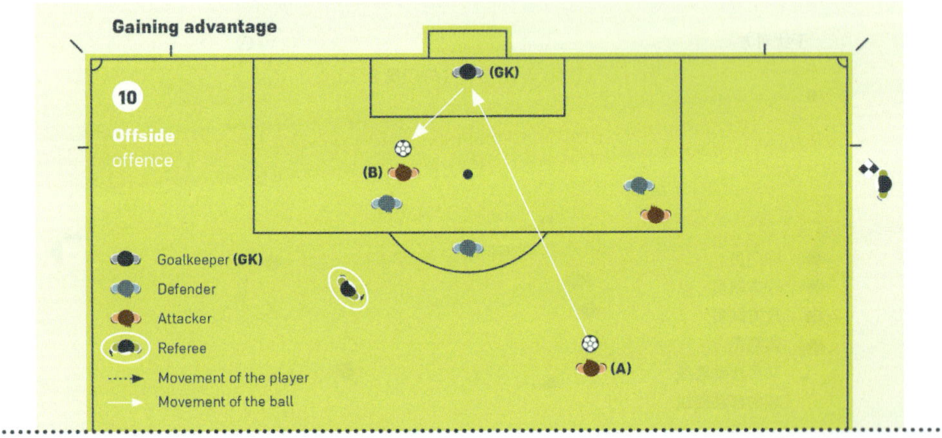

An attacker **in an offside position** (B) is penalised for **playing or touching the ball** that rebounds, is deflected or is played from a deliberate save by the goalkeeper having been **in an offside position** when the ball was last touched or is played by a team-mate.

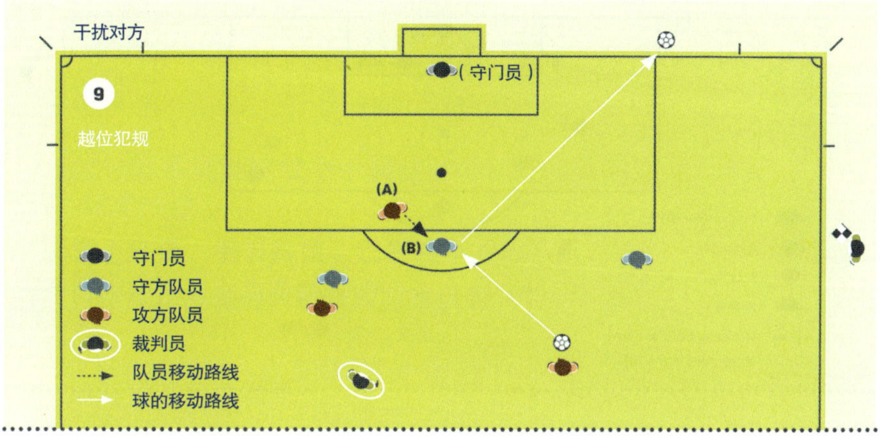

处于越位位置的攻方队员（A）跑向球并与对方队员（B）争抢球，妨碍了对方队员处理球或处理球的能力。队员（A）视为与对方队员争抢球。

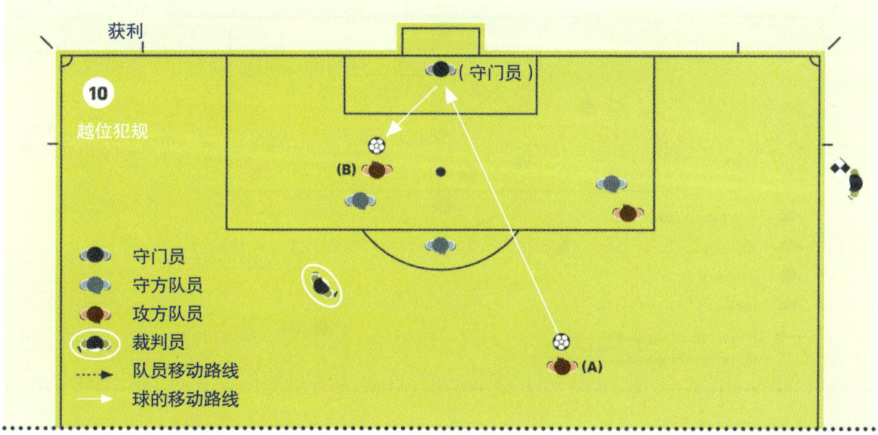

攻方队员（B）被判罚越位犯规，因其在同队队员**传球或触球**的一瞬间**处于越位位置**，且在球从守门员反弹、折射或经守门员有意救球后触球。

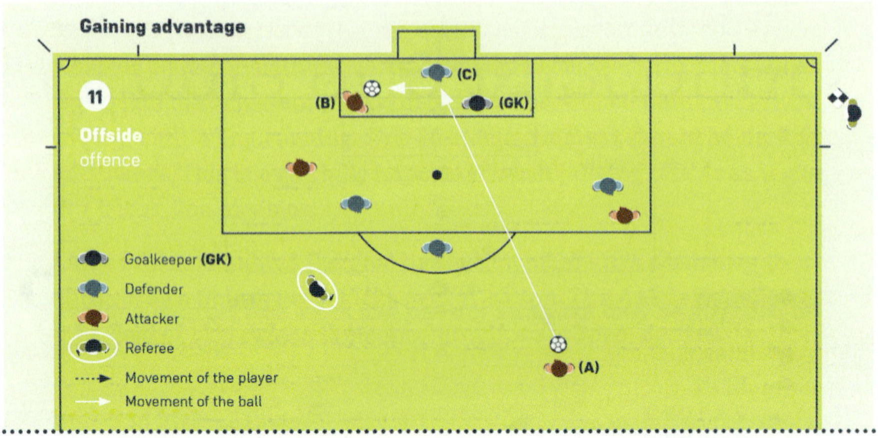

An attacker **in an offside position** (B) is penalised for **playing or touching the ball** that rebounds or is deflected from a deliberate save by a player from the defending team (C) having been **in an offside position** when the ball was last touched or is played by a team-mate.

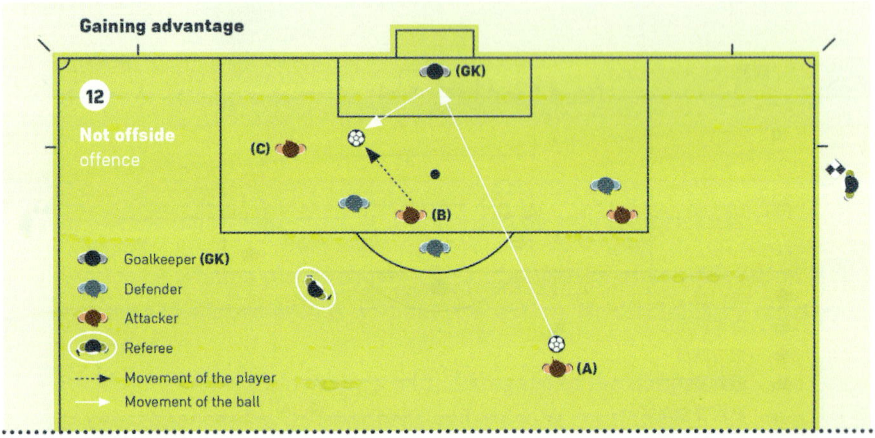

The shot by a team-mate (A) rebounds from the goalkeeper, (B) is in an onside position and plays the ball, (C) **in an offside position** is not penalised because the player did not gain an advantage from being in that position because the player did not touch the ball.

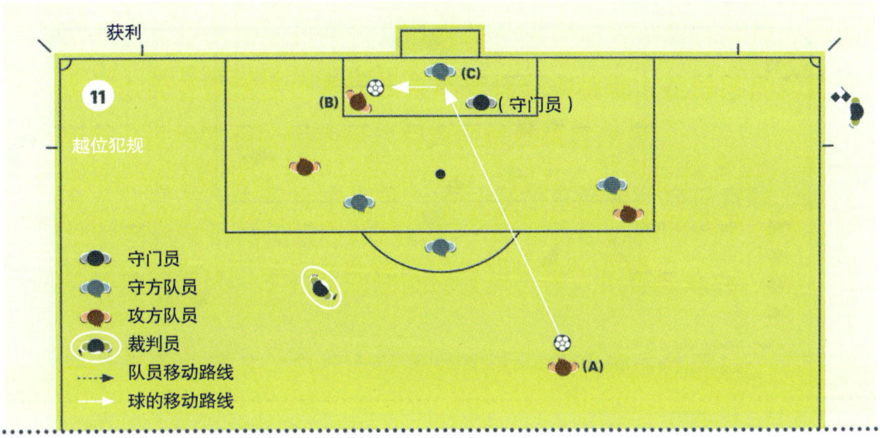

处于越位位置的攻方队员（B）被判罚越位犯规，因其在同队队员**传球或触球**的一瞬间**处于越位位置**，且在球从守方队员（C）反弹、折射或经守方队员（C）有意救球后触球。

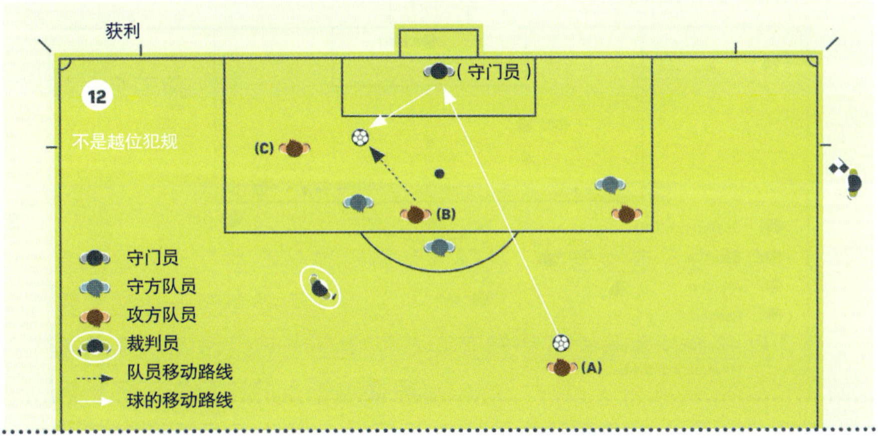

球经同队队员（A）射门后，从守门员处反弹，队员（B）处在不越位的位置，并且触球，**处在越位位置**的队员（C）不能被判罚越位犯规，因其未触球，并未从越位位置获利。

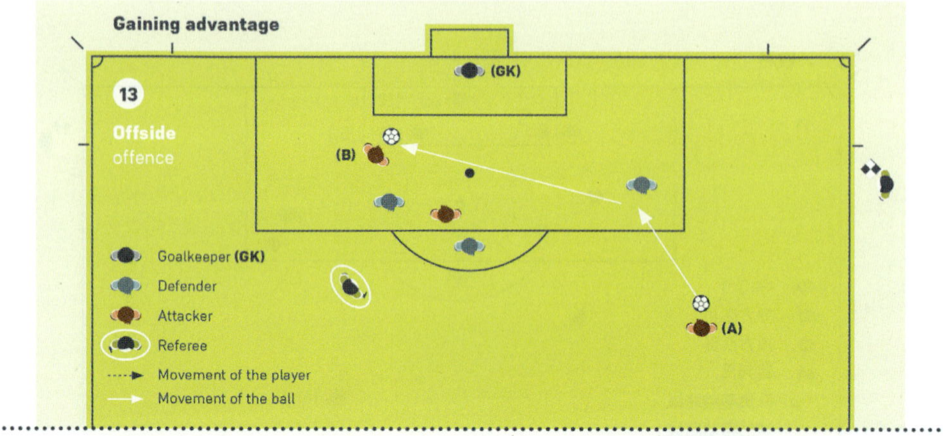

The shot by a team-mate (A) rebounds off or is deflected by an opponent to attacker (B) who is penalised for **playing or touching the ball** having previously been **in an offside position**.

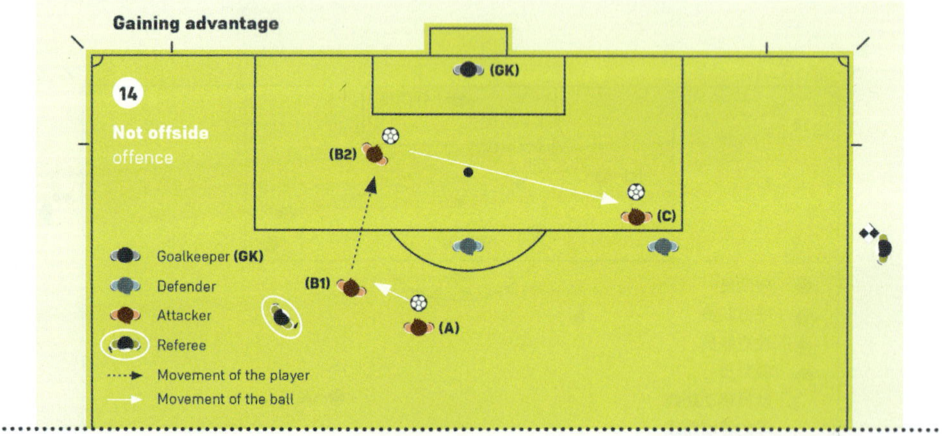

An attacker (C) is **in an offside position**, not interfering with an opponent, when a team-mate (A) passes the ball to player (B1) in an onside position who runs towards the opponents' goal and passes the ball (B2) to team-mate (C). Attacker (C) was **in an onside position** when the ball was passed, so cannot be penalised.

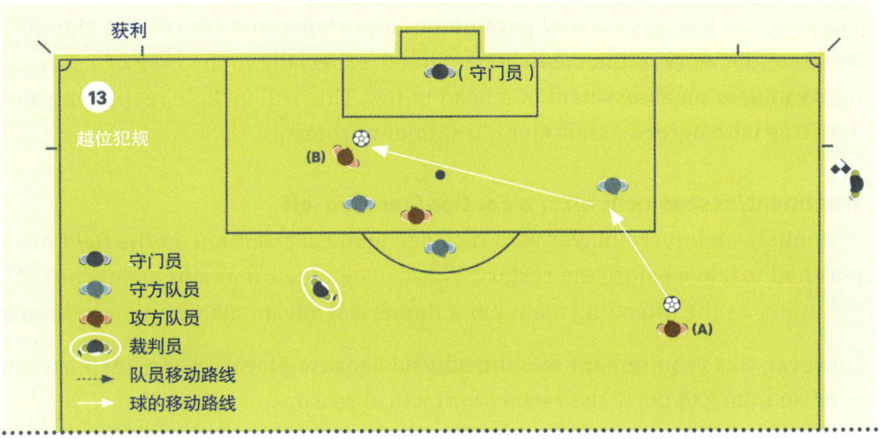

球经同队队员（A）射门后，从对方队员处反弹或折射，攻方队员（B）**触球**将被判为越位犯规，因其之前已**处在越位位置**。

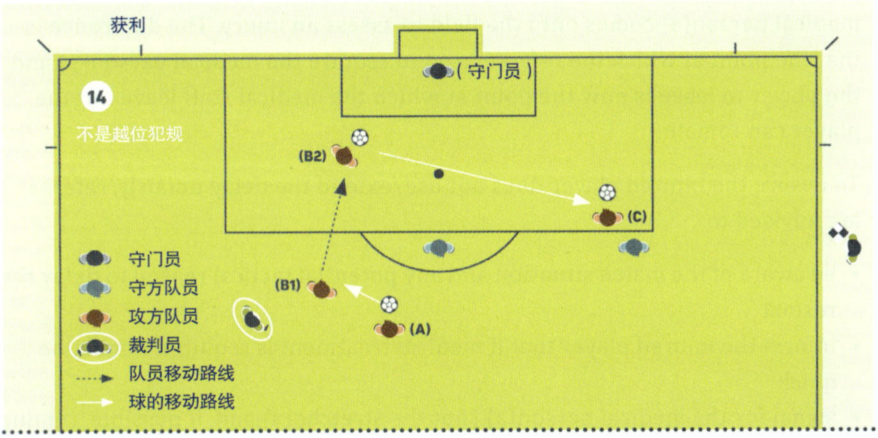

攻方队员（C）**处在越位位置**，未干扰对方队员。当同队队员（A）传球给处在不越位的位置，且向前插上的队员（B1），该队员在（B2）位置传球给队员（C），此时进攻队员（C）处于**不越位的位置**，因此不能判罚其越位犯规。

5. **Injuries**

The safety of the players is of paramount importance and the referee should facilitate the work of the medical personnel, especially in the case of a serious injury and/or an assessment of a head injury. This will include respecting and assisting with agreed assessment/treatment protocols.

6. **Treatment/assessment after a caution/sending-off**

Previously, an injured player who received medical attention on the field of play had to leave before the restart. This can be unfair if an opponent caused the injury as the offending team has a numerical advantage when play restarts.

However, this requirement was introduced because players often unsportingly used an injury to delay the restart for tactical reasons.

As a balance between these two unfair situations, The IFAB has decided that only for a physical offence where the opponent is cautioned or sent off, an injured player can be quickly assessed/treated and then remain on the field of play.

In principle, the delay should not be any longer than currently occurs when a medical person(s) comes onto the field to assess an injury. The difference is that the point at which the referee used to require the medical person(s) and the player to leave is now the point at which the medical staff leave but the player can remain.

To ensure the injured player does not use/extend the delay unfairly, referees are advised to:

- be aware of the match situation and any potential tactical reason to delay the restart
- inform the injured player that if medical treatment is required it must be quick
- signal for the medical person(s) (not the stretchers) and, if possible, remind them to be quick

5. 受伤

队员的安全是最重要的。裁判员应支持医务人员的工作，尤其是在出现严重受伤和/或对头部伤情的评估时。这种支持包括尊重与配合合理的治疗/伤势评估方案。

6. 出现可警告/罚令出场的犯规后对受伤队员的治疗/伤势评估

在以前的《足球竞赛规则》中，在比赛场地内接受治疗的受伤队员不得不在随后比赛恢复前离开比赛场地。然而如果受伤是由于对方的犯规造成，犯规一方在随后比赛恢复后会获得人数上的优势，这是不公平的。

这一条文的提出，是因为队员往往出于战术目的，以受伤为由不当地延误比赛恢复。

作为这两种不公平情况的平衡之法，国际足球理事会决定，仅当受伤队员在受到对方身体接触且可被警告或罚令出场的犯规时，可以在接受快速伤势评估和治疗后留在场内不必出场。

原则上，如果医护人员进入比赛场地内评估队员伤势，不应消耗更多时间。所不同的是，以往裁判员要求医护人员和受伤队员均要离开比赛场地，而现在只需医护人员离开，受伤队员仍可以留在比赛场地内。

为确保受伤队员无法以不当方式利用 / 延长受伤带来的时间损耗，建议裁判员：

- 留意比赛情况以及任何潜在的延误比赛的战术目的；
- 告知受伤队员，需要医护时，必须尽快完成；
- 示意医护人员（而非担架手），在可能的情况下尽快完成医护。

When the referee decides play should restart either:

- the medical person(s) leaves and the player remains or
- the player leaves for further assessment/treatment (stretcher signal may be necessary)

As a general guide, the restart should not be delayed for more than about 20–25 seconds beyond the point when everyone was ready for play to restart, except in the case of a serious injury and/or an assessment of a head injury.

The referee must make full allowance for the stoppage.

当裁判员作出如下决定后，比赛恢复：

- 医护人员离开比赛场地、队员留在比赛场地，或
- 队员离开比赛场地接受进一步的伤情评估 / 治疗（可示意担架手入场）

一般说来，当所有人员准备好恢复比赛后，延误的时间不应超过20～25秒，除非出现严重受伤和/或对头部伤情的评估。

裁判员必须对此类情况损耗的时间予以补足。